DATE DUE

EASTERN
EUROPE
IN
REVOLUTION

Eastern Europe in 1989

- ·—·—·— International Frontiers
- ············ Federal Republics in the Soviet Union, Czechoslovakia and Yugoslavia

EASTERN EUROPE IN REVOLUTION

Edited by **IVO BANAC**

CORNELL UNIVERSITY PRESS

Ithaca and London

First published 1992 by Cornell University Press.

International Standard Book Number 0-8014-2711-8 (cloth)
International Standard Book Number 0-8014-9997-6 (paper)
Library of Congress Catalog Card Number 91-57903

Printed in the United States of America

Librarians: Library of Congress cataloging information appears on the last page of the book.

⊗The paper in this book meets the minimum requirements of the American National Standard for Information Sciences—Permanence of Paper for Printed Library Materials, ANSI Z39.48-1984.

For Gaddis and Barclay

Contents

Preface

The articles assembled in this book represent the first thoroughgoing assessments of the East European revolution of 1989. More correctly, since the revolutionary processes were not completed—and in some cases not even initiated—in 1989, the authors have followed the time frame imposed by their case studies. But whether they discuss the Hungarian "refolution" that ended a decade of piecemeal retreat by the ruling Communists, or the strange turnabout of 1991 in Albania, where the revisionism of the Khrushchev era, the move toward a free market of the early 1980s, and the pluralist upsurge of 1989 were telescoped in an odd revolutio interrupta, they always seek to explain the sources, issues, and political contenders in the unheroic fall of East European communism. For never has an ideology and a system of power built on such vast pretensions and still greater human tragedies fallen so ignobly as did the red star that sought to unite the lands from the gray shores of the Baltic to the azure coves of the Adriatic within a single allegiance.

The downfall of East European communism was a heralded revolution, but its timing was resistant to prediction. As soon as the magnitude of the events became apparent, the Center for International and Area Studies at Yale initiated a set of conferences, lectures, and seminars with the common theme "East European Turning Points, 1989 and Beyond." The partial proceedings of one of these conferences, titled "East Europe in Revolution," which was held at Yale on November 5, 1990, and some additional material constitute the contents of this book. I thank the center and the Kempf Memorial Fund at Yale for providing the financial backing for our spirited meeting. Three members of the center staff, Nancy Ruther, the center's Associate Director, who worked heroically on the conceptual and financial planning of the conference, as well as Susan L. Lichten and Kathleen A. Rossetti, who administered the financial and publicity arrangements, respectively, have my special thanks. In addition, I am enormously grateful to Marko Prelec, my graduate student and assistant in myriad technical matters that attended the conference, and Kelly Allen, my administrative assistant, who kindly retyped several inelegant submissions. Paul Jukić, another of my graduate students, has my thanks for his assistance in bibliographical matters. The staffs of Sterling Memorial Library, Colony Inn, Mory's, and Pierson College helped make our meeting enjoyable as well as productive. I take pleasure in acknowledging the director, editors, notably Joanne Ainsworth, and staff of Cornell University Press for their customary support, for which I am more grateful than I can ever possibly let them know.

Finally, this book would not have been possible without the vision of Gaddis Smith, the Larned Professor of History at Yale and the Director of the Center for International and Area Studies. Gaddis and Barclay Smith have been dear and special friends for many years. It is a pleasure, writing from the third floor of that house on Park Street in their Pierson, to dedicate this book to them as a small token of my love and admiration.

IVO BANAC

New Haven, Connecticut
May 1991

EASTERN
EUROPE
IN
REVOLUTION

Introduction

From a suspect song: "O comrades, are you sad, the day
of parting is at hand."
                                        —Aleksandar Beljak

Communist Eastern Europe always had a politicized future. The expressionists and the resisters, who were not necessarily of the Right, were predisposed to recognize the weakness of Communist ideology and, hence, the conditional and inherently unstable edifice of Communist power. The cultural relativists and evolutionists, who were not necessarily of the Left, were predisposed to recognize an immense human capacity to adapt to anything that appears "natural." They therefore exaggerated the staying power of a political order (misunderstood as society) that has been adrift since the generation of its founders. In the words of the Serbian aphorist Aleksandar Beljak, "The new times are here again. We just plain have no luck."

Much ink has already been spilled in attempts to answer the question of who was right and who was wrong in assessing the strengths and weaknesses of East European communism. It would be graceless for the author of this introduction to cover himself with a magistrate's gown and render judgment on a phenomenon that will certainly continue to intrigue scholars and political theorists. All the same, now that the vapors have lifted after our raucous repeal party, we can see that the symptoms of the near approaching end should have been recognizable ever since the spring of 1989.

When did the decline turn into a stampede? The Round Table agreement between Poland's government and opposition in April 1989 made Lech Wałęsa's Solidarity a legal trade union, but also charted a system of semi-free elections that appeared to guarantee sufficient safeguards for the ruling Communists. When the elections took place on June 4 (second round on June 18), East European voters, albeit in a country noted for its anti-Communist resistance, rendered judgment on the Communists for the first time in over forty years. The results were stunning. Of the 161 seats (35 percent of all seats) in the Sejm, the lower house of parliament, which it was allowed to contest under the terms of the pre-election agreement, Solidarity won all of them. Even more embarrassing for the Communists, they managed to lose all but two of the thirty-five seats for which their ranking leaders, candidates of the so-called National List, ran unopposed. Among the National List candidates who did not manage to obtain the necessary 50 percent of the vote were eight members of the party Politburo and the leading reformer, Prime Minister Mieczysław Rakowski. The elections for the hundred-seat Senate, the restored upper house of the parliament, were entirely free (without quotas for the Communists), and Solidarity won all but one seat. The Polish voters did not distinguish between Communist reformers and Communist dogmatists. Their verdict seemed daring, especially as it came on June 4—the day of the Tiananmen massacre.

The Chinese terror astounded both the Communist reformers and democratic East Europeans. This was the first successful dogmatist rebound since the beginning of Gorbachev's *perestroika*. It cast a pall over what had seemed the irreversible process of democratization. It hastened the discussions between the Hungarian government and the Opposition Round Table, a coalition of principal nascent political groups. It gave special poignancy to the June 16 reburial of Imre Nagy, the martyr-hero of the 1956 Hungarian revolution, or "popular uprising" in the new parlance of reformist Hungarian Communists. It brought the Hungarian party to legitimate the tug-of-war between the radical reformers and the foot-draggers by electing the quadripartite leadership at the June 24 meeting of the party Central Committee. But it also gave heart to the entrenched dogmatists in East Berlin, Prague, and Bucharest. Though they had most to lose, they were as unsuccessful at reading the signs of the times as most Western observers.

A vital element was, after all, missing in 1989—the Soviet will to preserve the empire. More precisely, by the summer of 1989, the Soviet leadership clearly wanted to extricate itself from Eastern Europe. Beginning on June 12, Gorbachev's triumphal visit to West Germany turned the "Gorbymania" that has attended the Soviet leader in Western capitals into what journalists gleefully referred to as "Gorbasm." In the bonhomie of Gorbachev's meetings with West German leaders, substantive feelers were likely extended on Germany's future in the "common European house." As miners' strikes in Siberia rocked the Kremlin, Gorbachev was becoming increasingly suggestive in his public statements. His speech to the Council of Europe in Strasbourg on July 7 included reminders that he rejected the Brezhnev doctrine: "Any interference in domestic affairs and any attempts to restrict the sovereignty of states, both friends and allies or any others, are inadmissible." He all but blessed systemic innovations in Central Europe. At the same time his "allies" were contradicting him. Erich Honecker of East Germany kept denouncing any thought of Germany's reunification ("Nobody could have an interest in again having a state in the heart of Europe that would be hard to control") and Nicolae Ceauşescu of Romania even condemned President George Bush's July visits to Poland and Hungary ("an attempt at the destabilization of socialism").

Gorbachev's moment of truth came in August when the Polish parliament approved Tadeusz Mazowiecki, a leading Catholic and Solidarity activist with an oppositional pedigree dating from the 1950s, as Poland's new prime minister. At stake was the Leninist notion that the rule of the Communist Party cannot be reversed by peaceful means. At stake, too, was the Western notion that Communist parties never give up power without a fight. Not only was there no fight over the real revolution in Poland, but the makeup of Mazowiecki's cabinet, which emerged in September, lent weight to the thesis that the Solidarity government, for all its appearing a coalition, was actually forging ahead toward a full acceptance of Western economic and political models. The Polish changes, however, were overshadowed by the exodus from East Germany, as tens of thousands of people started escaping to West Germany via Hungary and even Czechoslovakia. When Hungary permitted the East German plastic Trabants to drive on to Austria, it broke the fundamental convention of the bloc—that states cooperate in restricting each other's refugees.

There was little time for recriminations. The deluge had started. On September 18 the Hungarian Round Table discussions brought forth an agreement between the Communists and the opposition for a "peaceful transition to democracy." On September 25, eight thousand people demonstrated in Leipzig, as several new organizations, notably the New Forum, began organizing for a more humane socialist state. Honecker's fortieth birthday party for the GDR, scheduled for October 7, was spoiled not only by thousands of demonstrators in East Berlin and several other major cities, but also by Gorbachev, who cautioned Honecker about the drawbacks of deferred reform. Only eleven days later, as popular demonstrations engulfed the whole of the hapless GDR, Honecker was replaced by Egon Krenz, a somewhat younger and crooning version of the old-style GDR bosses, who immediately promised a turnabout (*Wende*). Whereas only a few years earlier lesser trouble would have brought Soviet growls and threats of intervention, this time the Soviet leaders pointedly declared their disinterest. Soviet foreign minister Eduard Shevardnadze said on October 23 that the USSR recognized that every bloc country "has a right to an absolute, absolute, freedom of choice," something that a Soviet spokesman leeringly touted as the new Soviet "Sinatra doctrine."

The Soviet leadership's assumption still was that the growing popular movement in Eastern Europe, if given a glimmer of a full loaf in the distance, would settle in the near future for the half loaf of perestroika or reform communism. Instead, Krenz's "Ego(n)ism"—the protesters' reference to his quick "election" to the posts of the head of East German state and of the GDR national defense council, a passage that took Honecker five years to accomplish—and even Imre Pozsgay's radical reform in Hungary increasingly played to an empty house. As Poszgay's ex-Communists, renamed Socialists at the party congress in early October, started abolishing party cells in factories and disbanding the Workers' Guard, the party's private army, the opposition grew even bolder and demanded a referendum on presidential elections, thereby precluding Pozsgay's easy coronation in advance of multiparty parliamentary elections. (The opposition won the referendum on November 26.)

In the GDR, "Krenzman" (depicted by the demonstrators as a Batman with the smile of a Cheshire Cat) sacked the government, and the Politburo, initiated the bill that would permit free travel abroad, promised additional sweeping reforms, and on November 9 ordered the removal of the Berlin Wall. Three million East Germans, out of the population of 16.7 million, immediately took advantage of the concession to visit the forbidden West by breaching an ediface that was as much a symbol as an obstacle. The ruling Communists' goal was no longer reform communism, but an orderly retreat that would prevent obliteration. In the meanwhile, on November 10, Bulgaria's hard-line leader, Todor Zhivkov, responsible for the embarrassment of the vast exodus of Bulgaria's Turkish minority, was removed by his Politburo opponents (Petŭr Mladenov, Dobri Dzhurov, Georgi Atanasov, Andrei Lukanov) in what amounted to a well-orchestrated palace coup. And, already on October 28, the demonstration started in Czechoslovakia.

The Czechoslovak opposition was hesitant, spent too much time in testing the waters for a rematch with an incredibly obtuse government, and imitated the oppositional umbrella groups in the neighboring countries even in nomenclature (Civic Forum). Yet, for all of their faults, the Czechs and Slovaks still managed to accomplish the quickest turnabout in Eastern Europe. In part, the Prague Communist leadership was too stunned by the developments in the GDR and the Soviet abandonment of the old faith. More important, it had lost its will (though not its taste for delaying tactics). Concessions on travel policy and softness toward the accused dissidents in a Bratislava trial on November 14 gave courage to the opposition. The half-hearted use of force against the Prague demonstrators on November 17 compromised the government further, but did not restore the healthy fear that it once commanded.

The party tried the palace coup tactic by dumping Miloš Jakeš, the party's secretary general, and his Politburo allies on November 24. But ultimately as demonstrations and a paralyzing general strike reached a crescendo on November 27, the party simply blinked. The next day Prime Minister Ladislav Adamec started negotiations with the leaders of the Civic Forum, an odd conglomorate of students, intellectuals, and liberal Christians, augmented by economists from the Institute of Forecasting, which collectively represented an enormously wide political spectrum. The negotiators quickly agreed to a new government that would include members of the Civic Forum. The parliament would abolish all laws that gave advantage to the Communists, and the Soviet invasion of 1968 would be reassessed. The Czechoslovak regime, which was built by vintage Stalinists Klement Gottwald and Antonín Zápotocký and nurtured by the equally fear-inspiring Antonín Novotný and Gustáv Husák, collapsed in less than a fortnight. By December 29, Czechoslovakia had a new president, Václav Havel, the leading cultural and oppositional figure, and the new president of its federal assembly was Alexander Dubček, the dismissed party leader of 1968.

The remarkable tranquillity of most of the revolutionary year 1989—the smoothness of its "velvet revolutions"—probably would be so striking were it not for the exceptions. On November 20, Nicolae Ceauşescu opened the Fourteenth Congress of the Romanian Communist Party with defiant phrases condemning his fellow dictators for losing their grip: "What do we say to those who want to lead the way to capitalism? What were they doing when they were in positions of responsibility? The answer is they used their jobs to block socialism and did not serve their people." But Ceauşescu himself could offer no more than the timeworn tweaking of Moscow, obliquely questioning the 1939 Soviet grab of Romania's Bessarabia. Whatever the secret background of his remarkable and bloody downfall, which commenced less than a month later with the demonstrations in Timişoara and ended with his summary execution on Christmas Day, it is clear that the growing opposition within sections of Ceauşescu's party and army, helped along by well-wishers in foreign governments, came to the conclusion that the increasingly irrational dictator and his retinue could not be persuaded to depart peacefully.

Romania's National Salvation Front might very well be little more than a group of Communist chameleons, but Ion Iliescu and his friends, spurred by the fury of a long brutalized people, managed to restore a semblance of normality to a country that had been one of Eastern Europe's nastiest dictatorships. Freedom of assembly, the end of Ceauşescu's "systematization" plan, whereby dozens of Wallachian villages were razed, the end to the practice of exporting some 80 percent of Romania's foodstuffs in order to retire foreign debts, lights on the streets, and more heat in the houses may not be synonymous with Western pluralism. It is otherwise by Romania's standards. Much the same can be said of Albania, where the regime of Ramiz Alia had to contend with massive and dramatic flights of people in July 1990 and student demonstrations the following December. As for Yugoslavia, the republic-based split in the ranks of its League of Communists in January 1990 and the party's subsequent demise simply confirmed that the future of that country depended on the party's cohesion. Without the Titoist party, without a dictatorial core at the center, Yugoslavia could not survive as a coherent political entity. The effective dissolution of Yugoslavia meant that each of its republics found a separate path to a broad variety of post-Communist models, ranging from the Czechoslovak and Hungarian patterns in Slovenia and Croatia to the Romanian pattern in Serbia.

The first and perhaps foremost result of the revolution of 1989 was the end of the Communist monopoly in politics. Political pluralism meant the revival of party politics, although not all parties were new, and not all were politically influential and capable of competing equally with the remnants of the Communist apparatus. The temptation to root the Communists out of public office, indeed out of all positions of leadership, was tempered with concern for the requirements of an orderly transition and fear of perpetuating Communist methods. Inexperience and the atmosphere of mistrust (especially of joining political groups), dislike of party discipline and bureaucracy, and the quick proliferation of myriad parties all contributed to the bumpy start of new democratic habits. Yet, no matter how haphazard the electoral process and how difficult the course for the emerging parties, the first series of free elections in Eastern Europe since the war (excepting the early postwar elections in Czechoslovakia and Hungary) went ahead with great confidence.

Contrary to general expectations, these contests, whenever free of manipulation, could not be won by the Communists or even the broader Left. Not counting Poland's semi-free elections of June 1989, when the Communists protected themselves by agreement against a total electoral defeat in the lower house, or the electoral farce performed by Serbia's strongman Slobodan Milošević in November 1989 (when the 82 percent electoral support claimed for Milošević, added to the showing of the other three Communist candidates for the Serbian presidency, came to a total of 104 percent), the elections of 1990 in East Central Europe (not the Balkans) were generally won by the center-right parties. The tactical considerations of the Communist period, when opposition theorists kept devising ways of removing the Communists gradually, were no longer relevant. The electorate wanted a quick jump into pluralist democracy and an even quicker one into the hoped-for prosperity of free-market capitalism. Power-sharing and halfway solutions were disparaged. Instead of being greeted as the potential president of a Social Democratic German confederation, Willy Brandt found his campaign appearances in the GDR marred by inauspicious slogans, such as "Willy! Never again socialism."

At first it appeared that German exceptionalism was at work. The existence of the GDR was predicated on a systemic difference from "capitalist" West Germany. Small wonder that, in East Germany's elections of March 1990, the Christian Democrats ran on a platform of speedy reunification and even speedier introduction of West German currency to the East. West Germany's Christian Democratic chancellor, Helmut Kohl, stirred up East German expectations of an immediate changeover into the sort of society that obtained in the West, an anticipation that permitted his East German sister-party to sweep the go-slow, pro-neutralist, anti-NATO, and anti-unitarian parties of the Left. Ironically, it was the voters of the industrial south who gave clear majorities to the Alliance for Germany, a conservative coalition dominated by the Christian Democrats. The Alliance won in Leipzig (51 percent), Gera (59), Dresden (60), Suhl (60), Erfurt (61), and Karl-Marx-Stadt (61). The showing of the ex-Communists was no less surprising. They won as much as 30 percent of the vote in East Berlin and led the Social Democrats in Neubrandenburg and Dresden. Alliance 90, the party formed by the old GDR dissidents, including the New Forum, did surprisingly poorly, gaining less than 3 percent of the ballots. Overall, the first (and last) democratically elected

East German parliament (Volkskammer) had 193 deputies from the Alliance for Germany (48 percent), 21 (liberal) Free Democrats (5 percent), 87 Social Democrats (22 percent), and 65 ex-Communists (16 percent). The dominant force in East Germany was clearly the center-right Christian-nationalist bloc. The socialists of various hues represented almost two-fifths of the electorate. The liberals were in a decided minority.

It soon became evident that the East German electoral results were in some ways not exceptional. The Hungarian elections of March-April 1990 also favored the center-right Christian-nationalists, including the populist Hungarian Democratic Forum (43 percent), the Independent Smallholders' Party (11 percent), and Christian Democrats (5 percent), who jointly formed the first post-Communist government. But, in a reversal of the East German pattern, the Hungarian liberals turned out to be stronger than the Left. The two liberal parties (Free Democrats and Young Democrats) polled 24 and 5 percent respectively and became the main oppositional force. The Left fared poorly. The reformist ex-Communist Socialists won some 9 percent of the vote. The orthodox Communist Hungarian Workers' Party and the Social Democrats got less than the required threshold of 4 percent needed to win parliamentary seats under the proportional electoral law.

A similar pattern, though with a significantly better showing for the Communists and weaker gains by the liberals, obtained in Slovenia and Croatia, where the multiparty elections were held in April and May of 1990, but the trends are much more difficult to follow in these elections because of the peculiar three-chamber parliaments inherited from the Communists and the winner-take-all Communist-crafted electoral law in Croatia, which unintendedly helped the nationalist opposition. The Slovenian Christian-nationalist bloc won a little over a third of all votes and together with the Social Democrats (approximately 7 percent) and others formed the governing coalition. Slovenia's reformist ex-Communists (Party of Democratic Reform) gained 18 percent of the vote and the liberals some 16 percent. In Croatia, counting the results of the second round of parliamentary elections, the populist center-right Croat Democratic Union won 43, 41, and 23 percent of all votes in three chambers respectively, which, however, put it in absolute control of the parliament. The reformist ex-Communists (Party of Democratic Change) gained as much as 31, 32, and 27 percent respectively, and the liberals, various socialists, and traditional Christian Democrats insignificant percentages.

Elections in Czechoslovakia, in June 1990, departed from this trend only in degree. The country's governing, though unelected, protest movement—Civic Forum and its Slovak equivalent, Public against Violence—was really liberal in orientation, especially the wing led by Finance Minister Václav Klaus. Its showing, in the representative House of the People of the federal parliament amounted to 47 percent, or 53 percent in the Czech lands and 33 percent in Slovakia. Nevertheless, the Forum/Public chose to enter into a coalition with the Christian Democrats (9 percent in the Czech lands and 19 percent in Slovakia), showing that the liberalism of the anti-Klaus wing was hesitant in matters of privatization, or, as Havel put it, in "selling off the family silver." The Czechoslovak less-than-reformist Communists were relatively strong, at a level 14 percent in both the Czech lands and Slovakia, helped especially by the votes of Bohemia's rust belt, and the other Left parties were relatively weak. The elections in Bosnia-Hercegovina and Macedonia, as well as Lech Wałęsa's victory in Poland's presidential elections, in November and December of 1990, complete the success story of the center-right/nationalist trend in East Central Europe.

It was otherwise in the Balkan countries of predominantly Eastern Orthodox culture. Without any particular insistence on the cultural roots of the phenomenon, it must be stressed that reformed—and sometimes fully recognizable—Communists won clear electoral victories in Romania, Bulgaria, Serbia, Montenegro, and Albania. The tendency was not universal. Communists were strong, but did not prevail in predominantly Orthodox Macedonia, and Albania is not properly an Orthodox country. All the same, the trends in the Balkans demonstrated a less radical tendency in dealing with the remnants of the Communist regime. The Romanian case is particularly striking, as it points to all kinds of untidiness left behind by Ceauşescu, including the political behavior of former members of the Communist Party, the party itself having been banned by the revolutionary authorities. To be sure, the ruling National Salvation Front publicly has stood for multiparty democracy, social democracy ("Swedish model"), a market economy, and national reconciliation. Nevertheless, the Front was not just the home of former dissidents. It was more obviously the logical organization of Communist officials and military officers. More to the point, the Front has not encouraged pluralist discourse. Its treatment of political opponents, whom Iliescu typically dubbed "hooligans," has not been gentle. Front activists have disrupted opposition meetings, and several opposition campaign workers may actually have been killed.

Romania's opposition consisted of some sixty parties, but the only viable ones were the old prewar Liberals and National Peasants, both led by returned exiles. The issues were the Front itself and its electoral fairness. On May 20, 1990, the Front gained a clear victory. In parliamentary elections it won 66 percent of the votes and two thirds of the seats. Iliescu took the presidential election with an overwhelming majority of 85 percent. The Liberals and the National Peasants were left far behind, the second strongest party being the Democratic Hungarian Union, a party representing the Hungarian minority, which won 7 percent of the votes.

The Bulgarian elections were more nuanced, but nevertheless were the first clear vote for reformed communism. The old Communist organization was revamped and given the new Socialist Party label. Echoing everywhere else, the new/old Socialists argued for multiparty democracy and a market economy, but they continued to be entrenched under their old Communist personnel in their old centers, particularly in the provinces. The Union of Democratic Forces (UDF), the alliance of oppositional groups, consisted of some sixteen parties, notably the 1980s dissident organizations (Club for Glasnost and Democracy, free trade union Podkrepa, Independent Society for Human Rights, Ecoglasnost) and two historic parties (Social Democrats and the anti-Communist wing of the Agrarian Union). In the June elections for the single-chamber assembly, the Socialists won 52 percent of the vote and the UDF 36 percent. Nevertheless, soon after their victory the Socialists were embarrassed by revelations that one of their leading members, Petŭr Mladenov, the country's acting president, had argued for the use of tanks against demonstrators in December 1989. Mladenov was obliged to resign. He was replaced by the UDF leader Zheliu Zhelev in August 1990.

The overwhelming Socialist (ex-Communist) victories in Serbia and Montenegro (December 1990) were conducted under conditions of national mobilization, the opposition in these two Yugoslav republics being itself compromised by national exclusivism. The opposition that echoed Milošević's national communism was also (as a result?) significantly weaker than the opposition in Bulgaria. In addition, Milošević was helped by the electoral boycott of the Kosovar Albanians. The elections of March-April 1991 in Albania itself were safely won by the Communists (renamed Socialists), but not without embarrassments. The ex-Communists won 68 percent of the vote, to 25 percent for the permitted opposition, Sali Berisha's Democratic Party. Yet the Communist leader, Ramiz Alia, lost in his Tirana constituency. But is the unsure grip of the ex-Communists (or are they neo-Communists?) sufficiently strong to characterize the changes in the Balkans as no more than bogus revolutions?

That remains to be seen. Milošević and Alia, like Iliescu and the Bulgarian Socialists, are not presiding over the most stable polities in Eastern Europe. The real question is whether they will be able to satisfy the popular pressures for a semblance of prosperity. In East Central Europe, too, there was little thought of a market economy based on private property before the sudden collapse of communism. All sorts of halfway solutions—self-management, worker ownership, social ownership—were in vogue in Poland and Hungary before 1989. Yet these were radical ideas only a year before Poland's deputy prime minister in charge of the economy, Leszek Balcerowicz, imposed his bold and controversial stabilization program.

East European transition will depend on both boldness and common sense. Bold changes can be effective only in a responsive social and political environment. The absence of any great scheme that would replace Marxist-Leninist orthodoxies can initially be an advantage. The growth of the culture of tolerant citizens—a civil society, to use a useful, if mystified, buzzword—will take a great deal of time and effort. National independence will have to be strengthened before any possible integrations can be pursued. United Germany and a weaker Soviet Union, together with the demise of the Warsaw Pact, have recast the power relations in the region. With a bit of luck, the long-term effect will favor European and regional cooperation.

The dislocations endemic to systemic changes will keep Eastern Europe boiling for years. Are there any additional "subjective" destabilizing forces on the horizon? The "revival" of nationality conflicts is generally seen as a capricious development and an argument for apprehension about the East European future. But even in Yugoslavia, where national conflict has escalated into civil war, the issues are not irrational or evidence for the supposedly choleric temperament of the Balkan nations. The national question is an eminently political and ideological question. It was necessarily revived after the collapse of communism, since Communist regimes repressed every autonomy, including that of national groups. Can long-repressed nations be blamed for connecting freedom with independence? Instead of trying an ideological lobotomy of an a-national liberal sort, Western politicians and pundits would do well to analyze the real causes of national conflicts and to devise ways of relieving them. It must always be remembered, however, that democracy is not necessarily a panacea in the thorny area of nationality relations. Were it otherwise, by way of example, there would be no Irish question.

Non-Communist Eastern Europe will continue to have a politicized future. The expressionists and the new national establishments, who are not necessarily the Right, will find arguments for the restabilization of post-Communist polities. The cultural relativists and evolutionists, who are not necessarily the Left, will be predisposed to deny an immense human capacity to adapt to anything that appears "unnatural." In the words of the Serbian aphorist Aleksandar Beljak, "You do not have to lead us any further, the rest of the road is known."

Remaking the Political Field in Hungary: From the Politics of Confrontation to the Politics of Competition

László Bruszt and David Stark

Hungary in Comparative Perspective

The cataclysmic dissolution of Communist regimes and the clamorous awakening of the East European peoples in 1989 prompted observers to overestimate the strength of organized democratic forces in these events. The stunning electoral victory of Solidarity in June, the public drama of Imre Nagy's reburial in Budapest that same month, the street demonstrations in Leipzig in October, and the massive assemblies in Prague in November were all signs of popular strivings for democracy. But many observers mistook the enthusiastic expression of these aspirations as evi-

This chapter is based on the first stage of analysis of data gathered by the authors on the transition from state socialism in Hungary. The data include interviews conducted by the authors with the leaders of the major opposition parties as well as with numerous high officials in the Hungarian Socialist Workers' Party, including all members of the party's Presidium, the minister of foreign affairs, the minister of internal affairs, and the heads of the party's delegations to the Round Table negotiations; transcripts of the Round Table negotiations; detailed minutes of the opposition umbrella's strategy sessions; and data from public-opinion surveys conducted throughout the transition period. Data collection was supported by a grant from the National Science Foundation, and the data archive will be housed in the Hungarian National Archive and the Archive Department of Olin Library at Cornell University.

For comments on an earlier draft we thank Ellen Comisso, Monique Djokic, Peter Katzenstein, Victor Nee, Mark Selden, and Sidney Tarrow. Research for this paper was supported by a grant from the National Science Foundation and by a postdoctoral fellowship from the Joint Committee on Eastern Europe of the American Council of Learned Societies/Social Science Research Council.

dence of far-reaching democratic organization and misinterpreted the first stage of transition as the already-achieved triumph of citizenship and civic values.

This overestimation of the strength of democratic forces in 1989 was a direct consequence of an overestimation of the strength of Communist party-states in the previous epoch. If only months earlier the "totalitarian" regimes of the region were cast as powerful, stable, and immutable, their sudden demise could be explained only by equally powerful forces organized for democracy. Behind the metaphors of volcanic eruptions of democracy and popular revolutions sweeping aside powerful tyrants was the idea that strong states could be toppled only by strong societies.

The contrary view contains its own share of misunderstandings but is probably closer to reality: rather than strong states confronting strong societies, the more typical cases in Eastern Europe in 1989 were moments in which weak states faced weak societies. Instead of powerful party-states, this view sees cumbersome but weak bureaucracies, ineffective for achieving the goals of economic growth and social integration, headed by demoralized leaders whose belief in their own ideologies had withered apace with the exhaustion of their political and economic programs.[1] From such a perspective it is no longer necessary to invoke a "democratically organized society" as the agent that "overthrows" the old order. Of course, the citizenry of Eastern Europe did act in 1989. But, with the exception of Poland, these were extraordinarily weak civil societies without organizations strongly rooted in the citizenry, without leaders experienced in national politics, without elaborated economic and social programs, and without deeply engrained traditions of democratic habits and practices.

One modification of this "weak states/weak societies" approach would be to maintain some notion of the party-states of Eastern Europe as weak (with limited sovereignty and only feeble capacity to achieve stated goals) but to shift from a dichotomous view of civil societies as either strong or weak and instead regard the level of development of autonomous organization as a continuous variable.[2] A rough ranking of the societies of

1. These were states, moreover, with limited sovereignty, due, by 1989, not to direct control by Moscow so much as to dependence on foreign creditors and international lending institutions in Washington and Bonn.
2. The concept of civil society under state socialism here refers to the self-organization of society in spheres of activity relatively autonomous from the state. Civil society would be more or less strong depending upon the level of development of social and economic autonomy, independent political organization, and civic values. On the concept of civil society, see

Eastern Europe along such a dimension would yield the following (from high to low): Poland, Hungary, the German Democratic Republic (GDR), Czechoslovakia, Bulgaria, Romania, and Albania. Such a preliminary exercise suggests interesting hypotheses given that this rank order correlates directly with the ordering of transitional events and inversely with a ranking of the speed of the first stage of the transition in the countries in the region.

Despite the observation that the relative strength of civil society seems a good predictor of the timing and sequencing of upheavals in Eastern Europe in 1989, we would argue that this notion of strength and weakness still remains misspecified. In the first place, the degree of organization of civil society should be analyzed not simply relative to that of other cases but, more important, in relation to the forces obstructing (or promoting) change inside the ruling elite. We argue that these relations can be only partially captured by objective and static measurements of the relative strengths of hard-liners and reformers (inside the regime) and moderates and radicals (in the opposition). The critical measure of these capacities is not the analyst's but the actors', and the interactionist framework that we propose directs attention to their *perceptions* of the strategies of their opponents. Moreover, as we shall see below, these capacities, perceptions, and strategies are fluid rather than fixed. In fact, as our case illustrates, the political organizational identities of the major social actors change as they react to and interact with other competing strategies in the political field.[3]

In the same way that we shift the focus of analysis from relative strengths to strategic interactions "internal" to the particular national cases, so we shift attention from preoccupation with relative timing to interactive effects among the cases in the East European transitions. That is, the relationship among the various countries is not simply that some

John Keane, ed., *Civil Society and the State* (London, 1988), and, especially, Andrew Arato, "Revolution, Civil Society, and Democracy," *Cornell Working Papers on Transitions from State Socialism,* no. 90–5 (1990). On the "second economy" as a sphere of relative autonomy, see David Stark, "Bending the Bars of the Iron Cage: Bureaucratization and Informalization under Capitalism and Socialism," *Sociological Forum* 4, no. 4 (1990): 637–64.

3. For more detailed discussion of this interactionist model, see László Bruszt and David Stark, "Negotiating the Institutions of Democracy: Strategic Interactions and Contingent Choices in the Hungarian and Polish Transitions," *Cornell Working Papers on Transitions from State Socialism,* no. 90–8 (1990). This interactionist framework draws from the work of O'Donnell, Przeworski, and Schmitter. See Guillermo O'Donnell, Philippe C. Schmitter, and Laurence Whitehead, eds., *Transitions from Authoritarian Rule: Prospects for Democracy* (Baltimore, 1986); and Adam Przeworski, "The Games of Transition," unpublished manuscript, University of Chicago (1990).

cases come earlier or later but that experiences in earlier cases have demonstrable effects on patterns of change in the later cases.[4] But this learning process is actually obscured and distorted by diffusion or contagion models that present the experiences of the stronger (bolder) civil societies as charting the course to be emulated by citizens in countries where civil society was far weaker.[5] As we shall see, not only citizens but also actors within the old elite learned from observing the processes and outcomes of the interactions of rulers and opposition in other countries.

Attention to the ranking of the strengths of civil societies and the sequence and speed of transitions across the East European countries is further misleading because it perpetuates the widely held misconception that they represent simple variations on an underlying theme—as if there were some basic unitary phenomenon called "East European Transition" against which we could measure the particular cases as differing in degree, whether that be the intensity, speed, or level of development of the assertion of democratic impulses.[6] In our view, however, these cases differ not simply in degree but in kind. The year 1989 was one not of Transition in Eastern Europe but of a plurality of transitions with diverse paths to different types of political institutions.[7]

During the course of 1989, regime leaders throughout Eastern Europe faced various forms of organized confrontation from society. The particular interactions of rulers and opposition, however, yielded different paths

4. In the language of comparative methodology, purely structuralist comparative explanations using the methods of similarity of differences are inappropriate here because the country cases are not independent.

5. See, for example, Valerie Bunce and Dennis Chong, "The Party's Over: Mass Protest and the End of Communist Rule in Eastern Europe," paper presented at the Annual Meeting of the American Political Science Association, San Francisco, August 1990. For another review of the countries of Eastern Europe as cases of contagion, see Adam Przeworski, "Transitions and Reforms: East and South," unpublished manuscript, University of Chicago (1990).

6. Our perspective should similarly be counterposed to views of the East European cases as a unitary phenomenon in which "Gorbachev pulled the plug and the water ran out" (personal communication from a prominent area specialist). Our analysis of the Hungarian case in light of comparisons with Poland and other countries in the region indicates that there was not a single "Gorbachev effect" striking each of the countries with the same resonance.

7. For provocative discussion of the multiplicity of modes of transition, see Terry Karl and Philippe C. Schmitter, "Modes of Transition and Types of Democracy in Latin America, Southern and Eastern Europe," unpublished manuscript, Department of Political Science, Stanford University, 1990; and Juan Linz and Alfred Stepan, "Democratic Transition and Consolidation in Southern Europe (with Reflections on Latin America and Eastern Europe)," paper presented at the Conference on Problems of Democratic Consolidation: Spain and the New Europe, Madrid, July 1990.

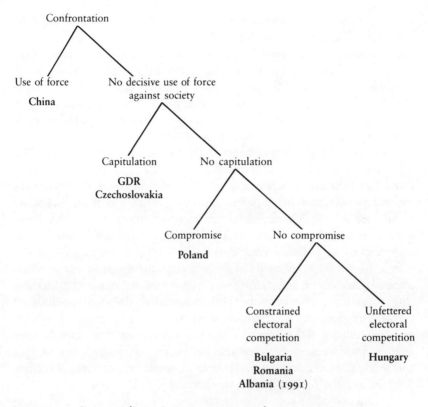

State socialist regime responses to confrontation in 1989

in the first stage of transition:[8] in some countries regime leaders capitulated, in others they attempted to maintain some hold on power (in part or total) through compromise or through electoral competition. The accompanying figure depicts these alternative paths in a preliminary typology. China is included among the "revolutions" of 1989 as that case

8. Following O'Donnell and others writing on Latin America and southern Europe, we make a distinction in this paper between the first stage of transition (of extrication from authoritarian rule and the establishment of new political institutions) and a second stage in which democracy is either consolidated or stagnates. (See Scott Mainwaring, Guillermo O'Donnell, and J. Samuel Valenzuela, eds., *Issues and Prospects of Democratic Consolidation: The New South American Democracies in Comparative Perspective* [Notre Dame, Ind., 1991]). In the East European cases, the critical aspects of the second stage of transition involve not only the question of whether democracy is consolidated but also the question of whether property relations and economic processes are transformed.

where state socialist leaders used massive force to crush the democratic opposition. Because of their very different geopolitical circumstances, regime leaders across Eastern Europe were unable or unwilling to bear the costs of the decisive use of force.[9] The limited use of force against some demonstrators in the GDR and Czechoslovakia, in fact, proves the rule: in the final moment of the crises of escalating public demonstrations, lacking either the ability or the resolve to use decisive force, these East European rulers capitulated and their regimes collapsed.

In the other cases, key segments of the Communist leadership did not capitulate. Instead, they negotiated compromise agreements containing provisions for institutional guarantees for some aspects of their power or entered into direct electoral competition without such guarantees. Poland is that case where Communist reformers struck an agreement that guaranteed their continued control over critical institutions not exposed to the uncertainties of electoral competition. In Hungary, Bulgaria, and Romania, by contrast, segments of the old elite attempted to use electoral competition as the very means to stay in power. Bulgarian and Romanian elites (and later, also the Albanian) managed to do so successfully (if perhaps temporarily) by renaming their parties, holding early elections, and maintaining tight control over key institutions that severely constrained their weak electoral rivals.[10] Hungary followed a different path and it had different outcomes. There the interacting strategies of the opposition and the ruling elite led to unfettered competition.

The different paths (capitulation, compromise, competition, and so on) of extrication from monocratic state socialism in Eastern Europe, moreover, have yielded different transitional institutions in the new polities of the region. That is, the strategic interactions of rulers and opposition (as well as patterns of conflict and alliance among competing opposition

9. The geopolitical differences include the full range of changing relations in the region, including not only the relationship to the Soviet Union under Gorbachev but also the weight of economic dependence on, and increasing political pressure from, the West. The peaceful character of the revolutions (Romania excepted, but see below) is one distinctive feature of the East European cases as a set. Discovery of an explanation for the absence of force (Gorbachev's unwillingness to send repressive assistance, the Communists' shattered morale, etc.) across the cases should not be mistaken as demonstration of the unitary character of these upheavals.

10. It might be objected that Romania does not belong under the same major East European branch of "no decisive use of force against society." Our reading of studies by Vladimir Tismaneanu, Gail Kligman, and Katherine Verdery leads us to see Romania as a case of intra-elite violence. That is, Bulgaria and Romania are similar as instances where one part of the elite orchestrates a coup against the oldest guard. Unlike Bulgaria's, Romania's palace coup was not peaceful and was coordinated with a popular uprising that in itself lacked leadership and organization.

forces) have created different political institutions and rules of the game across these cases. The rapid reconfiguration of the political field as a field of party politics in the Hungarian case of unfettered electoral competition, for example, differs dramatically from the Polish and Czechoslovak cases. Similarly, Hungary's parliamentary system contrasts markedly with Poland's presidential system. In short, the diverse (and possibly divergent) transitions in Eastern Europe are producing different kinds of political fields with considerable variation in the relationships within the political elite and between them and their respective societies. Attention to the differences in the broad contours of these restructured political fields might reveal not only that the cases differed in the intensity and forms of conflict during the period of extrication but also that the institutional arrangements in the first stage of the transition can have consequences for the capacities of these new political fields to consolidate democracy and to transform the economy in the second stage of the transition. In such a view, it is important that we study the recent past because the problems and prospects of the consolidation of democracy and the transformation of economic relations in the next stage of transition during the coming decade have been shaped by the broad configuration of political institutions (however transitory) established during the first stage.[11]

These important differences in institutional "outcomes," we argue, are not simply a by-product of differences in the relative strengths and weaknesses between power holders and oppositions in the respective countries. Instead, these differences can best be understood by focusing on the different dynamics of interactions between rulers and opposition (including their perceptions of strengths and weaknesses as well as perceptions of opponents' strategies), their changing perceptions of their geopolitical situations, and their learning from elites and opposition elsewhere in Eastern Europe.

Our task in this essay is to analyze these processes in the Hungarian transition with the aim of understanding the specificity of its route

11. The danger of studying the illusive "What will happen next?" (the correlate of seeing only stability and stagnation in the previous epoch) is particularly acute in the analysis of contemporary Eastern Europe. In our view, we still know far too little about what actually happened during the 1980s in the various countries of the region. Thorough comparative research about the recent past, moreover, is a necessary corrective to the tendency to over-emphasize discontinuities between state-socialist and post-Communist institutional configurations. In analyzing the results of the "fall of communism," we argue that the differences in how the pieces fell apart have consequences for how political and economic institutions can be reconstructed in the current period.

through unfettered electoral competition. It is precisely to encourage the reader to draw out comparative insights throughout our explication that we do not adopt the conventional formula of concluding with "implications of the Hungarian case" but instead open by highlighting some of the comparative issues that motivate our analysis. Stated differently, understanding the specificity of the Hungarian case requires some comparative reference points. All too briefly: in Poland and Hungary, leaders of weak party-states at the outset of the transition period attempted to increase their capacities for economic change by reforming but not entirely dismantling the political institutions of the old regime. In both cases, reform Communists eventually entered into agreements that resulted in the negotiated demise of Communist rule. But despite their similarities as negotiated transitions the Polish and Hungarian cases differ dramatically in the institutional outcomes of the first stage of transition. Our task will be to explain how the perceived weakness of the Hungarian opposition (in its interaction with hard-liners and reformers in the ruling circle) led to the creation of an uncompromised parliamentary system there—in contrast to the Polish case, where the perceived strength of the opposition yielded a compromised institutional arrangement marrying aspects of liberal democracy and one-party rule to produce a malformed parliamentarism as its offspring. In Hungary, reform Communists facing an opposition not only much weaker than Solidarity but also with a different organizational identity and different institutional configuration perceived an opportunity to stabilize their power better through direct electoral competition without guarantees.

We should not conclude from this observation, however, that the conventional wisdom is correct in seeing Hungary as a case where regime change was initiated from above. Quite the contrary, Hungarian reform Communists were spurred to action only when confronted by the organized opposition—whose earlier strategy of compromise was replaced by a strategy of mobilization and uncompromised confrontation in response to a direct challenge from party hard-liners. It was the opposition's strategy of mobilization and confrontation (provoked by threats to its organizational survival) that evoked images of larger-scale popular upheaval, catalyzed the polarization of the forces inside the regime, and precipitated the reformers' ascendance within it. Yet it was also the anticipated electoral weakness of these same oppositional forces that allowed reform Communists in Hungary to change the party's course from the politics of confrontation to the politics of uncompromised free competition.

It is this attempt by (renamed) Communist/Socialist leaders to take advantage of the perceived weakness of civil society that marks the point of comparison between the Hungarian, Bulgarian, Romanian, and Albanian cases. Only in the later cases (with their hastily called and arguably less freely contested elections) does this strategy succeed. But their success should not distract us from regarding the Hungarian case as the first example showing the possibility of using electoral competition to salvage Communist rule.

The Promise of Compromise

In the summer of 1988, Hungary appeared to be that country in Eastern Europe most likely to embark on political reforms of a compromised character that would have institutionalized some form of power sharing without questioning many of the basic prerogatives of the Communist Party in the political system. Hungary's organized opposition was vocal, visible, and a force to be reckoned with but was, nonetheless, far too weak to challenge the power of the party-state directly. Under these conditions, it seemed a willing and able candidate for a junior role in a reformed political system. The reform wing of the Communist Party, moreover, was certainly eager to engineer such a move. And although the reform Communists had not yet consolidated a hegemonic position within the party, compromise was unquestionably on the agenda in a country where even party hardliners based their legitimacy on the claim not simply to be "reformers" but to be the leaders on the path of change in socialist Eastern Europe. From all sides one could hear of the search for a compromise solution to the questions of political power in order to "unite all forces" to solve the nation's momentous problems. Talk of some forms of "institutionalized power sharing" was everywhere in the air.

This promise of compromise issued not from some surge of fresh optimism following the ouster in May 1988 of János Kádár and his retinue from the pinnacle of the Hungarian Socialist Workers' Party (Magyar Szocialista Munkáspárt—MSzMP) but from a growing sense of foreboding crisis.[12] Hard-liners, party reformers, and independents (who, it

---

12. On the removal of Kádár see George Schöpflin, Rudolf Tökés, and Iván Völgyes, "Leadership Change and Crisis in Hungary," *Problems of Communism*, September–October 1988, 23–46. For the best analytic description of change in the Hungarian economy during the Kádár era and criticism of the limitations of reform economics, see János Kornai, "The Hungarian Reform Process: Visions, Hopes, and Reality," in Victor Nee and David Stark, eds., *Remaking the Economic Institutions of Socialism: China and Eastern Europe* (Stanford, Calif., 1989), pp. 32–94.

should be emphasized, had not yet coalesced into an "opposition") shared a basic perception of the situation:

- Left unchecked, the widening scope and quickening pace of Hungary's downward spiral into economic, social, and political crisis could lead to chaotic threats to the social order.
- Reducing this threat called for large-scale economic changes of a qualitative character far beyond earlier efforts to reform the economy.
- The economic measures required to remedy the situation would unavoidably impose yet additional burdens on society and possibly further erode public confidence.
- Economic changes must, thus, be accompanied by some changes in the nation's political institutions.

The major political actors differed, of course, in the scope and type of political changes proposed as well as in the rationale for them. To increase the role of the market in the economy and reduce tensions in society, the conservatives positioned around Károly Grósz (the party's new first secretary) advocated weakening the direct role of the party apparatus, giving a freer (but not unconstrained) hand to the press, and strengthening the position of "interest organizations" (such as the trade unions, agricultural associations, and other similar satellite organizations). Unlike Kádár, who had remarked with bravado that "what Gorbachev is trying to do now, we already accomplished decades before," Grósz saw that Hungary was actually lagging behind the Soviet Union in the field of political reforms. He was acutely aware that by losing its image as "ahead of the pack" Hungary was losing millions of dollars and Deutsche marks in aid and credits during a period when its hard-currency foreign debt was doubling in only two years.

Placing greater emphasis on the importance of popular support to transform the economy, reform Communists in the circle around Imre Pozsgay stressed a liberalization of civil society that would allow greater scope for organizations that were genuinely autonomous from the party-state.[13] So great was their emphasis on dialogue ("a partner is needed")

13. Imre Pozsgay began his career as a party apparatchik in a provincial county. By the 1970s he had become a reformist minister of education and culture and had established close ties to the populist writers (who later created the Hungarian Democratic Forum) and to some reformist intellectuals. Later, as the leader of the Patriotic Front, a satellite organization of the MSzMP, he offered shelter to some newly emerging independent initiatives. By the second half of the 1980s, he was appealing to selective aspects of the legacy of Imre Nagy,

that they appeared at times to envy their Polish counterparts, who faced, in the still illegal Solidarity, a strong antagonistic but potential interlocutor. For their part, the leaders of Hungary's fledgling opposition movements (or "alternative organizations" as they were so labeled at the time) were vocal advocates of measures that would institutionalize their participation in affairs of state.[14]

The "alternatives'" arguments for institutionalized power sharing represented an important development in the evolution of the rhetoric of the Hungarian opposition. During its infancy earlier in the decade, its simple plea to the party-state to *Respect human rights* had become the call to *Constrain yourself* as it called on the authorities to separate state and society, to restrict state activities to those prescribed in rules of law, to allow some scope for societal self-organization, and to provide equal rights for small-scale private property. By 1987, with increasing frequency and volume, Hungarian critical intellectuals did not encourage the authorities simply to exercise self-restraint but voiced a qualitatively new challenge to the party-state: *Allow yourself to be constrained.* Rather than imploring the state to draw the boundaries across which it would not interfere with society, they now called on the state to allow society a voice in drawing those boundaries. The next step was to advocate that representatives of civil society autonomous from the party be able to cross those boundaries to participate in decision making inside state institutions. Rather than calling on power to limit itself, it now called on the state to *Share power.* Such co-decision would not be based on relations of parity; the meaning of power sharing was far from sharing power equally. In 1988 and still as late as early 1989 the rhetoric of compromise from the Hungarian opposition was voiced as *Your prerogative to have special discretionary rights will not be questioned, but our rights to a voice should be institutionalized inside the state.*

Compromise, moreover, was on the political agenda not only in principle but also in detailed blueprints for institutional change. Budapest was

---

who had identified the Patriotic Front as an institution for societal consultation. By the end of the decade he was moving publicly to appropriate the mantle of Imre Nagy, prime minister and Communist Party leader in the revolution of 1956.

14. In mid-1988 the number of "alternative" organizations was still under ten, but by the end of that year more than fifty organizations were listed in the first book that tried to map the "alternative scene," and many more were starting to form. Although some organizations had several thousand members, most had only a few dozen. The majority of these new organizations, movements, circles, clubs, networks, and independent trade unions were organized by Budapest-based intellectuals and their organizations did not extend beyond Budapest and several larger provincial cities.

full of compromise proposals circulating in networks of communication that crisscrossed the boundaries of opposition and officialdom.[15] Typical of these was the "Social Contract" written in 1987 by the editors of *Beszélö*, the most influential samizdat journal of the democratic opposition.[16] The institutional changes outlined in "Social Contract" resembled the transition from unenlightened despotism to a constitutional monarchy in which the party's Central Committee would be the reigning but constitutionally constrained monarchy with a two-chamber parliament giving special rights to the upper house (which, like the British House of Lords, would not be elected but *selected* from above) and allowing for the creation of a lower "House of Commons" with members elected via competitive elections.

Focusing on such concrete proposals provides insights into the very precise and specific ways in which a variety of political actors were attempting to design institutions for political power sharing. But to grasp the fundamental motivations underlying these intense preoccupations with finding a resolution of the crisis we must understand how the search for compromise solutions in 1988 was everywhere underscored by the legacy of 1956. Although suppressed from public attention, memories of the lost revolution of 1956 were never forgotten across the decades, and signs of crisis were the surest stimulant for recalling this haunting past. For the Communist elite, the ghosts of 1956 were the memories of the fury that can be unleashed when society has been pushed beyond its limits. It was above all the *fear of society* that so deeply inscribed in the Communist leadership an instinct to do everything to avoid another 1956. As the economic and political crisis deepened throughout 1988, so increased the references to 1956 in party leaders' speeches. In mid-November, for example, party ideologist János Berecz (certainly no liberal reformer) drew out the "lessons of 1956." Noting the growing "deterioration in the country's situation" and pointing to the mounting "crisis in confidence and pressure from the increasing social dissatisfaction," Berecz asked: "Will revolutionary restructuring [of political institutions] or will chaos provide

15. One precursor of compromise solutions was offered by reform economists inside and outside the Ministry of Finance. Their *Fordulat és reform, Medvetánc* 1987/2 supplement, was initiated in a series of semipublic debating forums under the auspices of the Popular Front. Political scientists and sociologists were quick to follow with detailed blueprints of institutional changes centering on Parliament and related constitutional questions. See, for example, Béla Pokol, "A politikai rendszer reformjáról," *Valóság* 1986, no. 12; and László Bruszt, "A többszólamu politikai rendszer felé," *Valóság* 1987, no. 5.

16. János Kis, Ferenc Köszeg, and Ottila Solt, "Társadalmi Szerzödés," *Beszélö*, June 1987.

an answer to the great historical questions of Hungarian development? We cannot avoid this question when we analyze the tragic experiences of Hungary's recent past. This dilemma emerged between 1953 and 1956 too, . . . and the fact that forces in the party and society which demanded renewal failed to meet in solving the conflict should serve as a lesson that is valid to this very day. The result: Hungarian blood flowed on each side." To halt the deterioration of political crisis into chaos, Berezc concluded, "Our nation's interests require us to find today the points of a national consensus which could represent the framework and substance of a compromise. . . . The party is unable to implement the political renewal on its own. There is no such force in the society that could carry out this task on its own. Thus, the need for collaboration and cooperation is an elementary consequence."[17]

If it was the fear of society—the fear of the transformation of the economic crisis into social and political crisis similar to that of 1956— that pushed the leaders of the regime to seek a compromise with the organized forces of the society, it was the lesson of the Russian intervention in 1956 that made the leaders of the newly emerging social and political groups hesitant to question the legitimacy of the regime and to seek, instead, a compromise with its leaders. Mikhail Gorbachev did not automatically alter those calculations, for the limits of his toleration were neither clearly articulated nor yet tested in this period.[18] Moreover, until the showdown with Egor Ligachev in October 1988, his political survival was itself a question mark.[19] As late as 1987 the authors of "Social Contract" concluded: "One cannot count on the Soviet bloc's disintegration within the foreseeable future. And there is no real chance of one or another of the satellite countries breaking away, either. But there is an opportunity for the satellites to increase their relative independence from the Soviet Union." Under circumstances where Gorbachev's stability was far from certain, they argued, "The more we are able to get the Soviet leadership to accept today, the more we will be able to defend later during

17. János Berecz in *Népszabadság*, November 19, 1988, p. 5.
18. Gorbachev and other Soviet leaders explicitly rejected the Brezhnev Doctrine and articulated the "Sinatra Doctrine" ("Do it your way") several times throughout 1988–89. But the first clear test of the end of the Brezhnev Doctrine was the Soviets' acceptance of the non-Communist Mazowiecki government in Poland.
19. Hard-liners in the MSzMP based their plans, similar to those of Bulgarian, Romanian, Czechoslovak, and East German leaders, on the hope of Gorbachev's fall. Their hopes were dashed when Ligachev lost his game against Gorbachev at the meeting of the Central Committee of the CPSU in October 1988.

a possible backlash."[20] Given these perceptions, some measure of cooperation and considerable willingness for compromise, if not outright coalition, seemed the wiser course.

Thus, with little exaggeration we can say that the end of 1988 still marked a period of the "long fifties" in Hungarian history. The legacy of 1956 and the contradictions of Kádárist policies from 1957 onward were still everywhere in evidence. Throughout the decade of the 1980s, nearly every major party program had begun with some variant of the formula: *We must make big changes in the economy to prevent the explosion of society. Society has reached the limits of its tolerance.* But execution of the policy changes prescribed in each of these programs was blocked in part by the fear of popular response to the growing burdens that would be the inevitable outcome of the policies.[21] By 1988 the economy was as bankrupt and exhausted as the theory of reform economics. It was no surprise to Hungarians that state socialism was an economy of shortage, but now there was also inflation and talk of unemployment. Stabilization and economic transformation would exact yet additional sacrifices from a society already short on patience. How could popular support for such changes be secured?

The situation was thus very similar to that in Poland. In both cases, leading opposition figures were ready to accept a compromise solution on the condition that it place limitations on the powers of the party-state and legalize and institutionalize the "right of society" to have its own autonomous representative organizations. In both countries, moreover, leading figures inside the Communist Party were talking about dialogue, cooperation, and the need for institutional changes to facilitate society's support for the economic changes. The difference in Hungary was that, precisely at the time that compromise seemed most likely, the reformers were still too weak to speak in the name of the regime and the opposition was much too weak to speak in the name of society. Although there was a perceived need, a justification, the political will, and concrete institutional programs for compromise, the two major political actors who most favored compromise in 1988 did not have sufficient political power to bring it about. But, as we shall see in the following sections, the closer that reformers and the democratic opposition came to establishing the conditions for negotiating a compromise, the more it became apparent that a

20. Kis, Köszeg, and Solt, "Társadalmi Szerződés."
21. Throughout the 1980s the government revoked each of its programs for economic stabilization because it feared the social tensions they would produce. The first program of stabilization to bring real results was the one endorsed by the opposition parties at the end of 1989—three months after the signing of an agreement establishing free elections.

compromise solution was an illusive and perhaps self-defeating strategy. In the end, both reform Communists and democratic opposition shifted from strategies of institutional compromise to strategies of unfettered electoral competition. But they did not arrive at that "solution" directly. The perceived weakness of the opposition made it an inviting target for the party's hard-liners, who favored institutional changes only as long as they controlled all the terms. It was the hard-liners' strategy of confrontation and the opposition's confrontational response that ironically strengthened the hand of the reformers and finally brought Communists and democrats to the negotiating table. Thus, in the course of only ten months, Hungry moved from the politics of impending compromise, to the politics of escalating confrontation, to the politics of electoral competition.

The Politics of Confrontation

The Strategy of the Hard-liners

If Imre Pozsgay and fellow reform Communists saw in the political crisis a pressing need to enlist the participation of the representatives of the organized political opposition, the conservatives who still controlled the party had their own ideas about the course to bring about "national consensus and cooperation." Basic to their strategy (in our view, definitional of hard-liners from late 1988 to mid-1989), was the notion that *a multiparty system could be created by the party itself* through political institutions that allowed for "consultation with society." The remedy for social crisis was limited liberalization within society and not democratization of the state. The desired result of these changes would leave virtually every fundamental political institution of the old order intact. The cornerstone of that strategy was confrontation through a variety of means, frequently combining frontal attacks and attempts at institutional incorporation in the time-honored practice of dividing and conquering.

The hard-liners first considered the option of attempting to eliminate the nascent independent organizations. The tactical maneuver of attempting to criminalize the opposition was brief (coinciding for the most part with the apparent resurgence of a hard-line faction in Moscow in October 1988) and half-hearted.[22] Cracking down on "dissidents," however invit-

22. It was during this period that the hard-line ideologist János Berecz (quoted above) referred to himself in an interview as the "Hungarian Ligachev" (*Reform*, 1988, no. 1). See also the infamous speech in which the party chief, Károly Grósz, referred to the opposition as portending the danger of "white terror."

ing to the hard-liners, would have sullied the "nice guys" image they had worked so hard to construct. To conform to the new "rule of law" line coming from Moscow and to keep their hands clean for IMF handouts, the Hungarian regime would have to tolerate the opposition and constrain them through legal means alone.[23]

If the autonomous political organizations could not be eliminated, the next step was to try to neutralize them. For the party hard-liners, the closing months of 1988 and opening months of 1989 were a period of defensive liberalization:[24] If some new political institutions are inevitable, then let us shape them as much as possible after our own image, seemed to be their thinking. First, they attempted to push through the parliament a new law on association that would give the party-state unlimited control over the formation of independent organizations. When the earlier ritualized practice of submitting the proposed legislation to "social debate" backfired, the hard-liners retreated and then, in an attempted outflanking maneuver, even accepted the principle of a multiparty system, pledging the party's commitment to its prompt realization at the February 1989 meeting of the Central Committee.[25]

Unsuccessful in their attempts to refigure the opposition to their own likeness and constrained by geopolitical circumstances to operate within strictly legal means, the hard-liners were then determined to ensnare the opposition precisely on the terrain of legality. They accepted a multiparty system but then proposed that the parliament (where 75 percent of the representatives were party members) adopt a new constitution allowing only for the existence of political organizations that accepted "socialism." The task of protecting the societal goal of developing socialism enshrined in the constitution, moreover, would fall to a special constitutional court whose members would be appointed for life by the Hungarian Socialist

23. In addition to their general moderating influence, foreign governments, creditors, and other international agencies often directly expressed their policy preferences to the Hungarian leadership. In part the protests of international trade union federalists and intensive negotiations between the Hungarian government and the ILO and the U.S. Department of Labor curbed the hard-liners' attempt to pass new regulations that would have restricted the right to strike and organize trade unions. For example, extending the protection of the Overseas Private Investment Corporation (OPIC) to U.S. investors in Hungary required certification by the AFL-CIO that the Hungarian labor code protected trade-union pluralism.

24. For a more elaborate discussion of "defensive liberalization," see László Bruszt, "Hungary's Negotiated Revolution," *Social Research* 57, no. 2 (1990): 365–87.

25. The Western media misinterpreted this decision when it called it a decision about "giving up the monopoly of power" of the Communist Party. In fact, the decision more closely resembled the following calculation: if our North Korean or East German comrades are able to thrive in "multiparty systems," why can't we make such accommodations?

Workers' Party. This court would rule on the constitutionality of legislation passed by a newly elected parliament and would have the responsibility for the registration, or nonregistration, of political organizations.

At the same time that it tried to weaken and marginalize the opposition, the hard-line faction also tried to incorporate, coordinate, co-opt, and corrupt the opposition. While some autonomous organizations were referred to as *ellenzék* (opposition), others were *ellenség* (enemies). The latter received only opprobrium; the former might be promised resources in highly selective bargaining on a one-by-one basis: "So, your party would like to get back its former headquarters from the pre-1948 period?" or "We hear that your organization is still in need of a telephone line."

More important than trying to pick off the various independent organizations through backroom deals, however, was another divide-and-conquer tactic of attempting to separate public negotiations. By February 1989, with the MSzMP committed to a multiparty system and with Polish Communists already engaged in their Round Table negotiations with Solidarity, it became obvious to all political actors that some kind of national forum must be convened to discuss the creation of new political institutions. To this end, the leaders of the Communist Party initiated efforts at a series of separate, bilateral negotiations with various organizations, including some of the independent organizations that were beginning to call themselves political parties. When this tactic failed to split the opposition, the hard-liners still hoped that they could conquer even if they failed to divide. At the end of March, the party's Central Committee issued a call to all the major social organizations (including its satellite organizations, such as the National Council of Trade Unions) and virtually all the major opposition organizations for the creation of a national Round Table to be convened on April 8.

The hard-liners' conception of a national Round Table of "harmonization and reconciliation" was to downgrade independent organizations to the level of its satellite organizations—as organizations representing only partial social interests. As the ultimate guardian of social order and national sovereignty during this difficult transition, the party's "historic role" was to act as the big broker. This emphasis on negotiation was thus a new development in the party's claim to "represent society"; yet it was but merely a step to a higher stage of paternalism.[26] Now no longer as the

26. On the concept of paternalism as applied to state-socialist political systems, see Ferenc Fehér, "Paternalism as a Mode of Legitimation in Soviet-Type Societies," in T. H. Rigby and Ferenc Fehér, eds., *Political Legitimation in Communist States* (New York, 1982).

monopoly holder of Truth but as the *prime negotiator* did the party claim to represent general societal interests. In assuming this posture, the hard-liners did not perceive themselves as a party to a two-sided negotiation between the representatives of power and the representatives of civil society. Instead, in their conception of a Hungarian Round Table the party, as prime negotiator, would resemble a teacher sitting before a class of unruly students or an arbiter before so many squabbling disputants in small-claims court.

But the opposition refused to accept such a paternalistic framing of the negotiations and issued a united refusal to attend the April 8 meeting. Formal negotiations between the Hungarian Socialist Workers' Party and an umbrella federation of the democratic opposition would be inaugurated only on June 13. In the interim, the reformers around Imre Pozsgay had gained the support of intraregime forces to confront the hard-liners with a new conception of the party's future. In challenging the party's old paternalistic representational claims, they established a framework for the Hungarian Round Table negotiations more closely approximating the civic principles of electoral competition in liberal democracies. To understand the ascendancy of the reform Communists, we must turn to analyzing the strategy of the democratic opposition in its interaction with the hard-liners' strategy of confrontation.

The Strategy of the Opposition

At the end of 1988, the independent organizations of Hungary's civil society were neither large nor cohesive nor fundamentally committed to challenging the legitimacy of the Communist regime. In fact, that the category of "opposition" could be used as a collective noun to refer to such a set of weak, diverse, and fragmented organizations would have occurred to almost no one active on the Hungarian political scene. As we shall see, the party hard-liners' strategy of confrontation acted as the catalyst to change all that.

In late 1988 the two largest autonomous political organizations, the Hungarian Democratic Forum (Magyar Demokrata Fórum—MDF) and the Alliance of Free Democrats (Szabad Demokraták Szövetsége—SzDSz), had memberships of just under 10,000 and 1,500, respectively.[27]

27. The Hungarian Democratic Forum was founded as a movement in 1987 by 160 moderate intellectuals, especially populist writers, many of whom had strong ties to the leading reform Communist, Imre Pozsgay (who himself attended the founding meeting at Lakitelek). The MDF reorganized itself as a political party in mid-1989. The Alliance of Free Democrats was the organizational offspring of the Network of Free Initiatives created by radical Budapest intellectuals, many of whom were outspoken dissidents in the 1970s.

With no institutionalized means to coordinate (or even communicate about) the activities of the proliferating alternative political organizations, the MDF and the SzDSz each offered to be the umbrella under which other movements and independent-minded citizens could stand as the two organizations competed for the right to speak in the name of society.[28] More urban, liberal, and secular, the Alliance of Free Democrats (together with the Federation of Young Democrats, or FIDESZ) was earlier inclined to a more radically challenging posture vis-à-vis the regime. The populist writers of the MDF, on the other hand, were more likely to give expression to the national issues and Christian traditions of Hungary's rural society, and its politicians were initially more cautious about directly confronting the authorities. The MDF leaders asserted repeatedly that they were neither an opposition nor aligned with power. In this moderate posture they were typical of Hungarian "alternatives" before 1989.

A measure of the opposition's willingness and ability to challenge the legitimacy of the regime can be taken by examining a series of public demonstrations from June 16, 1988, to June 16, 1989. On the latter date, one-quarter million Hungarians assembled in Budapest's Heroes Square to honor and rebury the former prime minister Imre Nagy and other heroes of the 1956 revolution on the anniversary of their execution. For the same commemoration only one year earlier in 1988, police easily dispersed a small crowd of only several hundred people when virtually all independent organizations chose to stay away from a demonstration whose premise directly challenged the legitimacy of the regime.

The beginning steps toward a more radical approach were taken in September 1988 when a group of environmentalists took the initiative to organize a demonstration before parliament that succeeded in gaining the endorsement of the major independent organizations in a protest against the construction of a dam on the Danube. The demonstration was the first major public questioning of the legitimacy of parliament, whose members had been chosen in elections that were competitive in name only. "Democracy or Dam!" the protestors declared. And, when the parliamentary representatives (including all the leaders of the party's reform wing)

28. By late 1988 there were over fifty organized independent groups. These included such organizations as the Federation of Young Democrats (Fiatal Demokraták Szövetsége, or FIDESZ) founded by young law school students in March 1988 as the first independent group to declare itself a "political organization." The first independent white-collar trade unions were created by scientific and cultural employees in the early summer of 1988, and the League of Independent Trade Unions was established in December of that year. The changing political field also saw the reemergence of parties that traced their lineages to some of the pre-1948 political parties. The Independent Smallholders' Party was organized in September 1988, the Social Democratic Party of Hungary in December 1988, and the Christian Democrats in early spring 1989.

bowed to the intimidation of the hard-liners and voted to continue construction, some of the "alternatives" organized successful public campaigns for the recall of several representatives.

If the environmentalists' demonstration illustrated the potential gains of more active mobilization, the hard-liners' threats provoked recognition of the potential costs of failing to do so. That is, it was the hard-liners' threats escalating confrontational policies that determined the urgency and the timing of the opposition's shift toward popular mobilization. By late 1988 and early 1989 the alternatives faced a conservative party leadership that was vilifying them in public, drafting piece after piece of legislation to exclude some organizations or tie the hands of those it legalized, and launching constitutional initiatives that promised to marginalize any surviving autonomous organization from any serious participation in political power. The alternatives could retreat, or they could change to a strategy of confrontation, popular mobilization, and efforts at undermining the legitimacy of the official political institutions. By the spring of 1989 most chose the latter course. And in mid-March the major independent organizations formed a loose umbrella federation to coordinate their activities.

Although it is clear how the hard-liners' assault could make it a vital issue of organizational survival for the alternatives to demonstrate their popular support, it is less immediately obvious how that attack contributed to bringing about considerable cohesion among disparate oppositional groupings. The fact that no single party or movement was sufficiently strong enough to challenge the party on its own might be seen as a factor pressing the alternatives toward mutual cooperation as an opposition. That is, perhaps it was the very fragility of the individual opposition organizations that provided the basis for their unity. But as any good game theorist or historian knows, the potential benefits of cooperation posited in the abstract are not sufficient to explain why some projects of collective action cohere and others dissipate. The problem is even more acute in this case where the party was promising resources to organizations that would defect from or never join an oppositional coalition.

The emergence of an oppositional umbrella federation becomes understandable when we consider the following: forced to conform to the formalities of *glasnost'* and to its own rules of "social debate," the various public forums that accompanied the party hard-liners' policies of defensive liberalization increasingly provided the occasions for opposition figures to assemble. Every draft of each new piece of legislation (the new law on strikes, the law on association, the proposed constitutional changes, and so on)—however restrictive in intent and however short the time given for public reaction—yielded another opportunity for the experts and organizers of the opposition movements to meet. More important, at these meetings, and then increasingly while working to prepare joint position papers, the opposition leaders punctuated their words in early 1989 with references to 1948. Entering the stage of declaring their groups opposition political parties, the leaders of the independents were led to reflect on the disappearance of opposition parties during the postwar period when Communists succeeded in the divide-and-conquer tactics their counterparts were attempting to emulate in the present. The alternatives' leaders reminded themselves and each other that although some opposition parties had been eliminated quickly while others lasted for a short time in coalition with the Communists, none survived. If they were not to repeat past mistakes, the nascent opposition groups would need to find some institutional means to coordinate their efforts. Whether the analyst uses the language of "iterative games" or of "collective memories," Hungary's young opposition parties had learned important lessons from a previous confrontation. Thus, increasingly over the course of the early months of 1989, public statements responding to this or that party initiative were circulated for endorsement by numerous independent organizations. In some cases the list of signatory organizations was longer than the text in which the independents collectively confronted the party with a blunt and dismissive challenge.

If the memories of 1948 provided the negative lesson, then the anniversary of 1848 celebrated on March 15 provided the occasion to manifest the opposition's shift in identity and strategy. Communist party authorities, of course, hoped to fit the anniversary into their plans of marginalizing the opposition by incorporating it. Under the auspices of the Patriotic Front, they issued an invitation to most, although not all, of the autonomous organizations to participate together in commemorating the Revolution of 1848. The national holiday could become a celebration of national unity in which everyone wanting "democracy" and a "multiparty system" could march together under the party's slogans for "renewal."

But in the streets of Budapest on March 15, 1989, not one but two commemorations were held. Twenty-four alternative organizations refused the party's invitation. Instead, they organized their own demonstration, which was attended by more than 100,000 participants and overshadowed the official ceremonies. That demonstration was the public signal that the alternatives could also play the politics of confrontation. In terms most concrete (Are you going to *their* demonstration or to *ours?*), it began the process of redrawing the boundaries of the political space along dichotomous lines between officialdom and the opposition. It was the act of standing with power or with those challenging power that created an "opposition." The March 15 demonstration was the performative action that made possible the mutual self-recognition of an oppositional identity transcending the boundaries of the various participating organizations. Eight days later, on March 23 in the building of the law faculty under the auspices of the Association of Independent Lawyers, representatives of eight independent organizations met to formalize this new identity by establishing a mechanism for coordinating their activities. Acknowledging their commitment to resolving differences in a framework of equality, they called their umbrella federation a "Round Table." Confirming their newly formed collective identity, they specified it as the "Opposition Round Table" (Ellenzéki Kerekasztal, or EKA). The stated purpose of the metaorganization was to create the basis for a common stance vis-à-vis the MSzMP, "the power holders."

The formation of the Opposition Round Table fundamentally altered the map of Hungarian politics. Its consequence was to unite and radicalize the opposition and eventually to polarize the political camps. At the beginning of 1989, even the more radical groups in the democratic opposition such as the SzDSz still made distinctions between reformers and hard-liners and discussed the possibility of alliance with the party's reformers. Their perceptions and depictions of the political landscape had changed dramatically by the time that EKA was founded only months later. In the lengthy debates and discussions that marked the first meetings of the new umbrella federation, the representatives of all the organizations of the EKA opposition (ranging from radicals to moderates to those who had only recently resigned their membership in the party's organizations) came to agree that there were only two political camps in Hungary: on the one hand, those who represent the "monopolistic power" *together with* those who want to make compromises with them, and, on the other hand, those who want to re-establish popular sovereignty. Against the party's paternalistic representational claims, the EKA representatives argued, first among themselves and later to the public, for an alternative legitimating claim based on purely civic principles: *The political and economic crisis cannot be solved by any kind of "power sharing." The solution to the crisis is not for power to be shared with society but for power to be legitimated by genuinely free, fully contested, elections. Anyone who disagrees with this principle, and anyone who is*

willing to compromise this principle, is with "them."[29] On the new political map being drawn by EKA there was no intermediate space, as there
had once been only months earlier, between "the paternalistic power"
and "democracy." Those who continued to speak about the need for
reforming the system and who claimed that they were using their power to
empower society for the future, the opposition argued, were but the Siren
voice of monopoly power, which only obstructed *transforming* the system
to one in which power resided in the citizenry. To the party's strategy of
attempting to delegitimate, marginalize, and divide the opposition, the
opposition now answered with its own strategy of delegitimating, marginalizing, and dividing the holders of power.

Although the opposition figures were committed to the escalation of
confrontation as the only means to arrive at a situation where they could
negotiate with the representatives of the regime on terms that recognized
them as major political actors, few were optimistic that these goals could
be achieved in a short time. Their plans for further demonstrations as
"tests of strength" looked to dates already marked well ahead on the
calendar. May 1 (Labor Day), June 16 (the anniversary of the execution of
Imre Nagy), October 23 (the anniversary of the revolution of 1956). They
could use these opportunities to challenge the regime's legitimacy and
expose its "naked power." Their reading of the changed geopolitical situation suggested that they could now move onto territory that was once
unimaginable, but also that they could do so only as long as Gorbachev
was in power.[30]

The Results of the Politics of Confrontation

The same perceptions that emboldened the opposition worried the
power holders in offices high and low. With the use of force ruled out as

29. The precondition for cooperation within EKA was acceptance of the principle that
the relative levels of support of the various parties of the opposition could be determined
only by free elections. That is, only free elections could adjudicate among the competing
claims to speak in the name of society. Acceptance of this principle, of course, could not
entirely suppress the problem of measuring the relative power of organizations within the
opposition. In the absence of free elections, other tests of strength could be attempted; but
they were illegitimate in terms of the explicit self-conception of the Opposition Round Table.

30. At the time of their negotiations from February to April, the Polish opposition still
did not trust the "End of Yalta," and the formation of their strategies was shaped by
considerations of some of the imperatives of the empire. Late in the spring, leaders of the
Hungarian opposition (encouraged in part by Gorbachev's apparent toleration of the Polish
developments) shaped their strategy on the assumption that they were—at least temporarily
under Gorbachev—"outside Yalta." Whereas the Polish opposition spoke about "self-
Finlandization," the slogan in Hungary was "Back to Europe!"

an option, with a more liberal law on association ensuring that opposition groups would not be eliminated, and with the hard-liners' policy of attempting to freeze out the opposition not only sputtering but backfiring, officeholders at the local level and members at the party's base were the first to voice concern.[31] Hungarian television had broadcast the parallel and competing March 15 demonstrations into every home. Local party officials could see which was the larger demonstration, and it was simple arithmetic to calculate from trends which side's numbers would grow in future demonstrations. To those sensitive to shifts in the political winds, moreover, the opposition's refusal to attend the Round Table of April 8 signaled the futility of the hard-liners' hopes of dividing the opposition.

As the first to feel politically vulnerable, local officials and party activists were among the first to respond to the newly drawn boundary lines. Local apparatchiks had been early to see the impossibility and absurdity of the orders coming from above to marginalize, co-opt, corrupt, or divide and conquer the independents. From their vantage point, the strategy of confrontation would not work when combined with deteriorating economic conditions and liberalized regulations allowing for genuinely autonomous political organizations. By late March and early April they were sending the message upward that *instead of trying to eliminate the opposition, we should be competing with them to offer better alternatives.*

Party members who were not officials in the apparatus were even more fearful that a cataclysmic rupture of the social order might threaten their personal safety or destroy their professional careers. Afraid that the party's leadership was headed toward the brink of disaster, they began to take organization into their own hands. "Reform Circles" within the party's local branches had already begun to emerge at the end of 1988; by April they were sprouting up everywhere and taking the local party organizations as their targets. From one provincial city to the next, reformist Communists ousted conservative leaders. From one county to the next, they battled successfully to hold party conferences to remove the staunchest supporters of Károly Grósz in the Central Committee. The Reform Circles were slowly, almost imperceptibly at first, but then more

31. The continued existence and growing legitimacy of the opposition parties were further strengthened when, starting from early 1989, Western delegations (presidents, prime ministers, party leaders, and parliamentarians) officially invited by the Hungarian government also held meetings with representatives of the opposition organizations. Increasingly as the spring progressed, such foreign delegations scheduled meetings with their Hungarian opposition-party counterparts before meeting with representatives of the government.

rapidly and visibly, encircling the party leadership. Their chorus: *the hard-liners' policy has become a most damaging liability. We cannot let ourselves be trapped with "them."* By late April some Reform Circles were not only calling for unconditional acceptance of the EKA's preconditions for negotiations but were also threatening to spit the MSzMP and create a new socialist party that would join the EKA opposition. The party was disintegrating at its base.

Defections from the conservative policy line were not limited, however, to local party organizations. Throughout the spring, an increasing number of parliamentary representatives indicated their independence from party discipline. Together with the growing visibility and unpredictability of the "Independent Faction" this demarcation of a dichotomous boundary inside parliament made things increasingly uncomfortable for "them." With each new day more and more high-ranking party officials and governmental bureaucrats were discovering that in their hearts they had always been reformers, and the press (now unleashed and hungry) was scarcely able to conceal its derision as it described yet another regime figure's conversion on the road to Damascus. So it was that on April 25, Prime Minister Miklós Németh (an appointee and protegé of Károly Grósz) took the unprecedented step of calling an evening television news program to repudiate a speech of Grósz and distance himself from the party hierarchy.[32] The *government* was clearly separating itself from the *party.*

May 1, the last glorious celebration of the highest (and only remaining) party holiday, marked the next stage in the polarization of the political field. With enough sense to avoid the traditional viewing stand located at the site where Stalin's gargantuan statue was torn down in 1956, the Communists had convened their May Day rally in the city's central park, where the party boss, Grósz, addressed the celebrants. But following the successful formula of March 15, the opposition also held a rally, this time organized by the League of Independent Trade Unions. Estimates vary— but the question was whether the opposition's crowd of 60,000 to 100,000 was ten times or only six times larger than the audience that came to hear Károly Grósz. With both rallies adjourning to separate public forums, the League used this opportunity to orchestrate the first

32. Miklós Németh was a leading representative of a new generation of young technocrats, mainly economists, who worked for rapid marketization of the economy but made compromises with the party apparatchiks in the 1980s by accepting important positions in the state and party bureaucracies. His public realignment with the party's reform faction was a dramatic indication of the party's crumbling hold on state institutions.

public appearance of the EKA representatives as a collectivity. Both forums were televised in question-and-answer formats; the Independent Unionists' contacts among television reporters, producers, and technicians yielded proportional coverage, perhaps as important as the content: fifty minutes for the ruling party, fifty minutes for the united opposition.

The growing defections from the ruling bloc accelerated exponentially throughout the month of May. Their timing was caused less by the events of the past than by those of the future. After the May Day celebrations, all the political actors began to orient toward the next public demonstration of political identity and strength in which they would be forced to take a position. The next date circled on the calendar was June 16, the anniversary of the execution of Imre Nagy. Under the pressure of public opinion, domestic and international, the Grósz regime had been forced to accept the reburial of Nagy and his close associates.[33] Although the results of complex negotiations between the Committee for Historical Justice and the authorities were publicly announced only on May 24, everyone in leadership positions had known for weeks that it was impossible to avoid granting permission for a public ceremony to honor the fallen heroes of the failed revolution of 1956. It was not difficult for them to imagine the possibilities for a dramatic declaration, demarcation, and enactment of the boundaries of "them" and "us." *Regardless of your cosmetic surgery and the new labels you now use for yourselves,* the opposition stated in effect, *you are still those who came to power with the Soviet tanks. You represent the interests of the empire and even now, when the Russians give us a chance to loosen the chains, you are still trying to salvage your power with reformist tricks.* With each day, the time bomb ticked louder, threatening an explosive release of the ghosts of 1956.

Thus, whereas the hard-liners' strategy of attempting to divide the opposition had the effect of pushing the independent organizations together, the opposition's strategy of attempting to portray hard-liners and reformers as conjoined had the effect of forcing an open division within the ruling bloc. For the party's reform Communist leaders it was now a race against time. They had forty days to show that instead of a well-meaning but subordinated junior faction they were in a position to exert the decisive, if not entirely uncontested, leadership of the government and the party. Hundreds of thousands were likely to be in Heroes Square on June 16, and a national audience would watch the funeral on television. Would

---

33. Károly Grósz had conceded to the reburial as a "humanitarian gesture" after repeated questioning by reporters during his visit to the United States in 1988.

they see a dichotomous line drawn between "society" and "power," between "democracy" and "paternalism," between "popular sovereignty" and "illegitimate rule"? Or, would they see ambiguity and blurred boundaries—government officials in the nation's colors mourning heroes slain by foreign aggressors, and Communists advocating popular sovereignty? To defuse the dangerous dichotomy and inject even the slightest ambiguity into the public drama, the reformers would have to do more than remind reporters that Imre Nagy, too, had been a Communist or that the party's official commission had recently concluded that 1956 was neither revolution nor counter-revolution but a "popular uprising."[34] They would have to demonstrate that they had the strength to turn the party's policies from regarding the opposition as enemies to regarding them as equally legitimate aspirants to holding governmental office, and they would have to bind themselves publicly to a course of negotiating the institutions of electoral democracy. To do so they would have to dethrone, or at least neutralize, the reigning conservatives and navigate a complex series of intense prenegotiations to bring the opposition's mobilization for June 16. That is, it was the anticipation of the calendrical event that produced effects preceding its occurrence.

One-quarter million Hungarians filled Heroes Square on June 16, 1989. They and the national television audience heard the morning's reading of the names of fallen martyrs and the afternoon's speeches honoring the executed prime minister and denouncing the still-occupying foreign army. But they also saw three politicians bear wreaths and stand silent beside the coffins: Imre Pozsgay, minister of state and representative of the government; Miklós Németh, prime minister; and Mátyás Szürös, president of the parliament.[35]

For the millions who watched the eight-hour television broadcast, June 16 did not prove to be an unambiguous demarcation of "us and them."

34. On the meaning of Pozsgay's efforts to recategorize 1956, see Bruszt, "Hungary's Negotiated Revolution," pp. 365–87.
35. Although the party hard-liners (represented by the Central Committee secretary György Fejti) refused permission for public reburials, the *government* (represented by Prime Minister Németh) endorsed the reburial and cooperated with the organizers of the public ceremony. In exchange for this cooperation, the government was able to send three senior representatives of the reform wing to Heroes Square. In his speech in Heroes Square, Viktor Orban, the leader of the Federation of Young Democrats, commented on their presence: "We young people are unable to comprehend that those who not so long ago were still reviling in chorus the revolution and its prime minister have suddenly come to realize that *they* are the continuers of Imre Nagy's reform policies. We also fail to comprehend that those party and government leaders who had decreed that we be taught from textbooks which falsified the revolution are now practically scrambling to touch these coffins, almost as talismans that will bring them good luck" (*Magyar Nemzet*, June 17, 1989, p. 4).

The divide between the representatives of naked power and those of popular sovereignty did not emerge. Although they were the last to be cognizant of the danger, by the end of May even the hard-liners saw the need to defuse the situation. So as not to be the last in the castle, they moved with uncharacteristic speed and solicitousness to reach agreement with the united opposition for direct and almost unconditional negotiations. On June 10—six days after the electoral debacle of the Polish Communists and six days before the reburial of Imre Nagy—representatives of the MSzMP and the EKA signed an agreement to enter into negotiations to construct the new political institutions of liberal democracy. The Trilateral Negotiations at which the new rules of the game were written opened on June 13 in the parliament building. The opening speech on the part of the EKA was delivered by Imre Konya, who had chaired the first organizational meeting of the opposition umbrella only months earlier. Speaking for the Communist Party was Károly Grósz, the architect of the party's confrontational strategy. At a Central Committee meeting ten days later, Grósz was officially placed under the tutelage of the party's three leading reformers, who were assigned the task of heading the party's delegation at the negotiations.

The Politics of Competition

Accepting Uncertainty

In the summer of 1988, we recall, Hungary had seemed a likely candidate for an institutionalized power sharing: leading figures inside and outside the regime could point to concrete proposals for a compromise solution to the generally perceived crisis. But reform Communists at that time were still too weak to grant concessions in the name of the regime, and the promising path to compromise was blocked by conservatives, who controlled party policy. By the early summer of 1989, these obstacles to compromise had been removed: the opposition had emerged strengthened by its confrontation with the party's hard-liners, and reform Communists had become the hegemonic (although far from exclusive) force within the regime.[36] The road of compromise now seemed clear and,

36. Although the reform Communist leaders were clearly in the ascendance by late May 1989, they had not yet succeeded in removing hard-line conservatives from their midst. Károly Grósz, for example, remained a member of the party's four-person Presidium, and his close associate, György Fejti, was one of the leaders of the party's delegation in the negotiations.

moreover, charted by their Polish counterparts, whose own Round Table negotiations had resulted in comprehensive agreements in April.

But the same processes that eliminated the old obstacles to compromise, in fact, produced new political identities, new goals, and new perceptions of opportunity structures that removed compromised power sharing from the political agenda in mid-1989. The closer reform Communists and opposition groups came to realizing the conditions under which they could negotiate a compromise agreement guaranteeing the ruling party control of designated institutions, the more they came to see compromise as self-defeating.

From the viewpoint of the united opposition, entering into a compromise solution would have undermined their own basis of legitimacy. During the months of confrontation with the old regime, the opposition had developed a coherent rhetoric that had come to serve as the basis of their own self-understanding and of their self-presentation to society. The basic principle that unified otherwise divergent organizations within EKA and the basic principle that orchestrated its appeal to the public during the spring of 1989 were the same: *there is no legitimate power in Hungary today; until legitimate authority is created through fully contested free elections, no organization—including those in the opposition—has the right to decide the nation's future political and economic institutions.* Unless it wished to undercut its own legitimacy, the opposition could not bargain about power sharing and institutional guarantees but could only negotiate about the creation of the institutions and rules of the game for free elections.

Of course, the opposition might have argued to itself and to the public that the balance of forces (domestic and international) were such that it had no other choice but to concede institutional guarantees as the only way to begin the process of democratization. In such a view, Hungarian society, like Poland only months earlier, would be forced to accept a two-step transition (compromise guarantees followed eventually by genuinely free elections) to democracy. But even if the opposition had been willing to retreat from first principles and mitigate the threat to its legitimacy by such arguments of realpolitik, both the Hungarian opposition and the reformers recognized an even more compelling argument against compromise. Imagine, went their argument, that the organized opposition is willing to ignore the illegitimacy of the regime, even temporarily, and agree to a deal. Some might think this will gain the regime time to solve its legitimation crisis, but it will only deepen that crisis. Institutional guarantees will only institutionalize the competing legitimating principles. They will make it dramatically obvious to the whole society that some offices are held on civic principles and others are derived from paternalistic principles—some from elections, and some from deals.

Moreover, they wondered, even if the opposition, from expediency, accepts the conditions of such guarantees, who can guarantee that *society* will accept them? Can the representatives of the organized opposition guarantee that society will not be outraged by a compromise? The independent organizations are strong enough to bring the representatives of the regime to the negotiating table, but they are not strong enough to ensure that society will comply. If compromise provokes an even greater crisis of legitimacy, that crisis will be "yours *and* ours," and when it sweeps the regime away, it will carry along anyone who made a deal with it.

The Hungarian situation at the outset of negotiations in the summer of 1989 thus contrasts markedly with the Polish Round Table launched in February of the same year. The basic premise of Polish negotiations, shared by all sides, Wojciech Jaruzelski no less than Lech Wałęsa, was that Solidarity represented society and spoke in its name. However curious it might sound, although Solidarity's *legality* was one of the subjects for negotiations, its *legitimacy* to speak for society during the negotiations and its credibility to speak to society after the negotiations in enforcing the conditions of the agreement were never in question. That is, in Poland the ruling party had to contend with an opposition that had already established its *claim* to represent society but which sought to reestablish its legal *right* to do so. Because of the perceived strength of the opposition's claims, both the ruling party and Solidarity agreed to compromised political institutions. The government could not risk freely contested elections; and Solidarity did not wish to participate in any. For the ruling party, the price of sharing political power was the recognition of a legal trade-union movement; for Solidarity, the price of legal recognition was the obligation to participate in less than free elections.[37]

In Hungary, by contrast, it was the very weakness of the opposition that forced it to be uncompromising. With their organizational membership

---

37. As Lech Wałęsa stated during the Round Table negotiations: "None of us want these elections. They're the terrible, terrible price we have to pay in order to get our union back" (quoted in Lawrence Weschler, "Reporter at Large (Poland)," *New Yorker*, November 13, 1989). After the June defeat of the Polish Communists, Wałęsa similarly observed: "by a stroke of bad luck, we won the elections" (quoted in Adam Przeworski, "The Choice of Institutions in the Transition to Democracy: A Game Theoretic Approach," paper presented at the Workshop on the Present and Future of Party/State Apparatus in Peaceful Transitions, Budapest, May 1990).

still numbering only in the thousands, and with their strength in society still untested, they could neither make an undisputed claim to speak in the name of society nor anticipate the capacity to call on society to agree to a compromise.[38] For these reasons, the united Hungarian opposition went into negotiations insisting that the goal of any agreement was the establishment of free, open, fully contested, uncompromised elections.

It was not this insistent strategy alone, however, but its interaction with the perceptions and strategies of the reform Communists that brought Hungarian negotiations to an outcome of unfettered elections. As they surveyed the confrontational politics of the spring of 1989, Pozsgay and other leading reform Communists granted that the opposition had demonstrated that it could draw crowds challenging the regime; the question now, however, was whether it could attract voters for its program and personalities. The reform Communists' conclusions were not discouraging. Their potential electoral opponents were young parties with few activists, meager organizational resources, no charismatic leaders, and only shallow roots in the society. If they could seize the high ground as champions of democracy, the reform Communists calculated that with their hands no longer tied by the Brezhnev Doctrine they could use their superior resources, organization, and nationally recognized candidates to defeat the opposition in a straight-ahead electoral contest with no strings attached.

If the basic perception of the electoral weakness of the opposition led reform Communists to conclude that there was no need for compromised institutional guarantees, the Polish election of June 4 was a warning sign of the dangers of compromise. With numerous parliamentary seats assured to them by the Round Table agreements, Polish Communists had proceeded, to the surprise and consternation of the leaders of Solidarity, to lose virtually every contested seat in the election. For the Hungarian reform Communists about to embark on their own talks of national conciliation, the lesson from Poland was not that they should secure even more guarantees but that guarantees can explode when society decides to reject the agreements. Given their electoral expectations, better to risk the uncertainty of free elections than to negotiate certainties that risk spoiling the chance to make a bid for legitimacy.

At the same time that the Polish elections signaled calamities to be

38. It should not be forgotten that Wałęsa had faced critics inside and outside Solidarity who opposed the compromise and even the negotiations themselves (e.g., Gwiazda's "Fighting Solidarność" faction). Wałęsa had succeeded in marginalizing these critics, but the Hungarian opposition could not be optimistic that they would have the means to do the same.

avoided, to the Hungarian reform Communists it also seemed to indicate an opportunity for the taking. By holding a fully contested election without guarantees, Hungarian reform Communists could reclaim the position, temporarily usurped in their view by Polish Communists under Jaruzelski, as the "frontrunners" among state socialist reformers. By winning such an election, moreover, they could achieve a historic precedent as the first Communists in the world to base their power on popular elections. The stakes were high, but the Hungarian reformers were confident that they could secure agreements for early elections and take advantage of a relatively weak opposition to win at least a plurality of the votes in a free election.

The reform Communists' basic perceptions of the opportunities, incentives, and advantages of shifting from a strategy of confrontation to a strategy of competition were bolstered by the results of the first surveys of public opinion on party preferences published in May 1989.[39] According to these early surveys, if elections were held immediately, the Communists would win a decisive plurality of the votes as 36 percent of the respondents indicated their intention to vote for the Hungarian Socialist Workers' Party. This was lower than the most self-confident leaders of the MSzMP had expected but still three times higher than the percentage of respondents choosing the next highest party (the Social Democratic Party).[40] The surveys also indicated that the opposition parties would be hard-pressed to field candidates for national office. A majority of the respondents did not recognize the names of the opposition's leaders, whereas Pozsgay, Németh, and others were not only widely recognized but also growing in popularity. In general, the surveys suggested that Hungarians in 1989 were deeply distrustful of all political institutions and organizations. And although the level of distrust of the MSzMP was so great as to frighten some of the more hesitating regime leaders, the level of support and trust in the opposition was not much higher.[41]

The reform Communists, of course, could not be certain that they

39. László Bruszt and János Simon, "Politikai orientációk Magyarországon a redszerváltás évében," in Bruszt and Simon, A Lecsendesített többség (Budapest, 1990).

40. According to various surveys conducted in the spring and early summer of 1989, the opposition parties were scarcely known to the public. Typically, one-third of the survey respondents could not name a single opposition organization, and another third could name only one or two.

41. In exit interviews conducted during the recall elections in the summer of 1989, the majority of those who declared that they had voted for the Communist candidates told surveyers that they distrusted the MSzMP. Similarly, more than half of those who voted for the candidates of the opposition declared that they did not trust the opposition parties. According to these same surveys, conducted while the Round Table negotiations were in progress, only 13 percent of the respondents agreed with the statement that the EKA represented the "interests of the society."

would triumph in the strategy of competition. But their perceptions of the weakness of the opposition and their assessment of their own electoral prospects gave them confidence to accept that uncertainty. With this they made the decisive step of accepting the principle of "certain institutions of uncertain outcomes" that is at the core of liberal democracy.[42]

Negotiating Uncertainty

By late May 1989 the question was thus how to create the institutions for generating uncertain outcomes. What should be the new procedures for elections and the new rules of the game for a competitive party system? All sides could agree to negotiations in principle, but they disagreed considerably about the scope and character of such talks. To get to the table, they had to resolve the basic questions of the range of issues that should be addressed and who should participate in the formal negotiations. Central to these questions about the framing of the negotiations were the competing legitimating principles of the various sides to the negotiations.

In the prenegotiating stage, the nine organizations of the EKA opposition sought to frame the talks as two-sided negotiations between the representatives of "power" and the representatives of "society." Their self-representation along civic principles dictated that the only issues for negotiation should be those directly related to establishing free elections (for example, party registration, access to the media, and the neutralization of the state's repressive apparatus).

Party conservatives, on the other hand, still insisted on framing the negotiations in terms congruent with their paternalistic representational claims. That principle dictated involving the greatest number of organizations to discuss the greatest range of issues including such distributive issues as housing, labor-market problems, social security, wage indexation, and the like. From the paternalistic vantage point, an immature society would be less interested in the details of legal paragraphs on the negotiating table than in what was to eat on the kitchen table. Hence the legitimacy of the negotiations should rest on the demonstration that "we care about your problems."

With their emphasis on competitive elections, the reform Communists around Pozsgay were making a dramatic departure from the paternalistic themes that had permeated the party's entire postwar history. In the Stalinist period, of course, paternalism had been expressed as *We know your*

---

42. Adam Przeworski, "Democracy as a Contingent Outcome of Conflicts," in Jon Elster and Rune Slagstad, eds., *Constitutionalism and Democracy* (London, 1988).

interests and take your future into our hands, as the party's claim to superior knowledge of long-term interests superseded shortsighted and narrow preferences. Under Kádár, paternalism had no longer been expressed as "we take your future into our hands" but as *We take your interests into account* with the party claiming to represent society as servants who cared about present preferences. Pozsgay's new formula, by contrast, was genuinely postpaternalistic. *We give you back the future as we lead you to democracy,* was his apparent message. This postpaternalistic principle dictated strict adherence to the appearance of democratic propriety, especially to formulas of equivalence of the participants— insofar as they could be made consistent with the latent image that among the equal participants there was an older brother with maturity and experience who could be called on in the most difficult times to lead the younger siblings through the dense forest of extrication from authoritarianism.

The Hungarian Round Table negotiations that opened on June 13, 1989, were ambiguously framed, as civic principles dominated but nonetheless coexisted with elements of late paternalism, reflecting the persistent, but by now minor role, of the hard-liners on the political stage. The range of issues on the agenda (worked out among the various parties in prenegotiation consultations at the beginning of June) seemed a formal, almost equitable compromise between the civic and the paternalistic frameworks: the detailed negotiations of the Round Table would be conducted in twelve subcommittees, six on political questions (constitutional changes, elections procedures, and so on) and six on economic questions (property reform, budgetary reform, and the like). But this apparent compromise was more a facade than the real structure of the negotiations, for the EKA umbrella had succeeded in excluding such immediate issues as wage indexation (in marked contrast to the Polish Round Table) from negotiations. Moreover, as negotiations proceeded throughout the summer, the work of the economic subcommittees receded almost entirely from view, and in the end, no agreements were reached on any economic issues.[43]

The patterns of exclusion and inclusion of participants to the negotia-

43. The opposition parties' relative passivity in the economic subcommittees is not, of course, due to their lack of interest in economic changes. Committed to marketization yet without a mandate to decide the precise arrangements for institutionalizing markets, they (and the representatives of the MSzMP) reached agreement about a most important economic question—but did so outside the economic subcommittees within the political subcommittee on constitutional questions. There they agreed to remove from the constitution the paragraph consecrating the dominant role of state ownership in the Hungarian economy.

tions yielded an apparently even more complex framework of coexisting principles. The negotiations that opened on June 13 were tripartite talks: on one side sat the representative of the MSzMP; on a second side, representatives of the EKA organizations; and on a third side, representatives of the satellite organizations of the party. As with the range of negotiable issues, the inclusion of these last-mentioned "social organizations" was more a face-saving gesture for the party conservatives than a substantive compromise of civic principles. The prenegotiation agreement reached between the MSzMP and the EKA specifically relegated the "third side" to a minor role by stipulating that any agreements reached by the first two sides could not be blocked by the third. From the opening plenary session, these were in actual practice bilateral negotiations, and when the most important representatives of the third side (the official trade unions) walked out of the talks later in the summer, their absence went virtually unnoticed.

More important than this readjustment of the sides of the negotiating table was the reconfiguration of the identities of the actors and of their self-legitimations of the negotiations. In a fundamental sense, the real negotiations in the Hungarian setting could begin only when both sides suspended their claims to represent society. But whom, then, did they represent? As the negotiations proceeded, the answer became clearer: they represented the would-be parties of an anticipated competitive polity. As they negotiated the institutionalization of uncertainty, they were making the new rules of the political game and defining it as *party* politics.[44] The Hungarian Round Table negotiations were the making of a new political class. This was a tremendous work of reconfiguration—not simply of remaking explicit rules and legal codes but of establishing codes of personal conduct with each other and of trying out new vocabularies, rhetorics, gestures, and clothing as party functionaries and dissenting academics became politicians. For this they had an entire summer, largely behind closed doors, away from the glare of publicity.[45] The new rules of

44. As the reform Communists jettisoned the paternalistic principles of the party's past in favor of the competitive principles of its future, the qualitative differences in legitimating claims (with fundamentally different scales for measuring the validity of their stature and weight) that had separated rulers and opposition gave way to the anticipation of a time when their relative strengths could be weighed by a common measure, a unitary political capital, a single currency—the number of votes received from the electorate.

45. A condition for talks had been that all sides desist from any further mobilizations; with good reason it could be seen that escalating the game of counting demonstrators would only interfere with reaching agreements on the electoral rules for counting votes. After the well-publicized inauguration of the talks, no further plenary sessions (and no subcommittee meetings) were conducted before television cameras, and neither side made serious efforts to inform the public about the details of the talks.

the game would be hammered out among those with the highest stakes—the potential winners and losers in electoral contests. Thus, it is far from surprising that the Hungarian Round Table failed to reach any agreements on economic issues. The economic negotiations were paralyzed by this framing of the Round Table structure in which the "parties to negotiation" were exactly that—*parties*, not capital and labor, not peak associations, not corporate groupings, not employers' associations, not trade unions.[46]

Hedging Uncertainty

With the basic triumph of civic principles on the near horizon and with their identities as electoral parties mutually confirmed during each day of the talks, the negotiators now turned to hammering out the specifics of the new rules of the game. There could be any number of institutional arrangements compatible with liberal democracy (a stronger or weaker presidency, direct constituency representation versus party lists, minimum percentages for parties to be seated in parliament, and so on). But each of these would have a differential impact on the actual political success of the various parties.[47] In principle, the opposition parties could participate in designing new political institutions from behind John Rawls's "veil of ignorance" in which none of the actors could know his assets in advance.[48] But as the chances of successful negotiations improved, each organization lifted that veil to scrutinize its potential electoral resources and began to negotiate accordingly. From arguing about principles, the parties turned to calculating the relationship between their interests and particular institutional outcomes. If these political organizations accepted the basic institutionalization of uncertainty, as political parties they each sought the best array of institutions and rules that would provide it some hedge against uncertainty.

Such calculations intensified when, several months into the negotiations, the new party leaders could read the results of actual elections for

46. On the actual economic changes that occurred in Hungary during 1989, see David Stark, "Privatization in Hungary: From Plan to Market or from Plan to Clan?" *East European Politics and Societies* 4, no. 3 (1990): 351–92.

47. Parties who expected to win only a small number of parliamentary seats, for example, would want lower percentage thresholds on exclusion rules. Similarly, parties who inherited historical names known to the public would favor national or regional party lists over local, single-member elections. But such calculations would be especially speculative in a case such as the Hungarian one in 1989, when none of the parties had any previous experience upon which to base their electoral expectations.

48. John Rawls, *A Theory of Justice* (Cambridge, Mass., 1971).

four parliamentary seats recently opened by the recall campaigns. The reform Communists lost every race. This crack in their electoral self-confidence led them to push even harder in the negotiations for the institution of a strong presidency and for scheduling early elections for the position. Perhaps they might not win a plurality in parliament, but with their candidate, Imre Pozsgay, as the only nationally recognized figure in the race they were sure to gain the presidency.

The defeat of the Communist candidates in the summer elections did not, however, raise the entire EKA ship: one party, the Hungarian Democratic Forum, had won all four of the contested seats. The Forum's negotiators now pressed for wrapping up the Round Table talks. As the Forum was the clear frontrunner, they were for striking an agreement and getting on with elections, tactics that coincided with the hopes of the reform Communists. The "smaller" EKA parties meanwhile pressed for relatively strong rights for minority parties in the parliament lest they be squeezed out by the MDF, the MSzMP, or the two in coalition. The resulting package, concluded expeditiously, would have established an eclectic set of political institutions consisting of, on the one hand, a strong parliament with provisions that almost all important legislation would require a two-thirds vote (thus strengthening the voice of minority parties) and, on the other hand, a presidency to be directly elected by popular vote before the parliamentary elections but without especially strong institutional authority. The agreement was signed on September 18, 1989, and presidential elections were scheduled for late November.

But one group of opposition parties examined the package and concluded that the timing and terms of this particular institutionalization of uncertainty would almost certainly lead to their marginalization. While claiming that the parties to the negotiations had no authority to create a new state institution (the presidency), the Association of Free Democrats, from vital self-interest, refused to sign the agreement and launched a national referendum challenging the presidential component of the Round Table package. They were joined in this challenge by the Federation of Young Democrats.[49] Little known to the electorate at that time, they calculated that their best hope to gain attention from the public was a frontal assault on the Communists and those who had "made a deal" with them. That arrangement, of course, had not compromised civic principles. If the reform Communists were likely to win the presidency,

49. The Social Democrats signed the agreement with the qualifier that they disagreed with the creation of the presidency. They and, later, the Independent Smallholders, who had signed the agreement, joined the "front of rejection" in campaigning for the referendum.

that expectation was situational and not an institutional guarantee. But the arrangement, SzDSz and FIDESZ hoped, might be portrayed as a deal. And it could be especially damaging politically if it could be tied in a referendum to three other problems represented as attempts by the Communists to "salvage their power": when they created the presidency, the Round Table signators had failed to exclude the Communist party from the workplace, to abolish the party's armed workers guard, and to provide a process for a public accounting of the party's considerable assets.[50]

In sponsoring the referendum, SzDSz and FIDESZ hoped to increase their recognition and the size of their constituency. Portraying themselves as *the* authentic anti-Communists was the ideal move because it would indirectly question the credentials of the MDF on exactly that score. The more they turned up the volume of anti-communism, the more uncomfortable became the MDF. As signators of the Round Table agreement they could hardly reject the presidential clause in that document. But the temporary coincidence of interests with the reform Communists was now becoming a liability. And so they asked their potential voters to stay home from the polls in the November referendum. SzDSz countered with an effective slogan: "Who stays home votes for the past." The referendum carried by the narrowest of margins.

The reform Communists lost much more, however, than the referendum. They also lost precious time. Had they not insisted on the presidency and moved, instead, into early parliamentary elections soon after the conclusion of the Round Table talks, they might have taken full advantage of the weakness of their electoral rivals, secured a place at least as the second largest party, and perhaps entered a coalition government. Instead, they entered a long winter of campaigning in which their opponents thrived week by week. In losing the referendum, they also lost the ability to use institutional leverage during the course of the campaign. Without control of a popularly elected president they, nonetheless, tried to use some advantages of being the governing party (control of television, for example) until the March elections. But with the public alerted by the referendum to any attempts at "power salvaging," these clumsy moves

50. These problems had been left unsolved because the MDF and the MSzMP reformers had not wanted to waste time in fights with the party hard-liners. The Németh government moved promptly to abolish the workers' guards, remove the party cells from the workplace, and clarify the party's assets before the plebiscitory; but it was already too late.

only sullied their other efforts to demonstrate a commitment to civic values—a key component of their strategy of uncompromised competition once they had abandoned the road of institutional guarantees. Finally, the referendum cost the reform Communists the ability to set the tone of the parliamentary election. Instead of emerging from the Round Table talks as the party that had successfully navigated the nation to the shores of democracy and that was now prepared to lead it into the future, the reformers were forced into a defensive posture as the opposition parties competed among themselves for the title of most authentic anti-Communist. Just at the moment they hoped to be rewarded by the citizens for giving them back the future, the reform Communists were confronted at every turn with their own awkward past.

Once hopeful of being the first Communists to win a popular election, the renamed Hungarian Socialist Party emerged from the March and April 1990 elections with only 8 percent of the parliamentary seats. The victorious Hungarian Democratic Forum, with 43 percent of the seats in parliament, formed a governing coalition with the Independent Smallholders (11 percent) and the Christian Democrats (5 percent). Within less than nine months the Association of Free Democrats had gone from less than 7 percent in opinion polls to becoming the second largest party in parliament. With 24 percent of the seats, it is a strong opposition party.

But the election results tell only one part of the story of the outcomes of the negotiated politics of competition. The institutional outcomes are perhaps even more important. Unlike the strong presidencies that have hijacked transitions from authoritarianism elsewhere in the world, Hungary now has a governmental structure with a weak presidency and a strong parliament.[51] Observers have marveled at the relative ease with which government and opposition settled differences and the speed with which parliamentary committees began extraordinarily smooth functioning. With only a few exceptions, this is a political elite with a high degree of agreement about the formal and informal rules of the game. Hungary's political institutions would appear to be a political science textbook recipe for democratic governance. But it is questionable whether this neat structure of political institutions and the new political elite occupying it

51. See Juan Linz, "Democracy: Presidential or Parliamentary: Does It Make a Difference?" unpublished manuscript, Yale University (1986); and Arend Lijphart, "Presidentialism and Majoritarian Democracy: Theoretical Observations," unpublished manuscript, Georgetown University (1989).

can successfully undertake the transformation of Hungary's inherited economic system and solve the fundamental problems that provoked the transition.

Conclusion

In 1990, the citizens of Poland discovered that compromises had strewn the road of their transition with enormous and difficult obstacles. Although a non-Communist government was in office, the presidency was still occupied by the martial-law general, and parliamentary seats were still being occupied by representatives with dubious legitimacy. Even after Wałesa's election, the major constitutional issues remained unresolved, and the final character of many of its political institutions was still undetermined. In Poland an initially undifferentiated social movement had come to power, and its breakup into a competitive party system will obviously not be without friction. Yet despite difficulties that seem to hinder the rapid consolidation of liberal parliamentary democracy, the events of the first year of the transition are far from discouraging from the viewpoint of regime transformation. Although Solidarity has been greatly reduced from its much larger base in 1981, its leaders still enjoy the trust of millions of members who accepted its goals through deliberation and identification with those leaders. Deeply enrooted in the society, these organizational ties were able to mobilize popular support for an ambitious economic program of stabilization, marketization, and privatization—at least in its first crucial period.[52]

In Hungary, by contrast, the transformation of political structures has been so rapid and comprehensive that its party system seems to whir like a finely calibrated and well-oiled machine. These parties developed in a hothouse atmosphere where the transition from social movements to political parties could be measured in months rather than years. If for a decade or more some of their leaders had been courageously calling on the state to change its ways, the period in which they addressed society

52. If not active support then at least passive acceptance was crucial for the Polish government's crash stabilization program (until mid-1991, the first and only such effort in Eastern Europe). The presidential election and the end of 1990 demarcated a new epoch in the Polish transition. The surprisingly strong showing of Stanisław Tymiński in the first round of those elections indicated the limits of such passive acceptance and points to the future volatility of Polish politics. For an argument that we need new categories to understand the next phase of developments in Poland, see Andrzej Rychard, "Passive Acceptance or Active Participation? The Ambiguous Legacies of Societal Opposition in Poland," *Cornell Working Papers on Transitions from State Socialism*, no. 91-3 (1991).

and mobilized it for a confrontation with the state was very brief; and the week that this mobilization crescendoed on June 16, 1989, was the same week that it began rapidly to subside. The summer of 1989 was not a season of organizing society but of negotiating with other political parties, and the fall and winter were devoted to electoral campaigning. Given the one-step uncompromised jump start into electoral competition, the preoccupation with party politics, however necessary, was not conducive to sinking deep roots into the society. Moreover, despite their short life and their shallow roots, the political parties have been remarkably successful in filling the entire political space. But this almost totalizing supremacy of party politics finds the society unorganized and still lacking intermediary forms of political organization such as trade unions, corporatist institutions, and broad social movements. As a result of this abrupt transition to entrenched parliamentarism, no organized extraparliamentary forces can challenge the dominance of the parties. But it may well also be the case that no one will be able to gain society's support for the government's economic policies.

To date, these economic policies have not been particularly innovative, coherent, or consistent. The most striking aspect of such policy as does exist has been its extreme cautiousness—as if the new political class is unwilling to call upon society to make the sacrifices that will necessarily accompany measures that address the fundamental problems of the economy. And well it should be cautious, for the absence of organizational ties into the society means that it has neither the means to know the limits of society's tolerance nor the channels to persuade it to make those sacrifices. Thus, although elections created legitimate power, such legitimacy in itself cannot evoke the social support to remedy the economic crisis that had provoked the transition to liberal democracy.

Looking at the Hungarian case from a distance, one might think that the absence of a strong politically organized civil society would make it easier for a new elite to reorganize the economy. Strong trade unions, for example, might prove an obstacle to marketization. But the Polish and Hungarian cases may yet demonstrate that vital trade unions not only mobilize but also demobilize and that the transition from redistribution to markets will be more difficult in their absence.[53] The relative weakness

53. On the other hand, the existence of a large and vibrant "second economy" in Hungary provides entrepreneurial skills and dispositions that may facilitate the growth of market relations under new conditions. For a sober assessment that cautions against over-estimating such possibilities, see István Gábor, "On the Immediate Prospects for Private Entrepreneurship and Re-Embourgeoisement in Hungary," *Cornell Working Papers on Transitions from State Socialism*, no. 90–3 (1990).

of the organized forces of civil society that made it possible for Hungary to travel the path of uncompromised competition in the first stage of transition might make it more difficult for it to transform its economy in the second stage.

But whereas Hungary's civil society looks weak in comparison to Poland's, it has a healthy, dynamic, thriving public sphere when compared with its counterparts in Bulgaria, Romania, and Albania. In those countries, elites within the old ruling order took advantage of the extreme feebleness of the opposition to schedule early elections, control the registration of their electoral rivals, and limit their access to the media. They were elected to office by extraordinary majorities. In this they learned from their Hungarian counterparts that it was not necessary to seek institutional guarantees but that renamed Communists might attempt to stay in office via competitive elections. The difference was that state socialist elites in the later cases moved with much greater speed and confidence and showed a clearer sense of knowing exactly the institutions they needed to control in order to succeed.

The above description parallels the conventional wisdom about how the citizens in the "later revolutions of 1989" differed from those in the earlier ones. The East German people moved with greater speed than the Hungarians, the Czechs were more confident and directed than the Germans, and so on—so goes the domino theory of mass mobilization. There can be no doubt that the citizens of Eastern Europe learned from the series of dramatic events of 1989. But the flaw of "contagion theories" is that they ignore the possibility, suggested in our comparison of Hungary, Bulgaria, and Romania, that elites also learned. The consequences of this learning is felt daily in Bulgaria and Romania. By ignoring the ways in which elites could modify their strategies on the basis of earlier experiences, by examining only the citizens (and discussing elites only in terms of their being supported or ditched by "Moscow"), and by neglecting the complex interactions between forces inside and outside the regime, contagion theories can only register the timing of "collapse" and not account for important differences in outcomes.

With little doubt, in the coming years the most widely repeated statement about the events of 1989 will be some variant of Timothy Garton Ash's comment that it took ten years in Poland, ten months in Hungary, ten weeks in the GDR, ten days in Czechoslovakia, and (it will probably be added) ten hours in Romania. The statement itself is irrefutable. But in light of our examination of the Hungarian case and of the comparative insights that are suggested by it, we should add an important qualifier. In the longer-term outcomes of the upheavals in Eastern Europe it might yet be the case that the shorter the first stage of the transition, the more protracted the second stage of economic transformation and democratic consolidation.

Poland: From Civil Society to Political Nation

Jan T. Gross

The notion of civil society has been elucidated over the last decade in numerous writings stemming from (and generated by interest in) East Central Europe. Narrowly constructed, civil society refers to society outside the framework of official institutions provided by the Communist state. It emphasizes, with perhaps a certain myopia (after all, official establishments ought to be given some credit for contributing to their own demise), that the emancipation of East Central Europe did not require taking over the extant institutions. From the Workers' Defense Committee, through Charter 77 and Solidarity, up to the Neues Forum and the Občanské Fórum, enclaves of freedom where collective action took place were deliberately constructed apart from and outside of them.

A new phase in the political articulation of liberty has currently taken hold of East Central Europe. It involves the enfranchisement of the state. The nations of East Central Europe, which at the civil society stage of their emancipation have demonstrated that they are real, living entities, are now constituting themselves as polities. They are in the process of authenticating their institutions. This is what I have in mind when I speak about the transition from civil society to political nation.

In these new circumstances an altogether different environment for the articulation of liberty has been created. For the change that has occurred cannot be exhaustively described by pointing out that people who used to be in the opposition are now in the establishment (we typically understand that such a transition involves a shift from the role of critic to that of proponent of a positive program and an assumption of responsibility for carrying that program out). What is crucial, rather, is that members of the opposition—let us call them Solidarity/human-rights activists—implemented liberty in an uninstitutionalized context (creating civil society in the process), while as establishment they are bound to operate within the confines of institutions (creating, in the process, a political nation).[1]

One of the striking features of the Polish revolution was the inability of observers and participants alike to predict outcomes. Professionally competent public opinion research, usually reliable instruments of measurement, confidently predicted that the Poles would participate in two crucial elections held in 1989 and 1990 at a rate 20 percent higher than they actually did. Events were consistently outpacing, or sidestepping, conceptualizations. As a result, despite carefully planned and negotiated arrangements, surprising political developments constantly required improvisation.[2]

Of course, I speak now with the benefit of hindsight. But when the political life of a nation undergoes radical change, hindsight is necessary to make sense of events. Critical situations engineered within the logic of an epoch's closing days not only mark the end of the old order but, largely unbeknownst at the time, are also a *legacy* with which the new epoch will have to contend. This dual nature of important moments contributes to the unpredictability of outcomes and is characteristic of revolutionary periods.

1. Let me state at the outset that what I propose here is not a purely theoretical distinction. One can point to an immediate, concrete, and dramatic manifestation of exigencies produced by the state-building phase that the Polish revolution has entered. I will argue that the challenge mounted by Lech Wałęsa to the first Solidarity-sponsored government led by Prime Minister Tadeusz Mazowiecki stems specifically from Wałęsa's failure to occupy an institutionally defined position of power or authority in the reconstituted framework of Polish statehood. Though his own statements should not be considered as final proof, he has repeatedly expressed frustration over this state of affairs.

2. The penultimate round of political changes in Poland, leading to the June 1989 elections and beyond, began in earnest with one such miscalculation by the ancien régime: Lech Wałęsa's appearance on national television on November 30, 1988, in a free-wheeling discussion lasting forty-five minutes with the leader of government-sponsored labor unions (who was also a member of the Politburo of the ruling Communist party), a certain Alfred Miodowicz. Why would the government agree to put Wałęsa on television unless it had some plan to show him up? The opposition's credibility was on the line, and when the lonely man carried it before the cameras even some of his closest advisers were fearful. As Poland watched, Wałęsa outargued, outwitted, and outcharmed Miodowicz. The spell cast in 1981 on Polish society by the state of war was lifted. People later drew parallels, *toute proportion gardée*, between the psychological effects of this debate and the first papal visit to Poland.

The architecture of today's political scene in Poland has its foundations in the 1989 Round Table discussions.[3] During these negotiations several hundred pages of protocols listing agreements and, more frequently, specific points of disagreement between the government and the opposition were signed. Yet the Round Table's true significance, of course, was not in its substance but in the fact that it was held at all. Opposition had thus been recognized.

Simultaneously with this quasi-legitimization of the opposition, another process was set in motion. Shared experiences bind people together, and participants in the Round Table negotiations were not immune to this simple rule of collective life.[4] Coming from entirely different directions they were caught up in the process of forging solutions to problems that had for years been viewed as insoluble. And, imperceptibly, they came to be running ahead of their constituencies. Deals were being worked out that only the Polish parliament or the judiciary or the National Commission of Solidarity could decide upon. Of course every step of the way the Round Table produced a recognition of some social claim until recently suppressed or neglected and a retrenchment of some regime prerogative. But, from the vantage point of outside observers, it appeared as if the rudiments of a new political class were being forged.[5]

---

3. On December 18, 1988, a group of over 100 eminent intellectuals founded the Citizens' Committee Associated with the President of the Solidarity Labor Union Lech Wałęsa—the Citizens' Committee for short. When the ruling Communist Party concluded its tenth plenary session with an invitation to Solidarity to discuss Poland's future (implicit in the invitation was that Solidarity would be once again legalized) and the National Commission of the still-illegal Solidarity accepted the invitation, the Citizens' Committee put together the negotiating team. The Round Table lasted for fifty-nine days, from February 6 till April 5, 1989. Thirteen working groups met in ninety-four sessions, often lasting till dawn. Two plenary sessions were held, as well as four "summit" meetings (the latter, in the seclusion of a government retreat in Magdalenka, between the chief government negotiator Minister of the Interior [i.e., of police] Czesław Kiszczak, Lech Wałęsa, and a group of their closest advisers).

4. It applied in particular to a narrow circle of about a dozen or two, who negotiated the most tricky obstacles in the seclusion of the Magdalenka retreat.

5. The specter of Magdalenka later returned to haunt the first Solidarity-sponsored government of Tadeusz Mazowiecki. Simultaneously with Wałęsa's challenge, beginning in the early spring of 1991, insinuations were passed around that secret deals advantageous to the Communists were made at Magdalenka. Presumably this cast a shadow on Mazowiecki's team and the left-of-center group of Solidarity activists and advisers—the Geremek, Kuroń, Michnik, Bujak milieu—which spearheaded the challenge to the old regime and masterminded the transition. It was conveniently forgotten that Wałęsa was present all the time at Magdalenka as indeed were key figures from the Catholic hierarchy. The atmosphere soured enough for the secretary of the episcopate, Bishop Alojzy Orszulik, to issue a denial on June 7, 1990, that any secret agreements had been concluded at Magdalenka. It did not help when his office simultaneously declared that no transcripts of negotiations had been kept by anyone. It is indicative of the public understanding and

Still, a larger and more consequential issue was at work there as well. The Round Table negotiations were set up outside the institutional framework of the Polish People's Republic. The participants were an ad hoc group that on the one hand embodied the authorities (the state/party decision-making circles) and on the other, society. I use "embodied" rather than "represented" because just as there was no delegation of authority from the state/party governing institutions to the group of government negotiators (there simply couldn't be—the parliament could not "delegate" its authority to make laws or amend the Constitution, for example), so their interlocutors were not, strictly speaking, representatives of society. There were no provisions under the law to construct such a representation, and the organization that was de facto sitting on the opposition side of the table—Solidarity—was illegal.[6]

In one sense we should appreciate that the illegality of this ad hoc arrangement was unavoidable. The Round Table was, after all, the instrument of a radical transformation of the extant regime (in fact much more far-reaching than *any* of the participants understood at the time), and as such it probably could not be accommodated within officially recognized procedures. Political regimes of a nondemocratic sort do not, typically, have legal arrangements to provide for their own extinction. And in the known arsenal of revolutionary means the Round Table's "illegality," its "lawlessness," was of a milder sort.

Thus, as an end to an era the Round Table was a most ingenious device, a "velvet revolution" indeed. But as it was also the foundation of a new era—the era of a *Rechtsstaat*, of a state based on law—its impact would reverberate with controversy. We can see this clearly when we consider what happened during the June 1989 elections.

The 1989 revolution in East Central Europe was driven by the idea of empowering society rather than that of national liberation. "Citizen," "civic," "society"—rather than "Pole," "Czech," "Hungarian," or "na-

---

perceptions of the process that rumors about alleged deals *compromising* Solidarity negotiators involved in these crucial and, by anybody's standard, phenomenally successful talks could be sustained for such a long time. It may very well be that a peaceful revolution, that is, one negotiated with a segment of a ruling elite, always makes the first successor team vulnerable to such accusations. The logic of transition and consolidation may be incompatible in that sense. But if this is a price for renunciation of violence, it is quite a bargain.

6. One consequence of illegality was that, since the first congress held in 1981, it did not elect its own governing bodies. In a way this did not matter. Wałęsa, after all, was the embodiment of the labor union and together with a group of advisers, Solidarity activists, and leaders of various independently thinking milieus (mostly Catholic intelligentsia) they were broadly representative of society. But the meaning and political consequences of this situation were rather complex.

tion"—were the key labels for what was going on. Appropriately, the favorite tool, the ultimate weapon, of velvet revolutions in East Central Europe was the election, since it is in elections that the enfranchisement (empowerment) of society finds its most complete fulfillment. But elections—or should we rather say, first free elections?—also shift the gears of the political process and usher in a new phase in community life. By legitimizing state institutions, free elections empower civil society to become a political nation. As such they stand at the end of an era, but also at the beginning of one. Once again, it is ambiguities having to do with crossing that threshold that drive current political life in Poland.

The June 1989 elections in Poland were not sought by the opposition. First of all, they were not exactly free. Simply, the idea of free elections in Eastern Europe—in February, March, and April 1989, when the arrangements were negotiated—was inconceivable. So the opposition agreed to participate in these elections *as a concession,* in exchange for the relegalization of Solidarity.

Naturally, the government's calculation of gains and losses (I use "government" and "opposition" as a shorthand, for each camp encompassed a whole spectrum of opinions, including vocal opposition to engaging in the Round Table process at all) was the reverse. It consented to the relegalization of Solidarity in exchange for the opposition's participation in the elections. Neither side anticipated a real shift in power as a result of the elections. Both sides apparently recognized the fiction of representation that the Polish parliament embodied.[7]

Both sides were wrong, and on both accounts. What the opposition gained (soon, it turned out, all power in the state) was won largely through elections. What the government lost was certainly not the result of re-legalizing Solidarity, which even today can neither recapture its membership nor reinvent its identity.

The Polish opposition, as is well known, accepted at the time a minority share of 35 percent of seats in the lower house of the parliament (Sejm).[8]

7. The opposition feared that ill-repute would rub off on anybody who crossed the parliament's threshold, but it calculated that the risk was worth the potential gain of consolidation of civil society that would accrue from the re-legalization of Solidarity. Nevertheless, several prominent figures refused to be nominated as candidates and, for example, Bronisław Geremek had to be threatened by Wałęsa before he consented. Of course Wałęsa himself did not run. "I will remain outside to defend you when abuse and blame will be heaped on you," he said. The government feared re-legalization of Solidarity but (supposedly) calculated that it might regain some legitimacy as a result of partially free elections or, at least, neutralize and split the opposition by drawing it into complicity of sorts.

8. Coalition seats were then divided between the PZPR (Polish United Workers' Party) and its affiliated organizations according to an agreed-upon formula. One more erroneous

Unexpectedly, during a meeting of the Round Table's political subcommittee, the government suggested a constitutional amendment to create the office of president with strong prerogatives in foreign policy and security matters. When the opposition flatly refused to consent, the government promptly proposed a package deal: the presidency could be reestablished and the second chamber, the Senate, could be restored to the parliament. Elections for the Senate, the government immediately agreed, could be altogether free.[9] Solidarity accepted.

Again we can see in hindsight that the justification for the whole arrangement was illusory. A strong presidency, an institutional device later adopted in the Soviet Union, was chosen as an instrument to establish a power base insulated both from the vagaries of electoral politics and the unsteerable behemoth of the party and government apparatus. In Poland it was also constructed as a guarantee of the stability and continuity of Soviet imperial interests. But the Soviets soon lost interest in their European empire, the party apparatus dissolved itself, and the only visible act of the "strong" president Jaruzelski was to protest, unsuccessfully, against abolition of a certain national holiday.[10]

As part of the electoral arrangements the government put up a so-called National List, where thirty-five candidates—all prominent figures of the regime, including principal participants in the Round Table negotiations—ran unopposed. To win a seat in the first round a majority of valid votes cast was necessary. In the second round a mere plurality was suffi-

---

assessment by the government: three months later, when General Wojciech Jaruzelski's presidential election was held in the National Assembly, the coalition parties' deputies could no longer be disciplined to vote as ordered. It insisted that for its minority share elections would be free. It refused to run its candidates on joint electoral lists with the government. It cautiously made sure that all procedural arrangements underscored its separate identity. As the opposition strove for clean, unambiguous identity the government camp aimed for disguise. It called itself "coalition" because it included the franchised Peasant and Democratic parties (ZSL and SD), the official labor unions (OPZZ), as well as assorted milieus of "progressive" Catholics (PZKS, PAX, and ChSS).

9. In principle, in the election to the lower house the government and the opposition candidates did not directly compete for the same seats, whereas in the elections for the upper house, the Senate, opposition and coalition candidates did compete directly for two seats from every district (voivodeship) except Warsaw and Katowice, which had three senators each. This arrangement provided for the overrepresentation of agricultural areas, and the difference between the most and the least populous voivodeship was of the order of one to seventeen. The procedure was deemed to favor the government since its opponent—Solidarity—was a labor union and thus, presumably, an urban-based organization. As with many other predictions about the course of this revolution this one proved to be wrong as well. The strongest pro-Solidarity constituencies were in the rural southeastern voivodeships.

10. The anniversary of the so-called July Manifesto proclaimed on July 22, 1944.

cient. Since they were running unopposed, there were no provisions for the second round of elections for the candidates on the National List.

Altogether, it was a truly confusing electoral procedure and the June election date left very little time, barely two months, for the opposition to get ready.[11] The opposition was considered to have been out-negotiated in the preliminaries, since it had to start its campaign literally from scratch.

But all these calculations proved irrelevant. A network of Solidarity citizens' electoral committees sprang up all over Poland, empowered by the original Citizens' Committee, which advised Lech Wałęsa to organize the campaign. The Solidarity logo, released from confinement, tapped into a font of emotional support even the union activists did not believe still existed.

Solidarity elected 99 out of 100 senators.[12] Not a single coalition (that is, government) candidate for regular mandates in the lower house (Sejm) obtained the absolute majority of votes cast in his or her district, and thus none was elected in the first round. Thirty-three out of thirty-five prominent members of the regime who ran unopposed on the National List likewise failed to obtain the necessary absolute majority. And because of a proviso of government-drafted electoral law (no second-round elections for National List candidates) they could not recuperate from the loss.

The failure of National List candidates to get elected (especially in light of the government's total loss in the Senate elections) unexpectedly and unacceptably reduced its agreed-upon majority in the parliament. The Solidarity leadership, mindful of the *raison d'état,* was likewise taken aback by the scope of its own victory. When Solidarity spokesman Janusz Onyszkiewicz and Wałęsa's chief political adviser Bronisław Geremek went on national television to comment on the results for the first time, they were somber, expressionless, and did not begin by thanking the electorate for the magnificent victory. They first spoke to reassure the government—Solidarity is committed to respect the agreed-upon 65 percent to 35 percent ratio of seats in the Sejm. It will support any reasonable procedure to allow the government coalition to fill the thirty-three seats lost by the National List candidates.

11. Voters had to cross off all but one name on each ballot for the Sejm, and all but two names (three in Warsaw and Katowice) on Senate ballots, or else their vote was declared invalid. The National List was the exception. Here one could leave or cross off as many names as one wanted without invalidating the ballot.

12. Its only successful competitor was a self-made billionaire, Henryk Stokłosa, not a party-supported candidate. For these results the government had nobody but itself to blame. If it adopted proportional representation in the Senate elections it would have secured not zero but some 20 percent to 25 percent of the seats.

The people were furious. They had just openly and overwhelmingly repudiated Poland's Communist regime at Solidarity's instigation and were not even appreciated for having done so. "Allow us at least to enjoy ourselves," wrote a prominent writer in *Gazeta Wyborcza* (Electoral Gazette, Solidarity's daily newspaper). When Solidarity consented to the law's being changed in the midst of the electoral process—to allow for the additional thirty-three coalition seats to be filled in the second round of elections—a storm of protests broke out and several members of the National Electoral Commission tendered their resignations. One month later, on July 19, the spectacle of General Jaruzelski's doctored presidential election was played in front of the entire nation (literally so, for parliamentary debates, broadcast over the radio and television, were diligently followed by the Poles). Because deputies from the so-called coalition parties would no longer be disciplined into voting for Jaruzelski, several prominent Solidarity deputies ensured his election by waiting until all the votes were tallied and then, after being informed of the count, deliberately invalidating their own ballots so that Jaruzelski could be elected by one vote.

Once again—this was a mild form of lawlessness by revolutionary standards. But as this was also a mild kind of a revolution, with a stated purpose to establish a *Rechtsstaat,* it mattered that in the process the successor political camp overtly manipulated the elections, the most important legitimizing procedure of the new polity. It was also not without consequences that the leading personalities identified with this manipulation were key figures of what later was to become the pro-Mazowiecki government wing of Solidarity. They are the ones who in the current conflict advocate strict observance of due process, slow pace of transformation, and support for institutions of the state as a good in itself. Against them, in turn, the pro-Wałęsa wing uses the argument of "acceleration" and the idea of an interventionist president ("running around with an ax," in Wałęsa's words) calling in effect for results at the expense of due process.

Thus, at the very beginning and in full public view a conflict emerged between formal and substantive, or procedure- and outcome-oriented, understanding of the public good. Public good in this case consisted, on the one hand, in the need to respect the law and accept the results of elections and, on the other hand, in making sure that outcomes of elections did not lead to the aborting of the whole transition process by the old regime, which still controlled the apparatus of coercion. In time, in a very short time, electoral outcomes, which the new political stratum deemed so important to ensure, would prove irrelevant. And the stunning success of the Polish revolution would reveal the ambiguity of the very strategies that brought it about; for while the outcome-oriented politics may have safeguarded its short-term interests, it did so at the expense of undermining its long-term goals, the realization of which, as it turned out, was not as far removed in time as everyone thought.[13] Consider how the situation in Poland evolved under the impact of international developments.

On this point there seems hardly anything to debate: unlike in 1980–81, when Solidarity came into existence, the 1989–90 developments in the surrounding countries were uniquely favorable to the Polish revolution. But when we draw back to consider the transformation of domestic politics in Poland under the influence of international events we notice a paradox. The USSR dropped its imperial claims with such alacrity, and Hungary, Czechoslovakia, and East Germany so rapidly shed their Communist establishments (these stunning developments in the Soviet Union and in Eastern Europe allowed for the depth of the Polish transformations and their irreversibility) that the mid-1989 strategy of the opposition was rendered obsolete. While Solidarity activists operated as if their task was to consolidate the gains of civil society, events thrust them already into the role of architects of a political nation.

At the outset of the Polish revolution the opposition was unwilling to take over institutionally defined positions of authority and power. I have already mentioned the reluctance to participate in the June 1989 elections displayed by key Solidarity activists. Similarly, until the very last moment, leading personalities within Solidarity were (with some notable exceptions) vociferously opposed to the idea of taking over the government. The future prime minister, Tadeusz Mazowiecki, wrote a scathing editorial in *Tygodnik Solidarność* (Solidarity Weekly) against Adam Michnik's provocative and prophetic front-page piece entitled "Your President, Our Prime Minister," published in the *Gazeta Wyborcza* only six weeks before Mazowiecki was tapped by Wałęsa to assume the very office on behalf of Solidarity.

13. Consider how this conflict between procedures and outcomes was soon replayed: when Wałęsa began to stake his presidential claims and the procedural issue concerning the mechanics of presidential elections came up, his allies initially favored election by the parliament. This seemed most expedient at the time. Objection was voiced that the parliament was not representative, because 65 percent of its lower house had been put there by the old regime. To this, the leader of the pro-Wałęsa political movement Porozumienie Centrum, Senator Jarosław Kaczyński, replied that "even non-representative bodies can produce representative decisions." The phrase never became popular in the flurry of rhetoric produced at the time, even though it was pregnant with meaning and boded ill for the future of the Polish revolution.

Most important, however—from the point of view of subsequent developments and the transition from civil society to political nation—Wałęsa kept himself free from institutional involvements throughout. Had he wanted to run in the June elections he would have become what Bronisław Geremek became, the leader of Solidarity's parliamentary faction. Without his consent Jaruzelski could not have become president in July. Had he wanted to become prime minister he could have assumed the office in August. The clearer it became that President Jaruzelski and Minister of Interior Czesław Kiszczak were willing to play along with the transition, that the Soviet Union had effectively abandoned its claims to Eastern Europe, and that sweeping changes were taking place in all neighboring countries—in other words, the more auspicious external circumstances proved to be for the Solidarity-inspired revolution—the more obsolete became the role of an outsider arbiter, mediator, and source of authority that Wałęsa had prudently cast himself into at the beginning of the process.

Solidarity's very success and its becoming a legitimate government party more easily and in a shorter time than it had anticipated—fractured the Solidarity movement. Suddenly, the rhetoric of several of the most outspoken and articulate revolutionaries—by then occupying parliamentary, governmental, or editorial offices—rang with a new idea: strengthening and preserving the state. A polity was in the making. Institutions were being authenticated; some people were in positions of power, while others were out. Issues of personality, or rather personalities, aside, the source of today's political crisis in Poland is institutional.

Let me now turn briefly to societal and economic problems. Restraint, indeed self-restraint, was an important theme in this process of social change from its inception. As Solidarity struggled to grasp its own identity in 1980–81, it defined itself (Jacek Kuroń, a leading left-wing oppositional intellectual coined the expression, I believe) as a "self-limiting revolution." Later when the state of war was imposed by General Jaruzelski, a contemporary witticism called it "a self-limiting counterrevolution." These clever and catchy labels were nevertheless misleading, because the virtuous moderation in the exercise of liberty and then of coercion was due in fact to the Soviet Union. As Poland's powerful neighbor withdrew its imperial claims to East Central Europe, the external justification of restraint was also withdrawn.

A curious phenomenon could be observed almost simultaneously. As the fear of Soviet tanks gradually withered, a new nemesis of Polish politics came to lurk in the background: the fear of people marching into the streets in despair. Society has been put on alert instead of the Soviet army. Those desperate, angry crowds looming in the collective imagination create a different dynamic of the political process from the Red Army's deployment on Poland's eastern border. A decade ago, the articulation of political and social revindications could have led to Soviet military intervention. Since June 1989 the hesitation, indecisiveness, and snail's pace formulation of a program of economic and political reconstruction have threatened to activate widespread social unrest. The appeal to *acceleration* is the only ideologically identifiable content of Porozumienie Centrum's and Wałęsa's challenge to Mazowiecki's regime.

"Acceleration" is a catchy slogan and a dangerous one. People who are accustomed to associate the condition of restraint with external limiting circumstances have not yet grasped that the condition of restraint is now indigenous, that it must be self-imposed, because internal conditions of politics have changed and Poland is no longer a civil society but a political nation in the making. Liberty, freedom in politics, has now become institutionalized and must flow through well-defined positions and procedures or else liberty will undermine itself. Quite a mental leap must be made: it is now all right to be a law-abiding citizen and one may quite effectively pursue one's self-interest in that capacity. Why, the current secretary of labor and social welfare, Jacek Kuroń, asked in despair, would people nowadays resort to hunger strikes and wildcat strikes to press their pay grievances when there is political freedom and every opportunity to act through legal means? Why indeed?

Poland, together with the rest of East Central Europe, has developed a rather ironic self-understanding of the political process it is going through. Having parted with communism and the vocabulary of Marxist analysis, it was captured by the fundamentals of Marxism. In the first place, economics revealed itself with a vengeance to be the key determinant of the political realm. To be sure, Marxist principles were reversed and private ownership appeared as an indispensable foundation for well-ordered politics, for a stable, normalized—if you wish, natural—condition of society. But the framework remains unchanged; circumstances of material life, indeed *property relations,* are posited as the foundation of politics. The kernel of economic reform in East Central Europe is privatization.

But we are learning now that privatization is a surprisingly complicated idea when applied to state-run economies. To begin with, reprivatization, that is, the return of confiscated property to the original owners, would not be much of a solution, since most of the national wealth has been created in the last 45 years. Should employees of state-owned enterprises be given shares in their own places of employment, then? But this would leave out those employed in the state administration or in the private sector and would favor employees of the most valuable factories, whereas over the years the entire nation bore the burden, and paid the price, of the folly of a state-owned economy. Should, therefore, everybody be given equal shares of state-owned enterprises? But this would dilute ownership and fail to create a responsible actor on the economic scene, whose creation is the very purpose of the privatization process after all.

The privatization debate will soon bloom with full force, and many strategies will be experimented with. For the purpose of our discussion— which grapples with the bearing of practices developed at the civil society stage on the requisites of the political nation-building phase of transition—it must be mentioned that one such strategy of privatization has been in force since the late eighties. It was initiated under the old regime and is known in the vocabulary of political debate under the awkward name "appropriation of nomenklatura" (*uwlaszczenie nomenklatury*).[14] Legal mechanisms were established for incumbents in influential positions in the government/party bureaucracy to take over—whether by franchise or directly—state-owned material property. Many joint stock companies benefiting these dignitaries were founded over the last three or four years. Members of the nomenklatura effectively bought, at prices set by themselves, their jobs.

This was as crass a case of the use of public office for private gain as there ever had been. And one hears voices protesting the practice and indeed blaming Mazowiecki's government for not having moved decisively against the beneficiaries.[15] But this is again a rather complex issue with many ramifications, because the mechanism could have been one of the keys to the peaceful and evolutionary character of regime change that took place and indeed continues to take place in East Central Europe. To the extent that members of the Polish or Hungarian ruling class acquired property, the political regime ceased to be the exclusive source and guar-

14. Nomenklatura was the real-life implementation of the "leading role of the party" principle, commonly invoked in the countries of real socialism. Out of the 12 million employed in the state sector of the Polish economy and government bureaucracy some 1.5 million occupied the so-called leadership positions. In this hierarchy of "bosses," about 250,000 plum jobs belonged to the nomenklatura; that is, their incumbents were selected by appropriate party committees.

15. The protests are pure demagoguery. Indeed, the office of the prosecutor questioned the legality of over two hundred nomenklatura joint stock companies (see statement of the government spokeswoman quoted in *Gazeta Wyborcza* on October 20–21, 1990).

antee of their present and future welfare. Hence they were threatened proportionally less by the prospect of a change of regime. We are witnessing a strange revolution indeed, but perhaps the flip side of the strategy of nonviolence espoused by Solidarity (and human-rights activists all over East Central Europe), which rendered it so effective, was that the outgoing ruling class would not get expropriated during the process. And the most significant political consequence of this phenomenon may yet come through its influence on the outgoing Soviet ruling class's perception of the relative costs of the peaceful relinquishing of power in the USSR.[16]

The primacy of economics in this revolutionary process permits yet another observation. What is the essential point of reference, the shorthand designation, the symbol associated today with the Polish revolution? It is not a Solidarity logo, or one or another of Wałęsa's irreverent bon mots. Rather, it is a certain blueprint for economic reform—the Balcerowicz Plan.[17] The 1989 East European revolution is still encapsulated in a set of technical prescriptions; it stands or falls, apparently, on the accuracy of experts' advice. I think this is a major theme that requires reflection, for such development represents a radical shift in the spiritual élan of the revolution, in its ideological impact (though it shies from the term "ideology"), and in its ability to produce new ideas and therefore sustain the involvement (not to say enthusiasm) of the population.

Revolutions used to be export commodities, presumably because the exporters had a blueprint for a better society to offer or, in any case, because they represented something new. This one, judging by the number of outside experts crisscrossing Eastern Europe (from business-school graduates to constitutional lawyers), apparently can be imported. Evidently, there is a know-how somewhere—experience, ability, resources, knowledge, certainly money—that simply needs to be transplanted to carry the revolutionary task to successful completion. It is so because, unlike those of its predecessors (that is, other great revolutions), the future, the destination, the end point of this revolution is well known. It actually exists. It can be reached by an overnight train. A lot of people from East Central Europe have seen that future. And it works.

Over the last fifteen years, as society was emancipating itself from the

16. Besides, from the point of view of economic considerations alone, in the absence of a clearly stated comprehensive theory of privatization, it is as good *a component* of privatization strategy as any other.

17. And I dare say soon it will be likewise for other countries of East Central Europe. The Czechoslovak minister of finance, Václav Klaus, is a likely counterpart of Leszek Balcerowicz with a reputation and a clout rising fast to match that of President Havel's.

constriction of imposed state institutions, the articulation of liberty in East Central Europe was an immensely intriguing and creative process, self-conscious of its novelty in gradually weakening the grip of Soviet imperialism and Leninist organization of power. In this civil society stage, a new vocabulary, a literature, a strategy of social action, and a good many well-deserved reputations were created. The East European revolution carried the day, refreshingly, against and despite the advice and diagnosis of assorted experts.[18]

Now the conceptual/spiritual/ideological referent of collective action has changed decisively. Poland (East Central Europe) knows where it wants to go. It said so, with so many voices, on different occasions. It wants to return to Europe. But that demand—truly challenging, multifaceted, and provocative when it was articulated in the context of subjugation to Soviet imperial rule—has today lost much of its energy. For, in effect, it says: we want what West European societies have, though, of course, in the foreseeable future we wouldn't expect to get exactly as much of everything.

The hidden message—we will settle for less—is thus, certainly, different from the one that sustained East Central Europe over decades, some would say over centuries, and that certainly was coded into this latest revolution through its beginning years. The earlier message proclaimed, with confidence, that Poland was undergoing a unique experience, that it was traveling a road nobody had traveled before, that it was somehow special. Can Polish society settle for becoming second rate? Can it mobilize for the sustained and demanding collective effort of reconstruction with such an aspiration? As we seek explanations of the public apathy, of the unexpectedly low voter turnouts, which indicate a disinterest in the experience of liberation throughout East Central Europe, we should try to give more nuanced answers than the simple observation that the people must be tired.

Let me now return to the beginning with some observations on the changing institutional characteristics of the East European revolution. When positions of power and authority in a state are filled by incumbents who have an authentic mandate, the realm of liberty extends enormously compared with what it had been when free association could manifest

18. As Henry Kissinger travels the high road of advising governments and big corporate clients on the future of international politics, let us remember his expert recommendation to President Ford not to receive Aleksander Solzhenitsyn in the White House. For this realpolitiker, Brezhnev and his successors undoubtedly embodied the future of the USSR.

itself only within the boundaries of civil society.[19] Strangely enough, however—even though, I stress, the sum total of liberty multiplies many times in such a polity—for political actors the transition is experienced as a move from abundance to scarcity. It is so because liberty in the framework of a political nation is institutionally well defined and its bulk, therefore, is available in a *finite* number of well-circumscribed positions. Consequently, its exercise becomes a zero-sum game and as such a new experience altogether. For while there was little liberty in the confines of civil society, its supply—because it could be created by spontaneous action—was infinite. Anybody could launch a new initiative then—whether a newspaper or a political action group—and, if successful, it would redound to the benefit of all by creating yet another precedent and enlarging the domain of free association, by empowering in some fashion yet another segment of society. Today, society is empowered all right, but that power is confined, predominantly, to a small number of well-defined positions, for which there is bound to be competition.[20] The necessity of competition is what makes the exercise of liberty in the confines of a political nation so radically different from what it is in the confines of civil society.

It proved very difficult, during the first year of liberty, to institutionalize competitive politics in Poland. In a strange convergence, though for reasons that were unique for each of them, the political legacies of Solidarity and of the Communist Party reinforced each other in this respect: both were inimical to institutionalization of political competition. Against broadly held expectations the so-called historical parties were also unable to reconstitute themselves (with a partial exception of the Peasant Party). Indeed the very term "party" (that is, political party)—and with it, of necessity, the concept itself—thoroughly compromised by its appropriation by the old regime, was banned from public discourse. The whole vocabulary associated with the functioning of a political party was suspect. And as different political milieus began to crystallize, they went overboard in calling themselves by strange names that would simultaneously convey the fact of association and political purpose—movement, committee, understanding, action—*and* dispel suspicion that they intended to do what political parties were doing.

19. One would typically speak of incumbents selected in free and competitive national elections. But there were no such elections in Poland for national office, even though the current government and parliamentarians have such a mandate.

20. Power can still be created by spontaneous association, of course, but this introduces only marginal differences, since there is too much of it in institutionally well-defined locations.

The first attempt to transform Solidarity into an explicitly political organization came with the attempt to put the network of Solidarity's electoral Citizen's Committees (which drew in the most active citizenry all over the country and were full of energy as a result of a job well done) on a permanent footing. The committees would have converted into a pro-Solidarity government party at a time when the old Communist establishment seemed still strong enough for Solidarity to define itself against, that is, as an alternative to the old regime.

Wałęsa hesitated—originally, it seems, out of fear that the committees would keep the best people from returning to the labor-union organization. The down-to-earth motive might have been that while he held Solidarity's machine more or less firmly in hand, he did not control the committees (in a sense, nobody controlled them; they had yet to be converted into a unified organization). And then, in a matter of weeks, rapid implosion of the remnants of the old regime took place, and Solidarity could no longer credibly define itself *a contrario*. Internal tensions came to the surface as it became clear, in addition, that institutionalized power in the country was in the hands of the opposition. Some discovered themselves to be in, others to be out. Wałęsa was now outside the institutional order.

For reasons that remain obscure the rift between Wałęsa and the institutionalized power segment of Solidarity widened. On several occasions Wałęsa acted in a rude and offensive manner to his then closest and best collaborators (by the manner in which he replaced the staff of *Tygodnik Solidarność*, the leadership of the Citizens' Committees, challenged Michnik's editorship of *Gazeta Wyborcza,* and forbade it to use the Solidarity logo on its masthead). On the other hand, this up-to-then enormously politically creative milieu failed to produce a vision of Polish politics including Wałęsa in a capacity acceptable to him. A populist party—Porozumienie Centrum (Center Alliance)—emerged to champion his candidacy for the Polish presidency. Now that the liberal-democratic ROAD (Civic Movement for Democratic Action) has emerged in response to Porozumienie Centrum, a two-party system has begun to take shape in Poland. Somewhat paradoxically the American paradigm of two large nonideological parties may have been actualized by Wałęsa, indeed by his refusal to go along with the attempt to transform the Citizens' Committees in the fall after the elections into a political movement. Despite his evident taste for personalized power he may have effectively preempted the possibility of Perónist- or Mexican-style presidential politics in Poland by forcing a split in Solidarity.

"Ich will hier raus": Emigration and the Collapse of the German Democratic Republic

Norman M. Naimark

The miraculous recovery of the German economy after the Second World War—the *Wirtschaftswunder*—took place in an atmosphere of fierce political struggle in both the Federal Republic of Germany (FRG) and the German Democratic Republic (GDR). Not only did the Soviet Union and the United States fight their cold war on German territory, but Germans themselves in the West and in the East battled for control of the destiny of the divided nation. Less well known, but equally important, were the political struggles that absorbed competing forces within each of the Germanys separately. In the Federal Republic, one of the most uncompromising rivalries in postwar European politics—that between the socialist SPD (Social Democratic party) leader Kurt Schumacher and the anti-socialist CDU (Christian Democratic Union) champion Konrad Adenauer—threatened to tear West Germany apart before the economic recovery could take effect.

Political struggle was also an ongoing part of the history of the Soviet-occupied zone (SBZ) and the GDR. But after the Stalinization of the GDR between 1947 and 1950, political struggle did not take place between rival parties, or even primarily within the Socialist Unity Party (SED), despite the periodic eruptions of intraparty rivalries in 1952–53, 1957, and 1971. Instead, political conflict took the form of an ongoing and systematic struggle for survival between the government, the party, and the police on the one hand and the nonparty masses on the other. Sometimes, the political will of the people was expressed by organized opposition groups, demonstrations, or community and civil action, but usually the struggle went on at the level of the individual or family. The West German journalist, government figure, and GDR specialist Günter Gaus suggested that the state had ultimately won this battle because it had forced East Germans into the isolated and intensely private lives of a *Nischengesellschaft*, a society of niches.[1] Other commentators were more attracted by the notion of a "Red Prussia," a place—as the joke goes— where Germans could make even socialism work.[2] In this mythical land, the Socialist Unity Party commanded respect and deference, if not admiration or enthusiasm; German *Gehörsamkeit* (obedience) and *Ordentlichkeit* (orderliness) ostensibly proved an excellent match for the needs of the Leninist party. In the 1960s and 1970s, Western analyses of the GDR focused on the party's ability to mesh its program of economic development with the modernizing ethos of the East German technical intelligentsia. The model of the GDR described in this literature was a well-oiled, highly functional social machine, one that was able, with rare exceptions, to meet the fundamental needs of its population.[3] Well into the 1980s, Western scholars insisted that, fundamentally, socialism worked in the GDR, even if Soviet, Polish, and Hungarian societies were rent by political conflict and economic failures.[4]

None of these models took much account of the tens of thousands of GDR citizens who desperately sought to leave for the West, who crossed the borders or the Berlin Wall legally and illegally, who served prison sentences or were expelled because of their political convictions. The refugees, prisoners, and émigrés were described as aberrant phenomena, exceptions to the rule, rather than part and parcel of an ongoing political struggle for control of the lives of GDR citizens. As the events of the summer and fall of 1989 unfolded, and thousands of young, working-class families stormed West German embassies in Prague and Budapest and crossed the "green border" between Hungary and Austria, most commentators agreed that fleeing had a political effect if not political content. But it was seen as a dangerous development, threatening not just "German-German" relations, but also the dynamic unfolding of the Helsinki process with its visions of the construction of a 'common Euro-

1. Günter Gaus, *Wo Deutschland liegt: Eine Ortsbestimmung* (Hamburg, 1983).
2. Jean Edward Smith, *Germany beyond the Wall: People, Politics, and Prosperity* (Boston, 1969).
3. See Norman M. Naimark, "Is It True What They're Saying about East Germany?" *ORBIS* 23, no. 3 (1979): 549–77.
4. See the collection, "The GDR at Forty," *German Politics and Society* 17 (1989).

pean house.' "[5] Literary giants like Christa Wolf and Stefan Heym in the East and Günter Grass in the West appealed for an end to the emigration, citing the dangers of a united Germany and the promise of reformed German socialism.[6] The apparent moral and political status of the predominantly reformist leadership of New Forum helped this process along, as did the popularity in both Germanys of Mikhail Gorbachev and his program of *glasnost'* and *perestroika*.

As the events of the summer and fall of 1989 unfolded, a scholarly, journalistic and, to a lesser extent, popular consensus formed around the idea that the GDR model could be saved by updating German socialism in the East, by reforming it and giving it a human face. The political goals of those who fled to the West played no role in this calculation because they had allegedly gone for mere economic reasons, this despite the fact that many had left families and friends, jobs, homes, and possessions behind in the East. Monika Maron, a particularly sharp-eyed observer of the events of the fall of 1989, and herself a former GDR dissident who had moved West, expressed her shock at the way so many West Germans categorized the new arrivals from the East as *Banana-Fresser,* or consumer refugees. First of all, Maron notes, it is not at all apparent that the new arrivals moved for the purposes of consumption. And second, why do the ultramaterialistic West Germans, of all people, publicly place the East German refugees "under suspicion" of the lowest motivations when the refugees say they want to live decently.[7] Ironically, the personnel of the Stasis (the East German Staatssicherheitsdienst, state security service) also attributed the desire of GDR citizens to leave to "false illusions about the living conditions in the capitalist West." But the Stasis understood as well that another motivation played a significant role: "the rejection of the social system" in the GDR.[8]

The purpose of this chapter, then, is to examine the German revolution

5. Heinz Timmermann, "Die DDR im Zeichen von Selbstisolierung und hausgemachter Destabilisierung," *Aktuelle Analysen* (Bundesinstitut für ostwissenschaftliche und internationale Studien) 43 (September 29, 1989): 1.

6. See the speeches by Christoph Hein, Stefan Heym, and Christa Wolf at the November 4 Alexanderplatz demonstration in *Die Tageszeitung,* November 6, 1989; reprinted in *DDR Journal zur Novemberrevolution: August bis Dezember 1989,* expanded ed. (Berlin, 1990), pp. 71–75 (hereafter, *Taz, DDR Journal*).

7. Monika Maron, "Warum bin ich selbst gegangen," *Der Spiegel,* August 14, 1989, p. 22.

8. Armin Mitter and Stefan Wolle, eds., *"Ich liebe euch doch alle . . ."* Befehle und Lagenberichte des Mfs, Januar-November 1989 (Berlin, 1989), p. 82. See also the results of a local independent investigation of Rostock Stasi activities: *Arbeitsberichte über die Auflösung der Rostocker Bezirksverwaltung des Ministeriums für Staatssicherheit* (Rostock, 1990), p. 313.

of the fall of 1989 in the context of the history of its initiators, those GDR citizens who fled to the West. It is important, first of all, to understand their actions against the background of similar movements dating back to the war. Second, I discuss the concrete domestic and international problems of the summer of 1989 that made the *Ausreisewelle* (wave of exits) possible. Finally, the revolution in the GDR—symbolized by the dramatic breaching of the Berlin Wall on November 9—needs to be examined as a product of the complex relationship between the political motivations and actions of those who left and those who stayed behind.

Political Struggle and German Refugees

By the end of the Second World War, an estimated fourteen million ethnic Germans were on the move. Refugees from East Prussia, Silesia, and Pomerania fled to the West to avoid the advancing Soviet armies. The Poles drove Germans out of their homes in Silesia, Pomerania, and parts of East Prussia; the Czechs were no more tolerant of the Sudeten Germans. Even when the war ended, the movement of Germans continued. Soldiers returned home from detention prisons and prisoner-of-war camps; politicians and cultural figures returned from exile; millions of Germans were underway in search of friends and family. There was no clear demarcation of war and peace as the Allies, each in their own way, sought to administer their zones. American authorities persecuted Communist anti-Fascist activists in the West and the activists thus not infrequently looked for jobs in the Soviet zone, where political parties, including the Communists, were already legalized in June 1945. Landowners in the East fled West, in fear of Soviet retribution at the end of the war, and others fled as a result of far-reaching Communist expropriations and land reforms in September 1945.[9] Industrialists and government officials from the Third Reich also fled to the West, some afraid that Soviet justice would be harsher than American, others looking for a new start under Western auspices. The lack of discipline shown by Soviet troops also prompted waves of German refugees to the West, though superior food rations and a less chaotic and inconsistent system of de-nazification in the Soviet zone sometimes motivated Germans to move from West to East.

The number of Germans who left the Soviet zone grew with the acceler-

---

9. See the *Weissbuch über die "Demokratische Bodenreform" in der Sowjetischen Besatzungszone Deutschlands: Dokumente und Berichte,* new ed. (Munich, 1988).

ation of a fierce and uncompromising struggle for power among the political parties. On the one hand, the uneven battle between the Social Democrats and the Communists in the East ended in the spring of 1946 with the so-called *Zwangsvereinigung* (forced unity), which convinced large numbers of Social Democrats to flee the Soviet zone for the West. On the other hand, the leaders of the Christian Democrats in the East (and to a lesser extent the Liberal Democrats [LDPD]) failed to halt the process of Sovietization. They led a gallant struggle against both expropriations and the artificial unity of "the bloc of anti-Fascist parties," but in the end they often fled to the West. The complete victory of the Communist-dominated bloc in 1947–48 did not signal the end of political persecution. As late as 1950, SPD activists who had refused to conform to the demands of "the party of new type" were purged from the SED. The CDU and LDPD also continuously purged their ranks at Communist instigation. That so many "bourgeois" politicians were arrested and sent to the still-functioning prison camps of Buchenwald, Bautzen, or Sachsenhausen only increased the flow of refugees to the West.[10]

The consolidation of Communist political power by the end of the 1940s made it possible for the East German government to increase its pressure on the private economy. In 1948, for example, thousands of small factory owners and employees escaped to the West when the German Economic Commission socialized the Thuringian and Saxon textile industry. In 1949 the new state-owned HO's (*Handelsorganisationen*) took over commercial institutions and trading houses, prompting yet another wave of emigration to the West. Professionals were under attack in 1950–51, on political as well as economic grounds. Many who belonged to the CDU and LDPD did not submit easily to command politics and were forced to leave the country under threat of arrest. Doctors, dentists, and druggists fled by the droves in 1951–52, when the health-care system was nationalized. When Walter Ulbricht, the general secretary of the SED, announced in 1952 that the GDR would move into socialism and began collectivizing land in the countryside, some 20,000 farmers fled to the West. During the second and final stage of collectivization, which began in December 1959, the state arrested families who failed to join the LPGs (*Landproduktiongenossenschaften*, or collective farms). The choice for farmers was clear: join the LPGs or flee to the West.[11]

---

10. "Die Straflager und Zuchthäuser der Sowjetzone," *Sopade Informationsdienst*, Denkschriften 55, pp. 14–15. See also Karl Wilhelm Fricke, *Politik und Justiz in der DDR: Zur Geschichte der politischen Verfolgung 1945–1968* (Cologne, 1979), pp. 72–75.
11. Herman Weber, *Kleine Geschichte der DDR* (Cologne, 1980), pp. 61–66.

Ulbricht announced in the spring of 1960 the socialization of the remaining private factories, trading operations, and larger workshops. The result of these measures was predictable; tens of thousands of East Germans fled to the West from every social category of the population. Self-employed farmers, traders, and mechanics left, as did workers and employers. During the years 1954 to 1961, the GDR lost 5,000 doctors, dentists, and veterinarians, 800 judges and lawyers, 17,000 schoolteachers, and roughly the same number of engineers and technicians.[12]

Torschlusspanik, fear of the closing door, an end to the opportunity to escape, played an important role in the mass exoduses of 1953, 1960–61, and, most recently, the fall of 1989. In August 1961 alone, before the Berlin Wall was put up overnight on August 17, 47,433 East Germans poured over the borders. Even in 1953, when a total of 331,390 fled from the East to the West, GDR citizens feared, noted one observer at the time, that they would "shortly lose the opportunity to take the last path out of the GDR." The year before a zonal border had been cleared along a heavily guarded stretch all the way from Travemünde in the north to Hof in the south. Now East Germans were already worried that the borders around Berlin itself would be cleared and made impassable by units of the People's Police.[13] It is hard to know in the end how many East Germans fled to the West before the Berlin Wall was built and the final escape hatch closed. Probably a million East Germans fled from the East to the West between the end of war, May 1945, and the creation of the German Democratic Republic in October 1949. Between 1949 and the building of the Berlin Wall, an additional 2.69 million, registered as *Flüchtlinge* (refugees), moved to the West.[14]

After the construction of the Berlin Wall, a new category of refugee was introduced, the legal emigrant. Many were pensioners; some were allowed to leave "for pressing family matters"; and some were "special cases" arranged by government agreement. Between 1961 and 1984, 245,888 East Germans left the GDR by these routes. During that same period, 176,714 people risked death or imprisonment by escaping illegally: they crawled through tunnels, hid in truckbeds, sprinted across forest borders, swam across rivers, and found a whole series of ingenious ways to escape by land, sea, and air. At least 177 people were killed (usually shot) at the border during this period, 71 of them while attempting to get across the Berlin Wall. Another 17,000 or so GDR citizens were

---

12. See "Flüchtlinge," *DDR Handbuch* 1 (1985): 418–19.
13. *Der Spiegel,* February 18, 1953, p. 8.
14. *DDR-Almanach '90,* ed. Günter Frischbach (Landsberg, 1990), pp. 33–34.

sentenced to prison terms for political crimes between 1961 and 1984, which normally meant they had attempted to leave.[15]

In her early didactic novel about the Berlin Wall, *Divided Heaven*, Christa Wolf explored the reasons people chose to leave and to stay. Rita, the loyal GDR heroine asks her lover, Manfred, who has fled to West Berlin, "What do you want, then?" Manfred answers: "I want peace and quiet. I just don't want to be bothered any more."[16] Wolf understands in this novel that East Germans are not fleeing by the tens of thousands for material reasons; the conditions and prospects in the West are not all that much better. Another GDR writer, Kurt Bartsch, put the problem in rather crasser terms. Wadzeck, the hero of one of his novels, says, "I am at the bottom and will remain at the bottom, but I'm not going to let them puke on my head."[17]

The Prague spring in 1968 had an initially uplifting influence on the development of German youth, who followed its successes with breathless excitement. It would not be an exaggeration to state that a generation of dissidents—Reiner Kunze, Wolf Biermann, and Bettina Wegener among them—was created by the invasion of Czechoslovakia by Warsaw Pact forces, including units of the National People's Army. The growing militarization of society and the pressures of the universal draft also drove East German young people into the opposition. The policy of *Abgrenzung* (demarcation), which defined the Federal Republic as a foreign enemy state, disappointed and angered those dissidents who wanted to stay in the GDR. In "The Six-Year Old," Reiner Kunze ably sketches the propaganda of militarism, demarcation, and hate.

> He sticks needles through the toy soldiers. He sticks them through the stomach and the point comes out the back. He sticks them through the back and the point comes out the breast.
> They fall.
> "And why these exactly?"
> "They are from the other side."[18]

Soon after the Helsinki Agreement was signed in 1975 with much fanfare by the GDR, some 100,000 to 200,000 GDR citizens applied for

15. For a variety of data on leaving and escaping from the GDR, see *Der Spiegel* 10 (March 1984): 16–19; *Die Zeit* 12 (March 1984): 4.
16. Christa Wolf, *Divided Heaven*, trans. Joan Becher (New York, 1981), p. 157.
17. Cited in Hendrick Bussiek, *Die real existierende DDR: Neue Notizen aus der unbekannten deutschen Republik* (Frankfurt, 1984), p. 224.
18. Reiner Kunze, "Sechsjähriger," *Die Wunderbaren Jahre* (Frankfurt, 1976), p. 10.

an exit visa. The GDR dissident writer Siegmar Faust wrote that this was only "the tip of the iceberg of those who wanted to leave."[19] Those who submitted petitions, citing the Helsinki provisions that guaranteed the right of free emigration, were hounded by the police, thrown out of their workplaces and schools, and isolated from public organizations.

In 1978 the maximum penalty for trying to leave the GDR illegally (*Republikflucht*), which fell under paragraph 106 of the GDR criminal code on antistate agitation, was raised from a five-year to an eight-year prison term. Large numbers of young people found relief from state repression in a variety of peace, ecological, and women's groups associated with the Evangelical (Lutheran) church. Many became involved in church activities: jazz services, peace prayers, meditations, and the like.[20] But for the most militant groups, like the peace movement in Jena at the beginning of the 1980s, the church provided little help. The Stasis broke up meetings, conducted house searches and interrogations, arrested and imprisoned demonstrators. The leader of the group, Roland Jahn, was forcibly deported from the GDR in June 1983. Other dissidents who were serving prison terms were sometimes transferred to the West by what Bonn called "the discreet private solving of problems in single cases," or "the trade in humans" (*Menschenhandel*) as the business was commonly called.[21] Whatever one called it or thought of it, some 25,000 people left the GDR in this way after 1963 at the cost of approximately one billion deutsche marks.

Despite the periodic liberalization of exit-visa policies during the late 1970s and early 1980s—sometimes two hundred a day were issued—the backlog of applicants never seemed to dry up. The thirteen to fifteen thousand exits a year did not relieve the pressure on the authorities. As a result both of Erich Honecker's ultimately successful attempt to visit the Federal Republic and of the new inner-German consensus on policies of "damage limitation," "community of responsibilities," and "security partnership," thirty-five thousand East Germans were permitted to leave the GDR in 1984. Many were dissidents, who had submitted applications to leave years earlier. Some were disgruntled peace, ecological, and women's activists who had lost hope of influencing East German society for

19. Siegmar Faust, *Ich will hier raus* (West Berlin, 1983), p. 15.
20. Ehrhart Neubert, "Eine protestantische Revolution," *Deutschland Archiv* 5 (May 1990): 706.
21. Horst-Günter Kessler and Jürgen Miermeister, *Vom 'Grossen Knast' ins Paradies? DDR Bürger in der Bundesrepublik, Lebensgeschichten* (Hamburg, 1983), p. 116. See also Michel Meyer, *Freikauf: Menschenhandel in Deutschland* (Hamburg, 1983), p. 196.

the better. Many left with mixed feelings and heavy hearts.[22] Many had
been associated with the Evangelical church (52 percent by one estimate),
especially with the Junge Gemeinde (young congregations) that played
such an important role in combating the growing militarization of GDR
society.[23] Despite the church's argument that they should stay in the GDR
and give up "dreams of self-realization" in the West, the exit continued.[24]
In fact new groups formed that demanded the right to leave. In Jena, for
example, a "White Circle" demonstrated together every Saturday, holding
their candles and signs in silence, until they were granted the right to
leave.[25]

Contrary to expectations in both the West and the East, the number of
applications for exit visas did not diminish with the increased opportunity
for travel to the West guaranteed by the FRG-GDR agreement of 1984. In
1987, there were 1.2 million GDR visitors to the West under retirement
age, and 3.8 million pensioners visited, many of whom traveled several
times to West Berlin. With 5.5 million West Germans traveling to the East,
GDR citizens had ample opportunity for contacts and comparisons. Yet
prior to the summer of 1989, fewer than 3 percent of the East German
visitors to the West stayed. Some seemed to have gone back to the GDR
with the determination to leave with their families. But they had plenty of
opportunity to choose. In fact, throughout the history of the movement to
the West, roughly 4.6 million people altogether, there was also substantial
movement to the East.[26] It has been estimated that 503,000 West Germans moved to the GDR between 1950 and 1964, in part as a result of
the persecution and outlawing of the KPD (German Communist Party) in
the West. But between 1966 and 1983, an additional 600,000 moved to
the East, primarily former GDR citizens who chose to return home.[27]

The New Wave

By the end of the 1980s, political tensions in the GDR increased the
pressure to leave. The reasons were many and tended to reinforce each

22. See the interesting reflections on East and West by a member of the 1984 group:
Monika Reuter, *Ihr da drüben: Briefe in die DDR* (Bergisch Gladbach, 1986).

23. Robert Goeckel, *The Lutheran Church and the East German State: Political Conflict
and Change under Ulbricht and Honecker* (Ithaca, N.Y., 1990), p. 265.

24. Ibid.

25. Bussiek, *Die real existierende DDR*, p. 229.

26. For official statistics on movements of Germans, visitors, refugees, and pensioners,
see *Materialien zum Bericht zur Lage der Nation im geteilten Deutschland* (Bonn, 1987), p.
649, and *DDR-Almanach 89/90*, p. 33.

27. Kessler and Miermeister, *Vom 'Grossen Knast,'* p. 117.

other. Poland, Hungary, and the Soviet Union had embarked on an un-precedented path of openness and reform, replacing old leaders with new, holding out hope for the renewal of society. Meanwhile, the GDR refused to consider the necessity of reform. Even more devastating than the flip remark of the party ideologue Kurt Hager that just because your neighbor changes his wallpaper doesn't mean you have to, was the clear and rea-soned argument of Otto Reinhold that the GDR could not experiment with reform communism or capitalism precisely because its Marxism-Leninism was what distinguished it from the Federal Republic. Besides, added Reinhold (and Hager), the GDR had already gone through its reform period at the outset of the 1970s, when the vaunted "unity of social and economic policy" was instituted.[28] Reinhold's argument was all the more devastating because the same logic was being used in the West. The senior Bonn official Horst Teltschik wrote: "The SED lead-ership knows that a second German state loses its legitimacy if the Marx-ist-Leninist one-party dictatorship loses its ideological foundations. But this is exactly what happens when human rights and freedom forge ahead."[29]

The solid conservatism of the party leadership was backed up by the repressive activities of the state. Freya Kleier and Stefan Krawczyk, both of whom had already been deprived of their jobs and were hounded by constant police surveillance, were arrested and expelled from the coun-try.[30] Police attacked informal clubs and organizations and subjected their members to repeated interrogations and jailings. In Leipzig, on Janu-ary 15, 1989, a Luxemburg-Liebknecht "counterdemonstration" was broken up by the police, and eighty civil rights activists were arrested. The East-West border also continued to claim victims. On February 6, 1989, a young man was shot to death attempting to run across the border; on March 8 a man was killed while trying to escape in a homemade bal-loon.[31] The church, meanwhile, could not handle the growing frustration of young people desperate to leave the country.[32] The state responded to the entreaties of the church by introducing a campaign that mixed threats and propaganda in order to persuade those who had submitted petitions

28. For Hager's remarks, see Fred Oldenburg, "Repair or Reform in the GDR?" *Berichte des Bundesinstituts für ostwissenschaftliche und internationale Studien* 53 (1988): 8. For Reinhold's remarks, see his "Kurs XII Parteitag-Kontinuität und Erneuerung in unserer Gesellschaft," *Geschichtsunterricht und Staatsbürgerkunde*, June 1989, pp. 406–7.

29. Horst Teltschik, "Gorbachev's Reform Policy and the Outlook for East-West Rela-tions," *Aussenpolitik* 3 (1989): 213.

30. See the reprinting of the GDR dissident newspaper *Grenzfall* 6 (1987) in Ralf Hirsch and Lew Kopelew, eds., *Grenzfall* (Berlin, 1989), p. 69.

31. *DDR-Almanach 89/90*, p. 102.

32. Marlis Menge, "Auf den Putz muss man hauen," *Die Zeit*, February 25, 1988, p. 2.

to leave—125,429 in the first half of 1989—to withdraw them. Not only did the campaign not work—only 1,190 took back their applications—but, wrote the minister of state security, Erich Mielke, "the number of applicants is growing who do not accept the state's regulations and procedures, not to mention its decisions."[33]

The local elections of May 7, 1989, proved a focal point for reform hopes in the church and society. In the nominating commissions, reformers engaged in courageous attempts to confront the major issues plaguing the country. Some church groups decided to boycott the elections; others insisted the voters cast a "no" ballot. Citizens groups attached to the church were able to monitor many polling places, registering the turnout as well as the "no" votes, which they estimated at 20 percent of the total. When Egon Krenz, chairman of the voting commission, announced the results, 98.85 percent of the vote for the National Front, deep pessimism and sullen anger spread through the informal groups. When a group of demonstrators tried to present a petition outlining voting irregularities to the state council, police blocked their entrance and arrested 150 participants.[34]

The GDR's positive response to the Chinese crackdown on students in Tiananmen Square added a note of fear to the already despondent mood of opposition society. *Neues Deutschland* wrote on June 5 that the bloodbath in Tiananmen Square was an appropriate answer "to the counterrevolutionary uprising of an extremist minority."[35] In stark contrast to West German coverage of the events, GDR television played over and over again a Chinese government documentary that praised the heroic response of the Chinese army and police to the perfidious inhumanity of the student demonstrators. The warning to possible GDR demonstrators was clear.

If the opposition and church groups were angry and depressed, the youth as a whole suffered an overwhelming sense of malaise. Jurek Becker, a writer from the GDR, put it as follows:

> I can imagine a case of a young person, who looks at his parents who also grew up in the GDR, who for thirty or forty years conformed either out of ostensible loyalty or from cowardice. For the sake of their

33. Mielke report of July 1989 in Mitter and Wolle, *"Ich liebe euch doch alle . . . ,"* p. 82.
34. Hubertus Knabe, "Politische Opposition in der DDR," *Aus Politik und Zeitgeschichte (Das Parlament)* vol. 1–2 (January 5, 1990), p. 25. See also Mitter and Wolle, *"Ich liebe euch doch alle . . . ,"* pp. 29–38.
35. *Neues Deutschland*, June 5, 1989, p. 1.

careers, they have held their tongues all their lives. They had hoped that their problems would be solved if they stayed still, but that didn't happen. They are old, ugly, bent; they've become dislikable, gnarled. All at once, the young people are afraid like the plague of such a biography. If these young people had reason to think that their lives might go differently, they might well stay. But that is not the case. They have been convincingly and threateningly assured: There will be no changes. You must capitulate.[36]

Monika Maron put it in similar generational terms: "Today, the children are carrying out the old, walled-in dreams of their parents."[37]

Rather than capitulate to the fate of their parents, young working people in the GDR took advantage of the first hole in the Iron Curtain since the building of the Berlin Wall. On May 2, 1989, the Hungarians tore down the barbed wire in the mostly forested border between Hungary and Austria. During the months of July and August, hundreds of GDR citizens attempted to cross the border illegally, camping out nearby in order to try and try again. Meanwhile hundreds of GDR citizens headed for the West German embassies in Budapest, Prague, and Warsaw, and to Bonn's Permanent Representation in East Berlin. The crowded and unsanitary conditions in the embassies did not seem to discourage them, nor did the pessimistic messages from the West that "the boat is full" and incessant propaganda from the East warning of unemployment, impoverishment, and West German animosity.[38] The West German warnings were especially troublesome. One senior Bonn official insisted that "the people preferably should remain in the East where they are, so that the reunification does not have to take place in the Federal Republic."[39] Politicians in the West complained about not being able to handle the new GDR refugees over and above the normal exit numbers. German refugees from Eastern Europe and the Soviet Union, not to mention those non-Germans seeking political asylum from all over the world, made the situation of the East Germans in the embassies even more problematic.

According to the *New York Times,* 1.5 million GDR citizens had applied for exit visas; as many as 5 million people (out of a population of 16.5 million) would be ready to leave if they could.[40] Meanwhile, the

---

36. Interview with Jurek Becker, in *Taz, DDR Journal,* September 25, 1989, pp. 19–20.
37. Maron, "Warum ich bin selbst gegangen."
38. It was reported that editors throughout the GDR were given explicit instructions to frighten off potential emigrants. *Der Spiegel,* July 31, 1989, p. 25.
39. *Der Spiegel,* August 14, 1989, p. 27.
40. *New York Times,* August 22, 1989, pp. A1, A3.

illegal flow continued. On August 20, 500 GDR citizens used the opportunity of a country fair on the border to get into Austria. On August 24, the Red Cross flew several hundred GDR citizens from the West German embassy in Budapest to the West. Some 5,000 East Germany citizens were able to cross the Hungarian-Austrian border during the month of August. The escape hatch grew wider as the Hungarian government decided on September 11 that its adherence to the United Nations agreement on refugees, which prevented their return to their country of origin, took precedence over its 1956 bilateral agreement with the GDR to turn over "illegal" visitors and those who broke GDR law by attempting to escape. Immediately, some 6,500 East Germans crossed into Austria. With altogether 60,000 GDR citizens in the country, and more coming all the time, there appeared a good chance that tens of thousands of East Germans would leave via the Hungarian border.[41]

The East German leadership was deeply embarrassed by the refugees and by the widespread publicity about their actions all over the world. On October 1, Erich Honecker personally authorized the exit of some 7,000 GDR citizens who had been in the West German embassy in Prague and in the Permanent Representation in East Berlin. During the month of October thousands of East Germans used visa-free travel to Czechoslovakia to make their way to the West. Finally, with Honecker gone, the East German government almost inadvertently opened the German-German border, Berlin included, on November 9. Initially meant as a way to control travel to the West and thereby provide some legitimacy for state institutions, the border opening prompted hundreds of thousands of GDR citizens to take their rights literally and to stream through the border during the first few days.[42]

Why did so many people want to leave? Stasi chiefs from all over the GDR met in East Berlin on August 31 to discuss the question with Mielke, the minister of state security.[43] In Leipzig, reported Lieutenant General Hummitzsch, "the mood is lousy" not just in the public but in the party organization as well. People are angry in Potsdam, said Major General Schickart. Some want the state and party leadership "to strike hard and never again open up the way to the FRG and West Berlin." A

41. Budapest Domestic Service, September 10, 1989, trans. in Foreign Broadcast Information Service Washington, D.C. (hereafter FBIS-EEU), 89–174, September 11, 1989.

42. Gert-Joachim Glaessner, "Vom 'realen Sozialismus' zur Selbstbestimmung," *Aus Politik und Zeitgeschichte (Das Parliament)* vol. 1–2 (January 5, 1990), p. 8.

43. See selections from "Dienstbesprechung beim Minister für Staatssicherheit (Auszug)" (Berlin, August 31, 1989), in Mitter and Wolle, *"Ich liebe euch doch alle . . . ,"* pp. 117–34.

large part of the population in Potsdam are in any case convinced that "things cannot go on like this." In Gera, Colonel Dangress added, one must speak of "general dissatisfaction" among the people. Lieutenant General Gehlert from Karl-Marx-Stadt (Chemnitz) mentioned—as did many reports from the GDR in September and October—the dangerous situation in health-care delivery given the large number of medical personnel who left for the West. Gehlert also noted that his men did the best they could to intimidate a group of four hundred applicants for exit visas. While the Stasis were able to keep most of them from taking part in demonstrations, no applicants would withdraw their petition to leave. Mielke asked Major General Schwarz from Erfurt how many escaped from his town. Schwarz responded that 355 left through Hungary, mostly young people. One could say "good riddance" to most of them, Schwarz added; they were problem youth anyway. "Unfortunately, there were some good kids along with them, who came from good homes and families—even from colleagues." Mielke himself demonstrated some appreciation for the seriousness of the situation. He was shocked and dismayed that so many were leaving, noting that "this is no isolated group that is leaving but it comes from within the population itself." At another point in the meeting, however, he stated that those who left were nothing but dirtbags (*Drecksäcke*); what was important was their large numbers and the fact they were of working age.[44]

While the Staatssicherheit analyzed the motives for leaving and state agencies were tallying up the numbers of teachers, doctors, and service professionals who left through Hungary, *Neues Deutschland* engaged in a typically counterproductive attack on the "ice cold trade with GDR citizens," implicitly accusing the Hungarian government of selling out to West Germany money in the "Nacht und Nebel" (night and fog) operation. As in 1953 and 1961, Western "circles" had been allegedly preparing long ahead for this "Day X" action against the GDR.[45] Under the false pretenses of slogans like "Freedom" and "Human Rights" the West concealed its real goal, "to destabilize the GDR." On one issue, the East German party newspaper was correct; it would be hard to call these East Germans "refugees" in a typical sense: "There is neither persecution, nor war, nor public disaster nor other life- or existence-threatening criteria."[46] What *Neues Deutschland* did not understand was that a safe life in

44. *Der Spiegel*, (September 4, 1989), p. 21.
45. *Neues Deutschland*, September 12, 1989, p. 2; Mitter and Wolle, *"Ich liebe euch doch alle . . . ,"* p. 23.
46. *Neues Deutschland*, September 12, 1989, p. 2.

the East was not enough. As one newly arrived Leipzig baker put it on West German television: "If you put a bird in a cage and give it something to eat, it still doesn't feel free."[47]

Recent sociological studies of the 343,854 refugees and emigrants who left the GDR in 1989 support the baker's observation.[48] Most of those leaving were young (41.1 percent were between twenty-two and twenty-nine) and from the working class. In the first phase of the large legal emigration, October 10 to November 8, 1989, many professionals left with their families; 3.1 percent of the total number were doctors or dentists. Later, the percentage of young single men increased. The two most frequently mentioned reasons for leaving in well over 90 percent of the cases were general political conditions on the one hand and the lack of political freedom on the other. Living standards were mentioned in 80 percent of the cases, relatives in the West in 60 percent, and poor working conditions in 50 percent. Poor health and safety conditions, as well as environmental issues, also played important roles in motivating people to leave. It is worth noting, in fact, that the incidence of emigration was higher from those regions with the most backward working conditions and the most severe pollution.

One sociologist who studied both the 1984 and 1989 cohorts of exiles emphasizes that it would be inaccurate to differentiate too sharply political from economic motivations. In both cohorts, those who went to the Federal Republic looked to grow in their work and professional lives without external, politically determined constraints. Certainly the refugees sought to enjoy the economic fruits of their labor, but it is inaccurate, he suggests, to attribute this desire to a simple consumer orientation and not see it as part and parcel of a general political stance.[49] In fact, politics were very much a part of their general attitudes. Twice as many of those who left the GDR considered themselves CDU or CSU voters as SPD voters. Virtually all the emigrants expressed strong anti-SED sentiments and claimed to carry nothing in the way of a "GDR-identity."[50] Some of the younger people, especially, expressed virulent anti-GDR feelings. Anita P., a twenty-two-year-old *Punkfrau* from the GDR was interviewed after six months as a "punklady" in West Berlin.

47. *Der Spiegel*, August 14, 1989, p. 28.
48. The following observations come from Dieter Voigt, Hannelore Belitz-Demiriz, and Sabine Meck, "Die innerdeutsche Wanderung und der Vereinigungsprozess," *Deutschland Archiv* 5 (May 1990): 732–46.
49. Volker Ronge, "Die soziale Integration von DDR-Übersiedlern in der Bundesrepubik Deutschland," *Aus Politik und Zeitgeschichte (Das Parliament)* vol. 1–2 (January 5, 1990): 43.
50. Ibid., p. 42.

"Why did you leave the GDR?"
"The GDR? Never heard of it."[51]

Opposition and Emigration

The mood among those who left contrasted dramatically with those who remained behind. Monika Maron wrote that going itself "served as an act of self-affirmation," as a deed that the emigrants could be proud of.[52] Meanwhile, the mood among those who remained grew ever more bleak. The State Security reported on September 11 that "large parts of the working class, especially in the factories," were grumbling. Some workers left the party; others complained bitterly about the contradictions between the ostensibly "healthy world" of the SED and reality. "There is a growing gap in trust between the party and the people," the report concluded.[53] The invectives hurled on the pages of *Neues Deutschland* seemed even more hollow than usual.

> In an unprincipled campaign of agitation and defamation against the GDR, citizens of our state are being led astray and deceived by the mass media and by direct interventions, including the misuse of the possibilities for travel and contacts. . . . This coup attempt against the GDR is part of the crusade of Imperialism against individual socialist brother states from Berlin to Peking, each according to a special recipe.[54]

Readers of *Neues Deutschland* could not help noticing the implicit threats to the recently liberalized travel laws. At the same time, it was apparent the party remained uninterested in reform. The Romanian and the East German parties expressed mutual solidarity, and *Neues Deutschland* carried a nasty personal attack against Boris El'tsin, who had stated on a trip to the United States that people have the right to live where they want. "That which is law and justice among us," the party newspaper snapped,

51. Cited in Kessler and Miermeister, *Vom 'Grossen Knast,'* p. 208.
52. Maron, "Warum ich bin selbst gegangen."
53. Report of September 11, 1989, in Mitter and Wolle, *"Ich liebe euch doch alle . . . ,"* pp. 149–50.
54. *Neues Deutschland*, September 12, 1989, p. 2. Attitudes of the GDR leadership had changed little since Ulbricht commented on the exodus of GDR citizens prior to the wall: "That's no political emigration, but a filthy trade in humans . . . psychological warfare and sabotage—directed against the German Democratic Republic" (cited in Kessler and Miermeister, *Vom 'Grossen Knast,'* p. 30).

"will be determined by the elected representatives of the people of the GDR."[55]

One could argue that in these critical days of September the party lost any chance it had to lead the reform movement rather than be left behind. The mood of the young people was especially unsettling. In their founding proclamation, the citizens' movement Democracy Now, unlike the party, recognized the crisis: "People rub themselves raw on the situation; others are resigned. Throughout the land there is a growing loss of confidence in what the GDR historically has become. Many are barely able to affirm their commitment to being here. Many leave the country, because conforming has its limits."[56] "So many went away," stated Rolf Nehrich, a founding member of the political club New Forum. "Of necessity the question for the young people here above all is: Why do I decide to stay in the GDR? They want reasons for this; [they want] a feeling of collective identity."[57]

Intellectuals and cultural figures, peace-group activists and "greens" from the environmental movement, women's movement circles and church-related activists, became increasingly determined in those September days to provide reasons to stay. On September 10, the so-called "Day of Those Left Behind," Bärbel Bohley and twenty-nine other cultural activists founded New Forum. The first meeting took place in the house of the long-time Marxist dissident Robert Havemann, who had died in 1982. More than five thousand people quickly signed the petition for legalizing the group, but the minister of interior turned it down because of New Forum's "Anti-state platform."[58] Other opposition groups, including Democracy Now and the United Left similarly joined the chorus for a critical examination of the GDR's path to socialism.

The intellectuals and church activists, especially, were mobilized to act by the continuing mass exodus of GDR citizens. Christa Wolf stated: "The way in which the responsibility for this situation is shoved off, though the sources of it lie in the contradictions in our land, is unacceptable to us."[59] The synod of the church similarly called for a thoroughgoing examination of the reasons for "the mass exodus of citizens of the

---

55. For El'tsin's statement, see the *Frankfurter Allgemeine Zeitung (FAZ)*, September 14, 1989, p. 1; for the party response: "Herr Jelzen auf dem Holzweg," *Neues Deutschland,* September 19, 1989, p. 2. For the predictable Romanian reaction to the refugees, see FBIS-EEU, 89-178, September 15, 1989, p. 62.

56. *Taz,* September 12, 1989, in *Taz, DDR Journal,* p. 9.

57. *Der Morgen,* October 28–29, 1989, p. 7.

58. *Der Spiegel,* September 25, 1989, pp. 18–19.

59. Ibid., p. 19.

GDR to the Federal Republic," because "so many, especially so many young people in our country, can see no more future for themselves."[60] The church's resources had been strained to the limit over the previous year by its combined efforts to encourage people to stay in the GDR and provide counsel and protection for those who declared their intention of going. Now the synod expressed its fears about the spiritual collapse of the society. "Families and friendships are being torn apart; old people feel left in the lurch; the sick are losing their doctors and nurses." The severe consequences to the economy cannot be measured, the church noted, and, while the size of the congregations are shrinking, pastors are not able to take care of all the human problems of the needy.[61]

Prompted by the GDR's desire to celebrate the fortieth anniversary of its founding on October 7 without the embarrassing coverage of East Germans camping out in West German embassies, Honecker authorized the transport of East Germans from Warsaw and Prague. But the government again compounded its problems with gratuitous name calling in the press. "Through their [the refugees'] actions," wrote Neues Deutschland, "they have stepped on moral values and have separated themselves from our society. There is no reason to shed any tears after them."[62] In fact, on October 4, as citizens of Saxony learned that a special train from Prague loaded with GDR citizens would roll through Dresden, Leipzig, and Plauen on its way west, they stormed the stations on route trying to get on to the train. In Dresden, three thousand demonstrator fought with riot police at the train station. A dozen demonstrators were injured and several were arrested.[63] During the first week of October, sporadic demonstrations took place in various parts of the GDR. In Leipzig, an October 2 demonstration, the first of many "Monday Demonstrations," included singing "We Shall Overcome" and the "Internationale" and slogans like "Legalize New Forum," "We are staying here," and "Gorbi, Gorbi."[64] The Monday demonstrations in Leipzig quickly became the bellwether for the growing sense of community and empowerment that GDR citizens experienced in the mass demonstrations throughout the country.

The most critical point of the revolution followed on October 7, 8, and

60. Taz, September 19, 1989, in Taz: DDR Journal, p. 18.
61. Ibid.
62. Neues Deutschland, October 2, 1989, p. 2. Honecker is alleged to have insisted on this last sentence.
63. Bärbel Bohley correctly assessed the situation when she noted, "The people's patience is at an end" (Der Spiegel, October 9, 1989, p. 21).
64. Alexander Zwahr, "Was ich am 2. und 9. Oktober in der Innenstadt erlebte," manuscript, Stanford, Calif.: Hoover Institution Archives.

9. On the seventh, Mikhail Gorbachev visited East Berlin and spoke at the ceremonies marking the fortieth anniversary of the GDR. More important than the Soviet leader's speech, which only gently encouraged reform while reiterating the principle of noninterference, was that of Erich Honecker, which made no concessions to the vastly changed mood of the country. Our goals are set down in our program, he stated. "They concern the further formation of the developed socialist society." Then, as if to seal the fate of his regime, Honecker concluded with the well-worn slogans: "Work together, plan together, govern together" and "Always forward—Never back."[65] Antigovernment demonstrations took place throughout the GDR on the same day. Especially in East Berlin the police cracked down on thousands of demonstrators, whom they accused of being "trouble-makers, incited rioters, and criminal elements." The Stasi chief, Erich Mielke, is reported to have encouraged the violence: "Give those pigs a sound beating."[66] In fact, many demonstrators were badly hurt and scores of others were arrested.

But the people were no longer intimidated and on October 8 demonstrations took place in Dresden, Leipzig, Berlin, Potsdam, and many other towns and cities. Mielke again ordered the breakup of the demonstrations because he—and the party—feared the revolutionary potential of the masses. "The manifestations are coming to a head and with them the related danger of the molding of the enemy opposition, as well as other enemy-negative and rowdyesque forces, with the goal of disturbing state security as well as the public order and therefore endangering the state and social order of the GDR."[67]

Matters indeed came to a head on Monday, October 9, as mass demonstrations were expected to take place in Leipzig. Rumors around the city that the government was planning "a Chinese solution" were confirmed by the reported movement of tanks, army troops, and armed factory units.[68] In fact, the LDPD chief, Manfred Gerlach, later reported that Honecker had indeed ordered that "the counterrevolutionary demonstrations" in Leipzig be put down "with any force necessary."[69] Despite fears of impending violence and the show of force by the government, seventy thousand demonstrators, the largest demonstration yet in Leipzig, marched through the inner city shouting, "We are the people," "We are

65. *Neues Deutschland,* October 9, 1989, p. 3.
66. Cited in Glaessner, "Vom 'realen Sozialismus,'" p. 6.
67. Report of October 8, 1989, in Mitter and Wolle, *"Ich liebe euch doch alle . . . ,"* p. 201.
68. Zwahr, "Was ich am 2. und 9. Oktober erlebte."
69. *Taz,* October 8/9, 1989, in *Taz: DDR Journal,* p. 40.

going to stay here," and "Gorbi, Gorbi" without any incidents.[70] Although Egon Krenz later claimed that he stopped the order to break up the demonstration, the evidence to date indicates that local SED officials in consultation with leaders of the popular movement, most prominently the conductor Kurt Masur, made sure that the Monday demonstration concluded peacefully.[71]

Within a week of the Leipzig demonstration, the Politburo met in a long session "to discuss the questions of our society" and on October 18 Erich Honecker resigned from his posts for reasons of health.[72] But the naming of Egon Krenz to take Honecker's place only exacerbated the tensions between state and society. Wolf Biermann spoke of his thoughts when told of Krenz's appointment: "That's the lousiest of all possible candidates. Krenz; oh you poor Germans, I thought, how things will really move powerfully forward backwards."[73]

The three-sided relationship between a barely reformed state leadership, an opposition that was growing in self-confidence, and the unabated exodus of young East Germans to the West called the survival of the GDR increasingly into question. Tensions between the opposition, or the *Dableiber* (Stayers), and those who chose to leave, the *Weggeher* (Leavers), undermined the former's attempts to construct a humanistic socialist alternative. Reinhold Schult the leader of "Church from below" correctly pointed out: "If everyone slips through the narrow openings [to the West], the others get no more air."[74] In "Red Magdeburg" Carl Christian-Kaiser wrote about the resentment against those who went among those who stayed: "The personal hurt grew to mourning, the pain to unadulterated anger, even hatred. Didn't so many go from whom one would have never expected it? . . . In this way deep wounds were suffered. And not least of all: those who leave weaken the soil from which the reform efforts can and must get nourishment."[75]

It soon became clear that the government would not use force against peaceful demonstrators.[76] In part as a result, the size of the demonstra-

70. Zwahr, "Was ich am 2. und 9. Oktober erlebte."
71. Christian Schmidt-Häuer, "Der Widerspenstigen Lähmung," *Die Zeit*, October 13, 1989, p. 3.
72. *New York Times*, October 12, 1989, p. A1.
73. *Der Spiegel*, October 23, 1989, p. 16.
74. *Taz*, August 15, 1989, in *Taz, DDR Journal*, p. 7.
75. Carl Christian-Kaiser, "Die Ruhe täuscht," *Die Zeit*, October 20, 1989, p. 3.
76. There can be no shooting under any circumstances, a local Rostock Stasi headquarters ordered its men: "even if their curses and insults make our hearts bleed and our trigger finger itches" (Report of October 26, 1989, in *Arbeitsberichte über die Auflösung der Rostocker Bezirksverwaltung des Mfs*, p. 275).

tions rose dramatically. The Leipzig Monday demonstrations grew from
15,000 on October 2 to 80,000 on the fateful October 9, to 150,000 on
October 16. On October 23, the first Monday after Honecker's fall, the
number of demonstrators grew to 200,000, and then on November 6 to
500,000. In Berlin's Alexanderplatz, a huge demonstration of more than
a half million people listened to the country's leading intellectuals plead
for the people to stay and help build a democratic socialist society.
Christa Wolf proclaimed that "the people stand on the tribune, and the
leadership marches by them." "Imagine there is socialism," said
Christoph Hein, "and no one runs away."[77]

The problem, of course, was that the people continued to run away in
large numbers. On November 5 huge lines of cars and chartered buses
filled with GDR citizens stood on the Czechoslovak border with Bavaria,
waiting to be processed. In the morning, the "leavers" had heard on the
radio that the Czech border was open and that it was not necessary to
apply to go or to have a visa. Thousands grabbed a few necessities and off
they went.[78] Young people, especially, did not believe that anything
would change in the GDR. They were even more convinced of this fact
when the new draft travel laws were announced with great fanfare by the
Krenz government. The authorities still reserved the right to deny individuals the freedom to travel. Currency restrictions remained and limits
were placed on the duration of the stays abroad.[79] As one anti-SED
student banner put it, "Your policies were and are there to run away from
[*zum davonlaufen*]."[80]

By the time the Berlin Wall fell on November 9 and hundreds of thousands of East German citizens in Berlin and all along the East-West border
were able to look at and explore the forbidden West, entreaties to the
youth to stay could not save the GDR. Christa Wolf was right to note that
the exodus made any internal solution to the GDR's problems less likely.
On GDR television on November 9, she pleaded, "Stay with us. . . .
Those who still go away lessen our hope. We beg you, do stay in your
homeland. Stay with us."[81] Bärbel Bohley of New Forum was upset that
the government had opened the Berlin Wall; genuine reform of the GDR
would now be more difficult. "The people have gone crazy, and the gov-

77. *Taz*, November 9, 1989, in *Taz: DDR Journal*, p. 74.
78. Claus-Einar Langen, "Den Betrieb, die Hühner, die Papagein zurückgelassen," *FAZ*, November 6, 1989, p. 2.
79. *Taz*, November 7, 1989, in *Taz, DDR Journal*, p. 88.
80. *Taz*, November 10, 1989, in *Taz, DDR Journal*, p. 92.
81. Ibid., p. 97.

ernment has lost its head."[82] The demonstrations were losing momentum to the East Germans' fascination with the West. Even West German intellectuals rued the fact that the borders were opened. Güenter Grass wrote that "the order in which the changes took place was wrong. The internal process of democratization should have been pushed further before the opening of the borders was announced."[83]

Sarah Kirsch, the GDR poet who had moved to West Berlin in 1977, noted that the only way to stem the continuing exodus to the West was to hold free elections in the East. But as long as this did not happen, she added, it made no sense for intellectuals to appeal to the people to stay.[84] They were tired of socialism and wanted to determine their own future. Very few who left in the fall regretted their decisions. Interviews with them in the West consistently provoked the same responses: "For us there was no future any more, either job-wise or any other way."[85] By the end of November, a new government led by Hans Modrow tried to save the situation. But already slogans for reunification—"Germany: One Fatherland," "We are one people"—began to appear at the Leipzig demonstrations. Perhaps best summarizing the sentiments of those GDR citizens who wanted to stay was the slogan "No more experiments! We are not laboratory rabbits."[86] In other words, the only way to keep the population in the East was to create the conditions of the West in the GDR, and unification was the fastest and perhaps the only way to accomplish this.

New Forum and reform Marxist intellectuals in the East and West were clearly left behind by these developments. It is inaccurate to argue, as does Timothy Garton Ash, that "the tiny minority of human and civil rights campaigners . . . contributed most to Germany's peaceful October revolution."[87] It is worth reiterating that those who left the country started the revolution, while those who demonstrated maintained it. "The intelligentsia played a small, nice, important role only later," writes Sarah Kirsch.[88] It was difficult for Christa Wolf and Stefan Heym, who had devoted their lives to the German socialist alternative, to understand the

---

82. *Taz*, November 13, 1989, in *Taz, DDR Journal*, p. 126.
83. Günter Grass, *Two States—One Nation?* trans. Krishna Winston with A. S. Wensiger (New York, 1990), p. 16.
84. *FAZ*, November 11, 1989, p. 27.
85. *Taz*, November 11, 1989, in *Taz, DDR Journal*, p. 117.
86. *Der Spiegel*, November 27, 1989, pp. 19–27; *Taz*, November 23, 1989, in *Taz, DDR Journal*, p. 149.
87. Timothy Garton Ash, "Germany Unbound," *New York Review of Books*, November 22, 1990, p. 11.
88. *FAZ*, November 11, 1989, p. 27.

joy and sense of accomplishment felt by the East Germans who found
their way to the West. It was harder still for New Forum to watch the
soldiers of the revolution desert to the West: "You are the heroes of a
political revolution, don't be silenced by . . . travel and consuming."[89]
But statements like this one demonstrated that New Forum understood
the needs of the East German people no better than the GDR authorities,
who issued 4.5 million visas on the one hand and on the other set up large
stations on the border for advising the trickle of GDR citizens who
wished to return.

During the Christmas holiday 1989, in response to the continuing exit
of GDR citizens to the West, the government of Hans Modrow—with the
help of Bonn—introduced full freedom of travel across the German-German border for the first time since June 1946, when the Allied Control
Council introduced zonal travel restrictions. One goal of the revolution
had been accomplished. Still, between January 1990 and the *Volkskammer* elections on March 18, another 150,000 East Germans left for the
West. The free elections marked the second accomplishment of the revolution. Only with the currency union in the summer and the joining of the
two German states in the fall did emigration finally lose its political
significance.

Epilogue

Once the euphoria of November had faded and the harsh realities of
German unification became increasingly apparent, West German commentators began to question the ability of East Germans to adapt to the
political and economic system of the West. East German workers were
criticized for being lazy and lacking initiative. Observers saw signs of neo-
nazism among East German youth and worried about the negative effects
of unification on the political health of Germany. Scores of other problems
were cited as well: from East German racism against Vietnamese and
Angolan guest workers to small-town provincialism and backwardness.

There can be little question that the former citizens of the GDR share
many of the problems of their neighbors in Eastern Europe that have
resulted from forty years of Communist rule. The SED—like its "broth-
erly" parties—sought to create a closed, well-ordered, and passive society; that society is now exposed to a wide variety of new experiences and

89. *Taz,* November 12, 1989, in *Taz, DDR Journal,* p. 132.

THE GERMAN DEMOCRATIC REPUBLIC

challenges. Unlike their neighbors, the East Germans will have the immense advantages of West German capital, know-how, law, and institutions to structure the transition to a market-oriented, pluralistic society. But even more than their neighbors, East Germans will have to learn to live in a different world, one with political uncertainties, unpredictable economic circumstances, and open social and ethnic antagonisms.

Despite the obvious difficulties of the transition, there are good reasons for confidence in the future of the [East] Germans. First of all, four million of them have already played a part in the history of the Federal Republic. Those who chose to leave have taken an important and sometimes dangerous step toward freedom. They will not give it up as easily as West German and foreign commentators seem to suggest. Furthermore, the East Germans have demonstrated that the *Obrigkeitsstaat* (the hierarchical state), which Thomas Mann feared fit the Germans too well, turned out—in its GDR form—to have alienated its citizens and provoked their resistance. Democracy in the united Germany can only be strengthened by their experiences.

Metamorphosis: The Democratic Revolution in Czechoslovakia

Tony R. Judt

In contrast with its Polish and Hungarian neighbors, Czechoslovakia in 1989 had undergone no gradual political liberalization, no partial economic reform. The regime put in place by Soviet tanks after 1968 was still there, its leaders and policies substantially unaltered. Conversely, the outcome of the country's "velvet revolution" was a dismantling of communism more thorough and complete than anything achieved, to date, by its fellow former Soviet satellites. A discussion of the context of these changes and the problems that remain unresolved follows a brief account of how this situation came to be.

Although precipitated by a single event, the revolution that began on November 17, 1989, was also the product of three related developments that accelerated during the course of the previous months. The structural weaknesses of the Czechoslovak economy had become both unavoidable and unmanageable—as noted in August by Miloš Zeman, a government employee at the official economic forecasting unit, who gave a television interview in which he offered detailed evidence of the coming economic crisis. He later lost his job as retribution for speaking so plainly, but no one, in or out of government, denied his data or his conclusions. The regime had previously made feeble attempts at economic decentralization (including some relaxation of the regulations governing foreign trade) but dared proceed no further for fear of inviting the political and social change that would inevitably accompany such a diminution of government control. It was thus reduced, in 1989, to announcing its intention to establish links with the International Monetary Fund (IMF) and the World Bank; had the intention been pursued, it would almost certainly have precipitated the very economic changes the regime sought to avoid by inviting foreign loans and assistance instead.

The growing public awareness of economic stagnation (associated in the Czech and Slovak minds with the impending ecological disaster obvious to all) gave additional fuel to the opposition, already in the summer of 1989 proving bolder and more diverse than for much of the previous two decades. No longer was public dissidence confined to Charter 77 and its now-famous signatories. Two years earlier there had been formed Democratic Initiative (DI), a group that distinguished itself from the Charter by its overtly political character. Now, in August 1989, the DI formally established ties with Hungary's Democratic Forum, making clear thereby both its political intentions and its general ideological leanings. A petition under the title "Just a Few Sentences" (echoes of the 1968 document "Two Thousand Words") gathered over forty-thousand signatories in support of its demand for democratization and, on September 15, twenty-two of its original and more prominent signatories (Václav Havel among them) sent a letter to Prime Minister Ladislav Adamec requesting talks between government and opposition on the reform and liberalization of Czechoslovak politics. Taken together with Obroda, the group of reform Communists, and the numerous smaller citizens' initiatives, this action was evidence of an expansion, diversification, and politicization of the hitherto numerically insignificant Czech and Slovak dissident community.

A third element in the prelude to November was of course the international situation. The neo-Stalinists in Prague were isolated within the Communist world, resentful of Mikhail Gorbachev and his disturbing example, at odds with the Hungarians, who were refusing to proceed with the building of an ecologically disastrous dam on the Danube, and exposed to embarrassing comparisons with the German Democratic Republic (GDR), whose citizens were streaming across Czechoslovakia en route to Hungary, Austria, and the Federal Republic. The confusion and unease these developments produced could be seen in public statements during the autumn of 1989 by Jan Fojtík (the party's leading ideologist) and by the party secretary, Miloš Jakeš, both of whom made a number of clumsy attempts to justify their refusal to follow suit in the reforms now crowding in around them. They convinced no one but did confirm a growing public sense that the regime was in a cul-de-sac and that something must change sooner or later.

Among the opposition, however, still of necessity semiclandestine and some of whose leaders (like Miroslav Kusý and Ján Čarnogurský in Slovakia) had just been arrested, there was no consensus on what to do. On the contrary internal division was growing, much of it crystallized around the problem of public demonstrations. Should the dissident community encourage mass turnouts in commemoration of significant past events (the immolation of Jan Palach, the declaration of Czech independence in 1918), or should it avoid possible confrontations with the police and confine itself to public statements and semipublic attempts to establish a dialogue with reform Communists? Just how little agreement existed can be seen in an interview Havel gave to *Lidové noviny* in September (when it was still, of course, an illegal publication), in which his own doubts and his sense of the internecine squabbling now emerging came through very clearly. In this uncertain context, following the arrest of some 350 people in an informal Independence Day celebration in Prague on October 28, and a further 100 at a march protesting the degradation of Prague's environment, there was staged on November 17 a rally to honor Jan Opletal, a student killed by the Nazis fifty years earlier.

What happened that day is now widely known. Some fifty thousand people, many of them students, occupied the center of Prague with, apparently, the acquiescence if not the approval of the authorities. Then, possibly at the urging of agents provocateurs, the students were led toward a detachment of riot police who cornered them in the archways of one of Prague's main streets and beat them up. The police were almost certainly operating under orders to overreact, though it remains unclear just who so instructed them, and why. In any event, and in the light of the growing confidence of the opposition in previous months, the outcome was not in itself surprising: the following day a group of students joined with intellectuals and artists (notably from the Prague theatrical community) and demanded boycotts in the university and a national general strike for November 27.

The hectic, unprecedented events of the next three weeks, Czechoslovakia's "gentle revolution," have been evocatively described by Timothy Garton Ash.[1] In outline, the process divides into three episodes. From November 18 through the strike of November 27 there emerged Občanské Fórum (Civic Forum—CF), whose appearance coincided with a huge demonstration in central Prague on November 19, when 200,000 people gathered to protest at the police violence against the students. For

1. See Timothy Garton Ash, *The Magic Lantern* (New York, 1990), pp. 78–131.

the next three days crowds continuously occupied Prague; by November 23 they had grown to over one-third of a million in strength. Václav Havel, who surfaced as CF's natural leader, addressed the crowds for the first time on November 21, two days before Alexander Dubček made his first public appearance in Slovakia in two decades. In Bratislava, Havel spoke to a crowd of 50,000, mobilized by CF's Slovak partner, Public against Violence (PAV), brought into being four days earlier by a similar coalition of artists and writers. The Communists were already sufficiently frightened by the scale of things to dismiss the president and secretariat of the Prague City Communist Party (held responsible for the events of November 17), but it was only with the unexpected success of the November 27 general strike that they really began to give way.

At this point the second stage of the revolution began, with the opening of talks between CF and the government, the Federal Assembly's voluntary removal of the constitutional clause guaranteeing the Communist Party a "leading role", and, on December 3, the inauguration of a new government with five non-Communist ministers. But Civic Forum, which since November 29 had been guaranteed airtime on Czech radio, pronounced itself unsatisfied with this concession and used its now overwhelming influence in the street to press the Communists for deeper concessions. Within seventy-two hours the Communists caved in, accepting a new government, with a Communist prime minister but a non-Communist majority. On the following day the party expelled the former secretary-general Jakeš and the Prague party chief Miroslav Štěpán, blaming them for the calamitous error of November 17.

Up to this point the revolution, despite its dramatic successes and the attendant humiliation of the party, remained essentially unsecured. Even after the voluntary disarming of the People's Militia on December 3, there were no guarantees that the Communists would not regroup and strike back. The only real power in the hands of the leaders of CF was their capacity to bring hundreds of thousands into the streets in support of their demands. Hence, beginning with the establishment of the new government under Marián Čalfa, there was a growing emphasis on the need to replace Gustáv Husák with a non-Communist president, the better to secure control of all levers of power, political and military. By now the only possible candiate for the post was Havel—Dubček, for all his popularity with the Slovaks and with the generation of the sixties, lacked both the appeal to youth (it should be remembered how important the younger generation was in precipitating and maintaining the impetus to change) and a clear non-Communist pedigree. Thus the third stage of the revolution saw an insistence upon the demand for Havel to be nominated to the president's office in the Prague castle—*"Havel na Hrad."*

On December 10, President Gustáv Husák swore in Čalfa, with his majority of non-Communist ministers, as the new government—and then resigned. For a few days the Communists toyed with the idea of nominating a reformist party figure to replace him but were once again overtaken by events, in this case the nationwide demand, voiced in thousands of local meetings, marches, and demonstrations, for Havel to accede to the post. On December 16 the erstwhile imprisoned playwright agreed to run, and it became very clear that any attempt to oppose him would spark off major demonstrations and much anger. The Communists thus reluctantly agreed to concede their last remaining constitutional stronghold, and at the end of the month the Federal Assembly voted to complete the remarkable series of political reversals that had marked the past month in Czechoslovakia. On December 28 Alexander Dubček was nominated to the Federal Assembly, and simultaneously sworn in as its chairman, and on the following day Václav Havel was elected by the same (Communist!) Assembly as president of the republic (Havel had made Dubček's election a condition of his own, conscious of the double need to please the Slovaks and maintain the support of the reformist fringe of the still-powerful party). The students, acknowledging that the election of Havel met their conditions, called off their strike, now six weeks old, and Czechoslovakia entered 1990 in a political and social condition that would have been unrecognizable and unimaginable just two months earlier.

At this point, and before we proceed to a discussion of the complexities of the Czechoslovak scene between the ascent of Havel and the elections of June 1990, it is worth noting a couple of important and peculiar features of the revolution in Czechoslovakia. The first is that the whole process took place with no distinct sense, on anyone's part, of political strategy or policy. Overtaken by events and in many cases just emerging from prison or the menial tasks to which they had been consigned by the "normalization" of 1969 (the classic case being Jiří Dienstbier, who went from stoker to foreign minister overnight—literally), the members of the opposition, in and out of Civic Forum, were as confused as the Communists whom they defeated and replaced. Only Havel seems to have had a clear sense of purpose, and his goals, as may be seen in his New Year's address to the Czech and Slovak people, his first as president, were predictably concerned with the nation's moral condition. But he did emphasize in this speech that the Czechs and Slovaks, for once, had made their own history.

In contrast with 1918, 1938, 1945, 1948, and 1968, 1989 had found Czechoslovakia in control of its own destiny, albeit in a favorable international environment.

Some small doubts remain on this score. It has been suggested that November 17 was in fact engineered by elements within the Communist Party, possibly in collusion with Moscow, as a devious means of discrediting the conservative leadership and replacing them with reformers on the Gorbachev model. It may be some time before we know how far this was the case. In any event, even if the police violence was a devious plot to discredit Jakeš and his gang, it in no way diminishes the achievement of Havel and his allies, who took advantage of it to bring down not only Jakeš, but with him the whole Communist apparatus, conservatives, reformers, and all. At the very least it must be said that Jakeš's opponents within the party were almost as isolated and remote from developments as he was, since they too were shocked by the ease with which totalitarian political power and control withered and shriveled before their eyes.

Last, it is worth noting that until November 27, students and intellectuals were nervous (and in some cases pessimistic) as to the degree of support they would get from the industrial working class. What chance did a revolution led by actors, writers, and students and focused upon Prague (and to some extent Bratislava and Brno) have in a country where 60 percent of the working population were still blue-collar working class and where the latter had been carefully cosseted and sustained in reasonable living conditions by the party, the better to isolate intellectual and political opposition?[2] In short, the intellectuals had tended to believe the regime's own propaganda and were almost as surprised as the Communists when the hundreds of little Civic Forums in the factories managed to mobilize huge support for the general strike. It was at this point that the credibility of the "Workers' State" collapsed and the confidence of the revolutionary leadership found firm ground.

In the frenetic months between Havel's ascent to the castle and the first free elections since 1946, Czech public life revolved around four unresolved issues: the need to (re)invent politics and political parties; what measures to take with respect to the Czech economy; how to situate Czechoslovakia in the new international context; and how to resolve a problem not much discussed in the euphoria of November—the heightening tensions between Czechs and Slovaks.

2. The Communists had deliberately maintained huge industrial factories and complexes, even against the advice of their own economists, in order to ensure the survival and cohesion of a sympathetic (or at any rate beholden) proletarian constituency.

In addition to Civic Forum and Public against Violence, which aspired unsuccessfully and rather naively to remain nonpolitical umbrella groups embracing the loose coalition of November, Czechoslovakia already had four political parties, not including the Communists. The Socialist Party, the People's Party, the (Slovak) Democratic Party, and the (Slovak) Party of Freedom had continued an embryonic and enslaved existence under the old regime, nominally independent but under Communist control via the so-called National Front. Of these the first two had begun showing signs of independent life before November, and the Socialists' newspaper *Svobodné slovo* had been one of the first to condemn the police repression of November 17. By mid-January they were joined by more than thirty new parties seeking registration as independent entities. The most important of these were the various groups that came together under the general heading of Christian Democracy, an alliance of the old People's Party, a new Free Peasant Party and the Christian Democratic Party itself, led by former Charter 77 and CF activists like Václav Benda and the dissident priest Václav Mály, together with Slovaks like Ján Čarnogurský, newly released from prison and a prominent minister in Čalfa's first government.

The Christian Democrats and the Socialists, together with various Slovak groups, soon began to show signs of resentment at the Forum's close links to power. They also expressed dissatisfaction at the makeup of the Federal Assembly, where 120 (mostly CF/PAV) activists had been nominated to replace forcibly retired Communists on January 30, and whose composition took no formal account of the changing face of popular politics. The necessarily unrepresentative (or at least undemocratic) structure of power in the country during this interim period helps explain the growing internal dissent within the Forum itself, and the appeal of some of these new parties, reflected in opinion polls that had proliferated since February. On March 12 the Socialists' Youth organization publicly attacked CF for claiming a special status for itself,[3] while in Brno there were unpleasant and public personal squabbles between Forum leaders like Jaroslav Šabata and more radical, populist men like his opponent Petr Cibulka. Although, as we shall see, these divisions and feelings did not directly weaken the electoral appeal of the Forum, nor strengthen that of its opponents, they illustrated the unexpectedly rapid unraveling of the 1989 coalition and point to future political divisions in a country whose opposition had once been united and cohesive.

With the exception of the Christian Democrats, some of whose leaders,

3. See *Svobodné slovo*, March 12, 1990.

like Benda, were genuinely right wing by any European standard, most of the emerging political spectrum was divided more by personal and institutional issues than by matters of practical government policy. This can be seen from the attitude of the interim government toward the major economic issues facing it. In essence these consisted of a long-term crisis, that of the nation's creaking economic structure, and a short-term one: how to begin the transition to a market economy without provoking a massive economic and social crisis. That such a transition should take place was universally conceded, even by the Communists (albeit in questionable faith). On the one hand there were those like the finance minister Václav Klaus, and his deputy Vladimír Dlouhý, who advocated a rapid, and necessarily painful shift to free enterprise, and those like Valtr Komárek (a former Communist) who favored a slower, less radical transition. By April, Klaus had won. As Dlouhý put it in an article at the time, there was to be speedy legislation to favor private enterprise, foreign investment, and an end to central planning. The currency should be made convertible, monopolies should be broken up, and price controls progressively removed. The public control or ownership of the means of production should be reduced to the minimum, and the inevitable risk of inflation should be faced.[4]

No one seems to have argued openly against this strategy, saving those who sought to spread it over a longer period or postpone its more unpleasant aspects until after the June elections. Thus the Czechoslovak Assembly passed some sixty laws between February and June, many of them provisional but all of them significant. Of these the most important (leaving aside morally and symbolically significant measures such as the abolition of the death penalty on May 2) were probably the law ending monopolies and that which established the right to free enterprise (voted on April 19), with no limit on the scale of a business or the number of its employees. The de-control of prices was set to happen in two stages, the first on July 1, 1990, the second in January 1991. The timing here is significant—the true costs of the dismantling of communism in Czechoslovakia were not to be felt until after the elections. This delay not only ensured a continuing public sympathy for the interim authorities but helped perpetuate a common front on economic policy; the result of this, for many observers during the spring of 1990, was a strange sense of unreality, as though no one really wanted to acknowledge the implications of large-scale economic reform, at least not just yet.

The other area of agreement concerned foreign policy. It had been a

4. See Vladimír Dlouhý, in *Le Monde*, April 7, 1990.

central theme of dissidence ever since the founding of Charter 77 that
Czechoslovakia must "return to Europe," and thus it is not surprising to
find that Havel saw as one of his major tasks as interim president the "re-
centering" of his country in a democratic Europe. In his address to the
Polish Sejm on January 25, and again in the Hungarian parliament the
next day, he urged a coordinated "return" to Europe, echoing consciously
the 1985 "Prague Appeal" by Charter 77. On April 9 he repeated this
theme in the opening speech at a meeting in Bratislava attended by the
presidents, prime ministers, and foreign ministers of Poland, Czechoslovakia, and Hungary. Of special significance was the presence, too, of the
foreign ministers of Austria, Yugoslavia, and Italy, emphasizing a common Central European vision of regional coordination and cooperation
across the old political and military barriers. Havel's concerns are echoed
in public sentiment in his country, where a concern to be part of a common European structure, protected by security systems that preclude
division and exclusion, is rooted in Czechoslovakia's unhappy and still-
fresh memories of the price it has paid whenever the Continent and its
great powers have been divided or in conflict. Havel himself also spoke on
these occasions to the special problem of Poland, squeezed between the
USSR and a uniting Germany and lacking the option of close links with
the Western democracies traditionally interested in the region (Austria
and Italy). It is not clear, however, how much his personal affection for
Polish politicians like Adam Michnik, and his concern for Poland's fate,
are also reflected in the thoughts of his fellow countrymen.

So much for areas of general agreement. In at least one issue, however,
it soon became clear just how much the political revolution in Czechoslovakia had opened up an old and painfully divisive issue. Czechoslovakia
is a country of some sixteen million people, of whom just under ten
million are Czechs (Bohemians, Moravians, and Silesians), while five
million are Slovaks (the rest are mostly Hungarians or Gypsies). Under
the Communist regime Slovakia received a lot of industrial investment
and modernized rather rapidly. Its long-standing resentment at Czech
domination, however, and the occasional aspiration to autonomy or even
independence, were suppressed. The democratic revolution, in which the
Slovaks played an active if necessarily minor role, changed all that. In the
opening up of the national past for public scrutiny and debate, it became
clear just how widespread Slovak national sentiment was, to the point
where it became normal to hear favorable commentaries on the regime of
Jozef Tiso, the puppet government set up by the Nazis and the only
"independent" state the Slovaks have ever had. Although Havel and his

Slovak allies publicly frowned upon efforts officially to commemorate a Fascist government that had sent more than sixty thousand Jews to their deaths, they sought in other ways to placate Slovak feelings and retain the alliance and cooperation of November. This was a difficult task, given that even the leaders of PAV were in many cases openly at odds with the Czechs—in the matter of religion, for example, where men like Ján Čarnogurský favored something like the establishment of Catholicism as a state religion, understandable in heavily Catholic Slovakia but anathema to most Czechs.

A symptomatic and symbolic expression of the Slovak problem was provided by the Federal Assembly's debates in March over a new name for the country. For the Czech representatives, it was sufficient to remove the word "Socialist" from the old form, leaving "Czechoslovak Republic," or "Republic of Czechoslovakia." But the Slovaks insisted upon distinguishing their nation from that of the Czechs, and after the last-minute intervention of a sick Havel, the Assembly on March 29 agreed on the ungainly neologism "Czecho-slovak Republic," the Slovaks being authorized to use the hyphen, but on condition that they retain "slovak" in the lower case. This unhappy compromise produced demonstrations in Bratislava the very next day, demanding a Slovak state, and within three weeks the Federal Assembly was forced to come up with a new compromise, "The Czech and Slovak Federal Republic." It is far from clear whether this way of resolving a deep division of sentiment will prove lasting. Nationalist groups that have sprung up in Slovakia in the postrevolutionary period, such as the Štúr Association, the Slovak National Party, and the Slovak National Renewal Party, are strong enough to keep the issue alive, buoyed by resentment at the treatment of the 120,000 Slovaks in Hungary and at what they see as Prague's patronizing dismissal of Slovak feelings and needs. Local support may be less important in maintaining their fervor than the money they can raise from the Slovak population abroad (over three million strong), which is especially receptive to requests for help in advancing the more extreme nationalist case.

The institutional significance of the Slovak issue was already clear before June, when all decisions however minor had to be taken at three administrative levels (the federal, the Czech, and the Slovak), with ministries, commissions, and administrators often triplicating one another expensively and to mutual disadvantage—hence, among other reasons, the incentive to postpone vital choices in economic, ecological, educational, and religious affairs. Just how much it will complicate the future of the country can be seen from the results of the elections held on June 8 and 9, which produced the assemblies that were to govern the country for the next two years and that have among other tasks that of writing a new constitution.

On February 28, the interim Assembly of Czechoslovakia passed an electoral law that established the ground rules for the coming elections. Any party seeking election had to show proof of either 10,000 members or 10,000 signatories in its support. By April, twenty-three parties had met this test, although many of them would eventually come together in coalitions, the better to take advantage of the list-based proportional representation system the Assembly had chosen. To be represented in the Federal Assembly a party (or list of parties) had to secure at least 5 percent of the popular vote (following the West German example)—a further incentive to coalition building. In the Federal Assembly there were to be 150 seats in the House of the People (101 to represent the Czechs, 49 the Slovaks), and a further 150 in the House of Nations (75 each to Czechs and Slovaks alike). In addition there were to be simultaneous elections to the Czech and Slovak National Councils (their respective state assemblies); the 5 percent barrier applied to the Czech National Council as well, but in Slovakia, as a concession to the smaller electorate and minor parties there, the bar was set at 3 percent of the popular vote.

According to the opinion polls from January to May, Christian Democrats and Slovak national parties were doing well, while CF/PAV, though still the most popular organization in the land, was declining, paying the price for its internal divisions and the role of its leaders in sensitive governmental positions. The Communists, after falling to a low of 9 percent in the Czech lands and 6 percent in Slovakia, seemed to be improving their position in the weeks before the election despite growing demands in some circles for a punitive purge.[5] In general, however, the election campaign was marked by an absence of political disagreement, each party or group preferring instead to emphasize its own qualifications to carry out generally agreed-upon policies of economic transformation, political liberalization, and a return to the community of European nations. It was as though all sides were waiting for the elections to clarify their own standing and to clear the terrain for "real" political life in the country.

In this respect the elections may have helped, although they resolved little else. In the Federal Assembly the CF/PAV coalition did better than

5. These figures are from polls taken in January 1990. By March the Communists had already recovered to a nationwide support of about 13 percent. For more details, see *Pravda* (Bratislava), February 20, 1990, and *Rudé právo*, March 15, 1990.

recent polls had suggested, securing a narrow overall majority in both houses (though not within the Slovak section of the House of Nations). In the Czech Republic it also did well, winning 127 seats out of 200. In Slovakia, however, while it led all other parties, PAV did not get an absolute majority and will have to govern in coalition, probably with the Christian Democrats. The latter did not do as well as they had hoped, despite the popularity and prominence of some of their leaders and the undoubted revival of religious sentiment in the country. In the Federal Assembly they obtained just 40 seats (against 170 for CF/PAV), doing a little worse than the Communists (with 47 seats); in Slovakia they did predictably better, emerging there as the second party, but in the Czech Republic the Christian and Democratic Union got just 8.4 percent of the popular vote.

Two other features of the election outcome merit attention. The Socialist Party and a re-emergent Czechoslovak Social Democratic Party did surprisingly poorly—neither of them securing enough votes to be represented in *any* of the federal or state assemblies. In a country with the strongest social-democratic tradition in Central Europe (until 1948) and a large working-class electorate, this points to the one unambiguous historical achievement of communism in Czechoslovakia: its (albeit unintended) success in obliterating all trace of the tradition of left-wing political sentiment in the land! Second, one should note the very real achievement of the national minority parties. The Hungarian Christian Democratic Party elected twelve members to the Federal Assembly, but of even greater significance is the fact that a Hungarian group scored 8.64 percent of the vote in Slovakia (as the Party of Coexistence) and will now have fourteen seats in the Slovak National Council. This resurgence of local sentiment even touched the Czech lands, where the Association for Moravia and Silesia obtained 10.3 percent of the popular votes and will have 22 seats in the Czech National Council (more than the Christian Democrats) and sixteen seats in the Federal Assembly. But the real victory may have been scored by the Slovak nationalists. They won fifteen seats in the Federal Assembly and twenty-two in the Slovak National Council (with 14 percent of the vote, the same as the Communists got in Slovakia). Because the new constitution will need to be approved by three-fifths of the deputies in the Federal House of Nations (as well as in the Slovak National Council), the Slovak nationalists will be able to help block its passage unless it contains real provisions for autonomy—or more. In this they will certainly receive the support of the Moravian and Silesian autonomists, and very possibly that of the Communists (voting as spoilers) and the Slovak Christian Democrats (seeking to improve their standing in the Slovak community). The future of the unified Czechoslovak Republic is by no means unclouded.

As a result of the elections, Havel named Čalfa to form a new government, and the newly elected Federal Assembly returned Dubček to his seat as its chairman. These moves, and the reelection of Havel as president on July 5, helped convey a sense of continuity and permanence—and indeed, the problems facing the new government and the various parliaments were much the same as those that existed before. Now, however, there was no longer the excuse of forthcoming elections to justify postponement of difficult choices. The first of these concerns the Communist Party. Had the party been obliterated at the elections it might have been allowed to fade quietly away, leaving behind an economic and ecological disaster and many bad memories but posing little threat to the future. But instead it scored a surprisingly respectable 13 percent, making it the second party in the Federal Assembly and the Czech National Council and a significant presence even in the Slovak National Council. Under these circumstances, and even though its appeal is certainly generational (its electorate being substantially older than that of all other parties), the debates surrounding it remain very much alive.[6]

The first of these debates concerns its responsibility for past crimes. The Czechoslovak Communist Party and the country it ruled were undoubtedly the most consistently Stalinist and repressive in Europe (leaving aside the special case of Romania in the later years of the megalomaniacal Nicolae Ceauşescu), and there is little sign that the party has genuinely sought to reform itself or to confess its grosser sins. Certainly Jakeš and the Prague party leader Štěpán were expelled, followed by Husák and the former prime minister Lubomir Štrougal in February. But this constitutes no more than the traditional Communist practice of identifying scapegoats, rather than any acknowledgment of the collective errors these men symbolized, and there has so far been no indication of any serious intraparty debate over its common past. The party retains, moreover, not only its identity (more so than its sister parties in Hungary and elsewhere) but also many of its resources: even after the loss (by March 1990) of one-

6. The Communists' election campaign, symbolically limited to the display of their new logo (a pair of cherries) and the assurance of good intentions, had at least the advantage of alienating no one. Their vote was drawn overwhelmingly from rural areas, where agricultural cooperatives had been fairly successful in recent years, and from the tens of thousands of men and women whose livelihoods, past and future alike, depended upon the patronage of the party.

third of its former membership, it was still, at the time of the elections, the biggest and richest political body in the land.

Hence the pressure, in some quarters, to purge the Communists and punish them, individually or collectively, for their misdeeds. On April 30 Tomáš Sokol, the Prague city prosecutor, sent a letter to the Central Committee of the Communist Party warning it that he was considering a prosecution under the law prohibiting "Fascist or similar" movements (article 261 of the penal code). Although the general prosecutor of the republic disassociated himself from this move and members of CF publicly criticized it, there was much public sympathy for Sokol's position. Meanwhile, Miroslav Štěpán, the Prague Communist leader, was tried in June for his part in the November 17 events, and on July 9 found guilty of an "abuse of power." He was then sentenced to four years in prison, a judgment he is appealing. How much further the new government will go is unclear. On May 21 the interim Assembly voted to expropriate the party of all the property it had been given or had "rented" under the old regime, a move that went into effect on June 1. But Havel and many of the CF leaders are known to oppose further purges and to prefer what they see as the path of "reconciliation."[7]

This path may prove to be difficult. During the election campaign a number of charges, some of them subsequently proven, surfaced against politicians active in the new political parties, like Josef Bartončik, leader of the People's Party, and even Ján Budaj, a prominent figure in Public against Violence. The essence of the accusations was that these men had collaborated with the old, Communist regime, usually as informers working with the Secret Police. In the case of Budaj this was apparently the price he paid, in 1979, to obtain a passport, and his sin seems at worst venial. But the deeper problem is that what is true of Budaj and Bartončik doubtless applies to thousands, maybe even hundreds of thousands, of other Czechs and Slovaks. After 1969 it was almost impossible to secure proper employment, much less services, advancement, and the education of one's children, without collaborating in some respect, however minor. The position of CF, and of Havel, in these matters seems reasonable: only where high public office is concerned should people's pasts be closely investigated, and then by some independent mechanism to be established.

7. This is one of Havel's reasons for reappointing Čalfa as prime minister. A reform Communist who left the party only on January 18, 1990, Čalfa is symbolic of the sort of person with whom Havel and many others believe it is necessary to work, if the country is ever to be reconciled with its recent history.

Anything short of this degree of amnesty risks exposing people to false accusations and revenge, or else providing occasions for political manipulation—as in the case of Bartončik, who was revealed as an ex-collaborator just before the elections, by government officials openly sympathetic to his election opponents in Civic Forum. At the same time, failure to bring out to the fullest degree the crimes and corruption of the Communists may leave the latter quite well placed to benefit in the future from discontent with the democratic regime and its policies.[8] The question remains unresolved.

That there will be discontent is not in dispute. In contrast to the Poles, or the Hungarians, the Czechs and Slovaks have the unwanted advantage of knowing (from their neighbors' example) what economic reform really means. Some of them also, probably, still share the illusion that in Czechoslovakia at least, Communist economics worked. As to the difficulties, they have already begun: on July 9, 1990, the price of some thirty thousand items (mostly foodstuffs) rose by 25 percent, and with currency reform and the further lifting of subsidies in 1991 there are more increases to come. Any attempt to keep prices low (to avoid hyper-inflation) will undermine new enterprises that have started up and will kill a lot of them off. Foreign interest has proved less enthusiastic than hoped, as Hungary offers an easier terrain for investment (by the end of 1990 the government in Prague had still not fully removed many of the stifling regulations surrounding trade and business activity) and German concerns have been diverted to unification. As for the things the Czechs do well—the foreign minister Jiří Dienstbier announced on January 25, 1990, that the country would soon cease to export arms. (During the eighties Czechoslovakia stood sixth in the world in the arms trade in absolute terms and took first place in the value of arms exports per capita of the population.) It is not clear how long post-Communist governments will feel able to sustain this sort of morally informed position.

Equally unclear is how Czechoslovakia will handle its ecological problems. The country is notoriously the most polluted one in Europe. The political community is especially sensitive to this point because, after industrial northern Bohemia, it is Prague itself where the pollution is at its worst. The poor electoral showing of the badly organized Greens (who just scraped above the 3 percent mark in Slovakia but are unrepresented in the Czech and Federal assemblies) should not mislead one into believ-

8. In the municipal elections of November 1990, the Communists took nearly 15 percent of the vote, considerably more in some districts, a result largely attributable to growing anxiety in the face of economic change and uncertainty.

ing that ecological sensibilities are low. It does not, however, follow from this that anyone has an obvious solution to offer. The worst instances of corruption and sheer abuse can of course be prevented now, but the structural problem remains: Czechoslovakia cannot afford to import oil and gas at world prices (including from the USSR) and will thus for the moment continue to produce and use the lignite (brown coal) that has so damaged much of its northern quadrant. Nuclear energy (controversial at the best of times) can at present provide only 24 percent of its requirements in electric power. Thus the new government, many of whose leading figures were ecological activists in opposition and remain sensitive on the issue, will not be able to do much to alleviate the causes (as distinct from palliate the consequences) of the country's sad physical condition, at least not for some years to come. The easy rhetoric of the dissident years and the revolutionary months is already giving way to disabused realism.

Another source of disagreement is religion. Superficially, this is not a contentious area. When Pope John Paul II came to Czechoslovakia on April 21 (two days after the reestablishment of diplomatic relations between the Vatican and Prague), he was met with huge crowds and much real affection—in Catholic Slovakia the capital Bratislava boasted a crowd of one million on April 22—nearly 20 percent of the entire population of the Slovak Republic! Havel has often stressed the importance of faith and spirituality, and he and the pope can sometimes sound remarkably alike; for all that, Havel is not thought of as a practicing Catholic.[9] Moreover, though not as much as in Poland of course, the dissident Catholic community played an important role in Charter 77 throughout the 1980s, as well as in the November revolution itself.

This said, there remain issues of real contention. On May 30 Ján Čarnogurský, at the time still a senior minister in the federal government, accused CF of failing to support the Catholics' demand that land and property seized from the church forty years before be returned to it. He seems not to have appreciated that if the church could claim such a restoration of its property, so could millions of families and individuals expropriated by the Communists after 1948. Or, rather, by ignoring the point he implicitly demanded for the church a special status in Czechoslovak society, and it is this demand that many Czechs refuse to acknowledge. The association of church with nation that so marks Polish history and is echoed in Slovakia is quite absent in the Czech lands (where,

9. In his major speech in Czechoslovakia, the pope took the opportunity to condemn "Western" secularism, hedonistic consumerism, practical materialism, and moral atheism. These are themes well worn in some of Havel's own writings from the early eighties.

indeed, a tradition associated with Tomáš G. Masaryk sees the Catholic church instead as the traditional enemy of Czech identity, the latter represented spiritually in the martyr Jan Hus). Furthermore, the peculiarly *religious* hue of Christian Democratic politics in Czechoslovakia (more marked than in similarly labeled parties in France, Italy, or Germany) has tended to distance the secular liberals of CF and PAV from men like Mály, Benda, and Čarnogurský, whose theocratic and conservative bent was no secret in the days of Charter 77 but was conveniently ignored or minimized by those whom it made uncomfortable. In any case, the antireligious stance of the governing Communists, the most intransigent among the Soviet European satellites, generated sympathy for persecuted Christians even among the nonpracticing.

In addition to disputes over the church and the major question of Czech-Slovak relations, the country is also afflicted with a spate of lesser conflicts surrounding ethnic and other minorities. None of these is new, but only with the liberalization of politics (and the onset of new economic difficulties) have they surfaced into public (and international) view. The Hungarian minority has already been mentioned. It is about 600,000 strong (some 4 percent of the total population, but about 10 percent of the population of Slovakia) and is concentrated in rural areas along the Slovak border with Hungary itself. Although it is not as badly off as the smaller Slovak minority in Hungary, it is certainly a disadvantaged minority, at the bottom of the economic heap for the most part and speaking a language frowned upon by officialdom in the Slovak Republic. Its reemergence from an imposed silence under the Communists coincides with a renewed interest in foreign-ruled Hungarians by the nationalistinclined Democratic Forum government in Budapest; this combination may make Hungarian demands more audible in Bratislava and Prague, but it is also helping to stoke the fires of Slovak nationalism in competition and reaction.

The Hungarian minority is still better off than the other large minority ethnic group in Czechoslovakia—the Gypsies. There are about half a million Gypsies in the country (possibly more, since official figures underestimate their number). They have always been poor, itinerant, unrepresented, and unloved. But only very recently have they been the target of open aggression. During April 1990 there were a series of attacks in northern Bohemia and in Prague, most of them the work of gangs of skinheads. These attacks culminated in a semi-riot on May Day, when a crowd of some two hundred skinheads in Prague went in search of Gypsies and Vietnamese (the largest foreign presence, about 35,000 in the country as a whole). The government's response was inadequate, to say the least—indeed, the only positive action taken by the Federal Assembly was to announce, on April 23, that by 1995 all foreign workers would have to leave Czechoslovakia. As an economic measure this may make some sense (the foreign work force in Czechoslovakia numbers 46,000, including the Vietnamese), but it is no way to handle growing ethnic violence and intolerance, and in any case does not address the chronic problem of the much more numerically significant Romany population. Havel himself proved inadequate on this occasion, attributing the attacks on Gypsies to "dark forces"—a depressing reminder of Communist-style explanations of all "unfortunate" social incidents of this kind. The forces may be dark, but they are not at all mysterious—there is growing racism and nationalism in the Czech and Slovak nations (one hesitates to add anti-Semitism, since there are only 6,000 Jews left, but it would not be inaccurate to do so), as there is among their neighbors. This is not the fault of the new rulers, but it will be their responsibility to combat it, and this they cannot do if they deny its presence.

So much for the problems facing Czechoslovakia's new leaders. What advantages do they start out with, in their unequal struggle with the past and its legacy? The first is their geopolitical situation. Although it is vulnerable to the backwash of the reunification of Germany, Czechoslovakia is a natural candidate for inclusion in existing and new networks of European nations to its south and west. To the south lies Alpe-Adria, a loose confederation of regions and states in northeastern Italy, Croatia, Slovenia, Austria, Bavaria, and western Hungary. Its economic and ecological coordination is still at an early stage (Alpe-Adria was formed in 1978), but as a token of the genuine reemergence of a Central European identity it has more than mere symbolic value.[10] To the west, Czechoslovakia can hope to benefit from its rapid transformation to political democracy (and the liberal political traditions on which that transformation built) to establish its candidacy for admission to an enlarged European Community, though probably not before 1993 at the earliest. The Czechs are aware of their advantages in this respect, and Havel has made a big point of encouraging his fellow Central Europeans not to forget about the Poles, but also not to isolate the USSR, not to "exclude" it from the new Europe, especially now that (following the Moscow agreement of February 26) nearly half the Soviet troops are out of Czechoslovakia and the

10. On May 20 Czechoslovakia joined the so-called Group of Four (later the Pentagonal Group), made up of Italy, Austria, Hungary, and Yugoslavia, whose primary purpose is to encourage mutual approaches to regional problems.

rest should be gone in the course of 1991. Some of this rhetoric may be attributed to the man and the country's occasional *folie des grandeurs,* nonetheless, Czechoslovakia does have quite strong international cards and clearly proposes to play them in as even-handed a manner as circumstances (and economic self-interest) permit.

To achieve such goals and in order to maintain the momentum of their revolution, the Czechs will continue to play their strongest card—Václav Havel himself. Havel's greatest success came at the very beginning of the revolution, in November 1989, when almost alone he appreciated the possibilities now open to the opposition. It was then that he insisted that they press their demands to the full, further and faster than anyone had hitherto thought possible. It was he, at the same time, who realized the need to avoid violence and above all to prevent political polarization—keeping lines of communication open to the Communists while giving the latter little option but to cede all real power. He was not alone in implementing these tactics, of course, and without students and workers he would have been nowhere. But the astonishing achievements of the "velvet revolution" are very much his own, and it is no accident that it was Havel whom the students and the Prague crowds propelled into the Prague castle.

This said, the man has undoubtedly made errors. Among these are his ill-advised visit to Salzburg on July 26, 1990, where he met the otherwise isolated Austrian president Kurt Waldheim. Havel's own Civic Forum colleagues advised against this move, as did former co-signatories of Charter 77, including his friend, the prime minister of the Czech republic, Petr Pithart. Then there was his New Year amnesty, which freed so many common criminals that the giant Škoda works had to reduce its working hours because it was deprived of the prison labor on which it had hitherto depended, like many other Czech heavy industries.[11] Havel has also been a trifle too enthusiastic in his condemnation of the expulsion of the Sudeten Germans, taking the opportunity of every encounter with President Richard von Weizsäcker of Germany to affirm his horror at this affront to human rights. He may be on strong moral ground, but he is almost certainly not in step with the innermost feelings of an older generation of Czechs. Finally, there was his rather obvious support for CF/PAV

---

11. There has been a rise in crime since the overthrow of the Communists, in Czechoslovakia and elsewhere. This can be attributed to a number of factors, but at the very least Havel's well-meaning release of so many prisoners will make him vulnerable to the charge of having contributed to the general increase in insecurity.

in the June elections, inappropriate if understandable when coming from a president supposedly above politics.[12]

Taken all in all, these actions suggest a man of admirable moral consistency for the most part, driven to conciliate and unite, both at home and abroad. They also hint, on occasion, at a sanctimonious and naïve sensibility that was well suited to the work of resistance, revolution, and political reconstruction, but which may leave Havel less equipped to lead his country through the more practical and mundane difficulties it is about to encounter.[13] His oft-expressed contempt for materialism and the crasser values of the West will not sit well with his countrymen as they try to weather difficult economic times, and it is an omen of what may lie ahead that there have been hints of popular resentment at his personal wealth (a resentment that will doubtless be fanned by Communists and Slovaks alike). It is doubtful whether he would be well advised to repeat in future years the theme of his 1990 New Year address, where he suggested that Czechoslovakia's best potential contribution to international politics in the future might be the "radiation of the power of love and spirituality."

These reflections notwithstanding, Havel's language and his ideas do capture something about the November revolution that is peculiar to Czechoslovakia. Nowhere else was so much achieved so quickly, at so little human cost and with so strong a chance of success. The atmosphere in Prague in December 1989 *was* charged with something spiritual, even if love is a little excessive as an account of it. The Czechs and Slovaks came from further behind and have moved further ahead (except in economic reform) than any other formerly Communist country. Much of this can still be attributed to the advantages of history—a strong liberal and democratic tradition sustained by an economic and social infrastructure not altogether destroyed by the Communists even after forty years. This history, and the confidence it has bred in even the most persecuted of

12. This may seem rather an unfair charge. In the still-uncertain circumstances of the spring of 1990, Havel could hardly be blamed for having put his weight behind the only political movement in the land capable of maintaining the momentum of the revolution it had done so much to bring about. It illustrated the fragility of his position, and the extent to which his personal heroism and moral credibility remained his chief (and perhaps his only) assets. In any case, for the moment there is no one else.

13. This is not to say that he is unaware of the scale of the hurdles to be overcome. On August 21, in a speech to mark the twenty-second anniversary of the Soviet occupation, he warned his compatriots against dwelling on the difficulties, against giving in to pessimism and treating the revolution as a "failure." The old structures remain, he said, and it is up to us to eject them. We must open new businesses, remove the old bureaucrats, change the parasitic and dependent habits of our countrymen. Everything remains to be done, the revolution is not yet finished. See report in *Le Monde*, August 23, 1990.

Czech democrats, is their best hope for a secure future. It is also their weak point, since Czechs especially are inclined to dwell on the advantages of their inheritance and ignore or underplay those aspects of the Central European heritage they share with their less-fortunate neighbors. The degree to which they come to acknowledge and address their domestic divisions and difficulties will determine not so much the survival of post-Communist Czechoslovakia—which seems reasonably assured—as the "quality" of its political life. In this as in other matters, the Czechs face an ecological crisis, one from which they can no longer turn away, however elegant and sympathetic the face they thereby present abroad.

Romania after Ceauşescu: Post-Communist Communism?

Katherine Verdery and Gail Kligman

> Since last December, things have not changed very much.
> —Romanian President Ion Iliescu, July 1990

What "really happened" in Romania in December 1989, when the twenty-five-year rule of Nicolae Ceauşescu was violently overthrown? For the moment, for the present authors, and, we believe, for most if not all members of Romanian society, it is simply impossible to say. Certain things are, of course, clear enough. The dictator and his wife fled, were captured, and were executed. A group calling itself the National Salvation Front assumed formal governance over Romanian society. Political parties, including the "historical" Liberal, National Peasant, and Social Democratic parties, quickly emerged to compete in the political arena; their representatives shared power with the Front from the formation of a provisional parliament in late February until the May 20 elections, which resulted in an overwhelming victory for President Ion Iliescu and a substantial one for the Front. What is impossible to say about these (and many other) events is precisely *how* they came about, who the decisive actors were, and what the events imply for the future course of events in Romania.

In this essay, we raise far more questions that we answer; we leave unresolved the contradictions among accounts we heard or have read; and we are hesitant to predict the future course of events. Indeed, our strongest claim is that for Romania, any account pretending to greater certainty than we offer is questionable. We address four areas: the "revolution" of December 1989, the much-discussed matter of whether it and the elections produced a neo-Communist restoration, the postelection

118 Katherine Verdery and Gail Kligman

weakness of Ion Iliescu's broadly mandated government as evident in events of June 13–15, 1990, and the broader issue of continuity and change in state-society relations.[1] Our principal message is that the situation is generally chaotic, is fraught with contradictions, and will in all likelihood worsen before improving.

The "Revolution" of 1989

The "movement of rage" (in Ken Jowitt's phrase) that overthrew Nicolae Ceauşescu on December 22, 1989, ushered in a monumental power struggle that had not been resolved more than a year later. From the near-unanimity of the social opposition that toppled his rule there emerged increasing fragmentation and strife, as various coalitions and groups struggled to fill the power vacuum left by Ceauşescu's exit. Cunning politician that he was, Ceauşescu had regularly cleared the terrain of contenders, successfully undermined all foci of opposition, and devastated other groupings that might eventually have challenged his place. His regime had overseen a remarkable atomization of Romanian society, in which fear and distrust became the currency of human relations, obviating all but the most localized and circumscribed solidarities. In any era other than that of a *glasnost'*-ravaged East European communism, his overthrow would probably not have happened when and as it did.

Western viewers saw on their television screens the first "revolution" witnessed live on mass media. What we thought we saw was a popular uprising: unarmed masses being fired upon in the streets of Timişoara (December 16–18) and then Bucharest (December 21–25), and ferocious exchanges occurring reportedly between the army, which had switched to the side of the people, and the Secret Police (Securitate), which had remained loyal to Ceauşescu until his televised cadaver persuaded them to renounce their mission. Gruesome photos of mass burials and signs of torture seemed to confirm the Securitate as the villains, the civilians and their army allies as the heroes. Dissident writers and others opposed to Ceauşescu jubilantly emerged from months of police surveillance to join the post-Ceauşescu government; the slogan "Down with communism!" completed the image of the event as a genuine revolutionary overthrow not only of Ceauşescu but also of Communist Party rule in Romania. It

1. Owing to limits on space, we have cut details and summarized many points and events for which full understanding would require longer exposition. We also note that this essay was written in November 1990 and reflects developments up to that point.

was by far the most stunning, brutal, and radical of the regime changes in the socialist bloc. Or was it?

Questions arose almost immediately, fueled by inconsistencies in the death figures reported from the revolution—initially as high as 60,000, then progressively lower (to an official count of 1,033, in July 1990).[2] Tapes of early government meetings registered the comment of the revolutionary General Nicolae Militaru that the National Salvation Front had already existed for several months, suggesting that the "revolution" was in fact a disguised coup. This view appeared most fully in an article in the French newspaper *Le Point*, which argued that what seemed a spontaneous uprising was a plot existing since 1971, its Timişoara outbreak liberally assisted by Hungary and by the conspirators' Soviet connections.[3] Its apparent struggle between army and Securitate had been staged, claimed *Le Point*, so as to enable the plotters to recapture for neo-Communist rule the power the popular revolution threatened to drain away.[4]

Although we lack space to expand upon this scenario, we wish nonetheless to observe that the *Le Point* thesis epitomizes the "plot mentality" characteristic of virtually every Romanian's description of events prior to, during, and after December.[5] It also poses questions that challenge the first "official version" of those events as a street revolution aided by the army. The socialist-planning mindset, the internalized tendency to blame every problem on "plots" or "outside forces," and the climate of suspicion so thick in Romania, together made it a reflex to see an organized action behind many events that may be adequately explained by confusion, self-interest, and improvisation. The Iliescu government continued this legacy,

2. The figure of 1,033 was given by President Iliescu in an interview (see "Preşedintele Ion Iliescu răspunde la întrebările 'României literare,' " *România literară*, July 5, 1990, p. 14). This figure left out, however, the dead in several major cities, and when pressed as to whether 1,033 was the exact number, Iliescu replied that it was the number "based on data verified up to the present time."

3. The original article, written by Olivier Weber and Radu Portucală, appeared in *Le Point*, May 21, 1990. The version we have consulted is a Romanian translation under the title "România—complotul iese la iveală" (*Expres*, no. 24 [July 4–11, 1990], pp. 4–5). Two other articles of the many in which the idea of a plot is discussed are Eugen Popescu, "Cine se ascunde în spatele morţilor noştri?" *Nu* 1, no. 18 (1990): 5, and Florin Iaru, "Poporul era să fure revoluţia Securităţii," 22, May 11, 1990, pp. 8–9.

4. In taking this line, *Le Point* seconded Ceauşescu's own diagnosis of what was happening: "It's an attempt at a coup d'état, a maneuver of our enemies both in the west and in the east."

5. The descriptions come from the authors' 1990 field trips to Romania; Kligman (February 8–28 and June 6–August 15) spent most of her time in Bucharest and a few days in northern Transylvania, and Verdery (July 6–27) spent two weeks in Cluj and villages in southern Transylvania, and a week in Bucharest.

identifying several suspected "plots" in its environs early on. Similarly, persons in the opposition proclaimed "Communist plots" lurking beneath the government's actions, while various other events were attributed to "plots" by Hungarians.[6] Details of the December "plot" proliferated as its putative members—especially General Militaru and the Front member Silviu Brucan—expanded upon their role in it.[7]

While there had indeed been opposition to Ceauşescu since the 1970s by people who would have liked to take his place, we find it unhelpful to speak of *a* plot active as early as 1971. Between 1971 and December 1989, Romanians hatched enough "plots" to kill the dictator a thousand times over. Diverse plot scenarios must be placed in the context of ongoing power struggles in which legitimacy rests on upholding the popular revolution, such that talk of plots undermines the legitimacy of the supposed plot members still in power. In this regard, we note that among the most active proponents of a supposed plot were persons once at the center of the Front leadership who had been marginalized.

We find it both unnecessary and unlikely that the Timişoara demonstrations were organized from above and afar, as the *Le Point* scenario holds. One need not posit such organization to explain the revolt of people living near Romania's border with Yugoslavia and Hungary, who had been watching Yugoslav and Hungarian television programs for two or more years, who were heading into their seventh winter of freezing homes and below-subsistence diets, and who had been listening to foreign radio posts for months and knew what was happening in the rest of the bloc.[8] Sparked by advance disclosure of the impending arrest of the antiregime pastor László Tőkés, their uprising ignited readily. Whether or not conspirators helped to spread the disturbance to Bucharest, there were a number of other, *un*organized channels through which it spread: international media, army reservists sent in to Timişoara from elsewhere who then returned home—intermingled with Timişoarans and migrant workers who fled the city with them—and railway workers, who transmitted news via the only telephone lines that had not been cut off.[9] And one need not explain the inflated death count by conspiratorial purposes: decades

6. See, for example, Ion Cristoiu, "Ce se ascunde dincolo de evenimentele din 13, 14 şi 15 iunie?" *Zig-Zag*, June 19–26, 1990, pp. 16, 2.

7. See, for example, D. Novăceanu's interview with Militaru and Brucan, "Adevărul, numai adevărul," *Adevărul*, August 23, 1990, pp. 1, 3.

8. A young factory worker reportedly agitated the crowd on December 16 with the words, "All Europe has given us an example to follow: Poland, Hungary, the USSR, Czechoslovakia, Yugoslavia, Bulgaria! What are we still waiting for?" See Miodrag Milin, *Timişoara: 15–21 decembrie '89* (Timişoara, 1990), p. 32.

9. Ibid., pp. 155–58.

of wildly inflated figures and of total reliance on rumor for information made those initial figures plausible, just as the government's effort to reduce the appearance of its crimes against the people would later cause it to lower those figures so astonishingly.

The questions raised either by Le Point or by other publications compel us, nonetheless, to recognize an internal conspiracy as contributing to Ceauşescu's overthrow, alongside many other factors. Why was the television broadcast tower not disabled, despite heavy gunfire, nor its power supply cut off, when to do so would have been not only easy—especially for a Securitate renowned for its commando training—but also a major setback for the persons holding the Front in power through their presence there?[10] How was it possible that Ceauşescu was not restrained from calling the disastrous December 21 meeting in Bucharest's Palace Square, which anyone—including his personal guard—could have told him was risky? Is it possible that this idea was actually suggested to him by his Securitate handlers? Why were two brigades of specially trained commandos massacred by the army in front of the Ministry of Defense, as they arrived to assist the troops? Why have there been no visible moves, comparable to the process initiated in East Germany, to dismantle the old Securitate apparatus? Why were the generals who were implicated in firing on the populace in Timişoara promoted in rank? Why did one of them soon become defense minister? If the army was struggling to defend the new government against Securitate loyalists, why were all buildings in Palace Square severely marked with bullet holes except the Central Committee building, in which members of the provisional government were sitting? What happened to the so-called terrorists who were captured and then either disappeared from their hospital beds or were freed untried? This list barely opens the questions that can be put to the "official version" of a popular revolution clinched by the army's fire against the Securitate terrorists. What conclusions can we draw from these confused, often conflicting possibilities?

First, it is virtually certain that without the popular uprising, a coup d'état would have had great difficulty overthrowing Ceauşescu (unless aided by foreign troops), and, at the same time, without the support of not just the army but at least a portion of the Securitate, no popular uprising could have succeeded. In our view, the revolution came from a fortuitous convergence of several elements: superpower interests, events in neighboring countries that permeated Romania's borders via the air waves, some

10. This question is particularly salient given that broadcasting *was* interrupted in June when the station was "attacked"—without the help of artillery.

sort of conspiracy at the top, and a long-incubated "movement of rage," culminating in a genuine popular uprising. None of these elements alone would have been sufficient.

Second, it is beyond doubt, as stated above, that the events of December 16–22 initiated a fierce struggle for power. A part of this struggle has been for control over the apparatus of governance and another part has been to control the basis of its legitimation: clear title to having brought off the revolution. No group could hope to exercise power effectively unless legitimated by a heroic role in the revolution; hence the battle over the revolution as symbol. The army—despite its having in fact fired on crowds in December—was more successful in this battle than the Securitate, owing in part to widespread hatred of the latter, long regarded as the incarnation of evil. The power struggle intensified in January, when the bulk of the Securitate was administratively subordinated to the army. This aggravated the already marked reversal of the earlier balance between the once-privileged Securitate and the neglected military, a reversal Securitate members have striven to rectify.

Third and finally, we must ask why the idea of the revolution's "confiscation" became so important for some groups in Romania—whom does such an idea serve? Allegations of a coup clearly imply betrayal of the street revolt, which suggests that some group other than the ruling members of the Front should be in power. Such allegations are, thus, in part a surface form of the power struggle. We find it prudent to be equally skeptical of "plot" stories and of the official image of an army-assisted popular revolution.

The Election Results:
Post-Communist Communism?

On May 20, 1990, Romanians elected Ion Iliescu president with 85 percent of the vote, giving the National Salvation Front 66 percent of the seats in the Assembly of Deputies and 67 percent of those in the Senate. This was an overwhelming success for an organization that had initially said it would not participate in the elections, had provoked outrage when it changed its stand, and had not yet held a party convention to define its politics.[11] Besides the Front, eighty-two parties competed in the elections.

11. The former Front member Silviu Brucan rationalized the Front's change of heart as stemming from its members' belief that the elections should give Romanians a real choice— lacking in a field in which the principal parties were defined as center-right. "If none but the parties had stood for election, [this would have left] a political vacuum, a political void. Since the majority of these parties are on the right, the center and left would not have been

Principal among them were two of the "historical" parties, revived from
the interwar years—the National Liberal Party (PNL) and the National
Christian Democratic Peasant Party (PNȚ), both of which ran Romanian
émigrés as presidential candidates. There were also many new parties,
such as the Ecology Movement Party and the Hungarian Democratic
Union of Romania (which, with 7 percent of the vote, emerged stunningly
as the largest opposition party). Foreign observers judged these elections
legal and fair, thereby lending the Iliescu government international acceptance and increasing its hopes for foreign aid. But inevitably there were
charges of fraud, especially by the Romanian émigré community and the
major opposition parties.[12] While we cannot fully corroborate or discon-
firm these charges, we can describe a few respects in which we find the
electoral procedure wanting (whether by design or not) and in which it
must be improved in future elections.

To begin with, it is undeniable that the elections were held too soon for
other parties to organize themselves effectively, given the complete disar-
ray of all oppositional forces a scant five months earlier (in contrast to
Poland or Czechoslovakia, for example). A the same time, a delay of three
or four months would not have dramatically altered this situation but
would have prolonged the provisional character of a political authority
that badly needed a legal basis. More critical, the Front's control over
television and its refusal to permit independent stations, unexplained
irregularities in the delivery of electoral propaganda for the other parties
in the provinces, and restrictions on electoral mobilization in some
provincial villages all prejudiced the ability of the other parties to get their
message to voters. For instance, we heard reports of villages in which
some local official or "someone from county headquarters" had torn
down posters for parties other than the Front, saying, "It has been decided
that there will be only one party in this county." We heard a variety of
stories from people holding subscriptions to the newspapers of the other
parties (for example, the Peasantists' *Dreptatea*), or to papers taking a
position critical of the Front (for example, *România liberă*), that their
copies were rarely delivered to their houses or villages. Similarly, friends

---

covered" ("In dialog: revoluția la răscruce," 22, February 16, 1990, p. 12). This is a somewhat specious argument, since the Liberal Party was more centrist than right and since at
least two Social Democratic parties fielded candidates, although admittedly neither had a
social base.

12. See, for instance, the London-based newspaper of the PNȚ candidate Ion Rațiu, *The
Free Romanian*, June 1990, p. 1 ("How Iliescu and Co. Gagged Free Speech"), and the
Franco-American Romanian émigré publication *Lupta*, June 15, 1990, p. 9 ("The Elections
in Romania"). Kligman heard consistently disturbing accounts of vote fraud in the north,
particularly against the PNȚ. This said, there is no doubt that Iliescu and the Front would
have won the elections, by a somewhat smaller margin, even without such fraud.

in villages said that leaders of the collective farms had warned that if the National Peasants or Liberals won the election, collective farms would be disbanded immediately and villagers would lose their farm pensions. In other villages, people told of obstructive tactics used on election day, ranging from ballot-stuffing and exploitation of the illiterate to physical confrontation.

It is difficult to prove that all these obstructions were actively ordered by the Front's political organization. We need not blame centrally organized intimidation to understand why collective-farm leaders, relying on the existence of the collective farm for comfortable livings, would wish to mobilize support against the parties advocating agriculture's privatization. The Front's steadfast vagueness concerning its intentions for agriculture made it the best bet for people holding executive positions in the system of socialist farms. Supporters of opposition parties claim to have photographs of bales of the Peasantist newspaper (for instance) being taken straight from the train station to the pulping mills, presumably by order of the Front. The "presumably" is important here, for once again, as with the collective-farm executives, city and county political officials knew full well from the electoral promises of the opposition parties that all persons with pasts in Romania's Communist Party apparatus would have no place in a Romania dominated by Liberals or Peasantists, whereas the Front would clearly be less exigent in this regard. For such persons, it was surely desirable to restrict access to electoral material from the opposition parties, even without party orders to do so. We also heard reports that opposition papers failed to reach their destinations because delivery boys and mailmen often stole them to sell at scalper's prices.[13] Although there is evidence of the Front's obstructing oppositional views, it is impossible to know how much was directed from the top and how much came from local-level maneuvering. That people *assumed* the diabolical work of a unified Front in these outcomes is yet another example of the widely prevalent "plot mentality."

The Front's main electoral base consisted of former party officials, peasants, and unskilled workers (many of whom live in villages). The campaign made good use not only of "lemons, meat, and gas," as the saying went, but also, paradoxically, of many ideas from Ceauşescu's time. These included the notions that the other parties were "traitors" and would "sell the country to foreigners," that they were organized and supported "from abroad" rather than from within, and that the Liberals

---

13. See also Emil Munteanu, "Ancheta 'R.L.: Cine şi cum fură presa?" *România liberă,* July 14, 1990, p. 3.

were out to reestablish the old landed aristocracy and restore great differences of wealth. This "dirty" campaigning and the Front's appeal to emotions rather than ideas are not, however, things about which Americans have any right to moralize. Xenophobia, together with decades of Communist teachings against the interwar parties and in favor of social equality, gave the "historical" parties a decidedly uphill fight, aggravating their disadvantage in the Front-controlled broadcasting media.

Despite legitimate questions about the electoral campaign, foreign observers concluded that the election results were sufficiently close to fair and did not warrant challenge. This judgment is separate, however, from the question, much discussed by both Romanians and outsiders, as to whether Romania's more or less legitimately elected new leadership was or was not a victory for "neocommunism." The answer to this question is complicated.

Some Romanians were convinced as early as February 1990 that the "revolution" had not, after all, overthrown communism, and they made this the basis of protests and demonstrations.[14] As one commentator put it, "The deterioration of the revolution's image began with the outbreak of the struggle for power, a struggle in which certain elements of the old Apparatus prevailed. From this emerges the paradox of the revolution: its having a clearly anti-Communist character while 'legitimating' a government that is far from that."[15] In a harsh assessment of the election results, Pavel Câmpeanu made the same point:

> The electoral victory of the Front is in good measure the victory of the old apparatus, whose economic and social impact on the population has remained considerable. For this reason May 20 could constitute the moment of a change in the relations between the new power and the old apparatus, in favor of the latter. Based on this change we might be finding ourselves in—or be moving towards—a stage in which the power born of the anti-Ceauşescu revolution does not control the Ceauşescu apparatus, but rather the Ceauşescu apparatus controls the power born of the anti-Ceauşescu revolution.[16]

14. See, for example, Stelian Tănase, "Ceasuri liniştite," 22, February 16, 1990, p. 1, and "Octavian Paler: La aceste alegeri a învins trecutul din noi," Parlament 1, no. 2 (1990): 9. In addition, one well-placed member of a ministry told us that as early as the end of February it was clear to him, from the fate of proposals he sent to his superiors for reform of his ministry, that the old apparatus was regrouping against such transformative measures as his. In his view, the "revolution" was the spasm necessary for the apparatus to retain control in Romania, even at the cost of sacrificing its ruler.

15. Stelian Tănase, "Imaginea revoluţiei," 22, April 20, 1990, p. 1.

16. Pavel Câmpeanu, "Despre învăţ şi dezvăţ: F.S.N., Criza victoriei," 22, June 15, 1990, p. 20.

These statements underscore a basic paradox that had come to be reflected in political stances as the electoral campaign proceeded. The December events were first and foremost an anti-Ceauşescu revolution. Being anti-Ceauşescu may have meant being anti-Communist for some (hence the slogan "Down with communism!") but not necessarily for everyone. Although the Front immediately declared the end of Communist rule, its leadership remained full of reform Communists. Thus, when it later announced its candidacy for the May elections, many Romanians felt betrayed and outraged. The Front's reversal signified to them a return to the old pattern of lies and suggested that Communists were trying to "steal" the revolution. With this, public action hitherto rooted in anti-Ceauşescu sentiment was transformed into anti-Communist activism.

When asked what the dreaded "restoration of communism" could mean, Romanians were likely to answer, "Dictatorship and a system of terror and repression," denying that Marxist-Leninist principles had anything to do with it. This requires us to distinguish between, on the one hand, the legitimating *ideology* of communism as defined by the Bolshevik Revolution and, on the other hand, the structures and practices that characterized Communist Party rule in Eastern Europe and the Soviet Union. Communism as an ideology has been thoroughly discredited throughout the region. As for structures and practices, those of the socialist systems are securely distinguished from those of other, non-Communist authoritarian and repressive systems—Idi Amin's Uganda, South Africa, Argentina under the generals, Duvalier's Haiti—only by the socialist state's near-complete monopoly over the means of production, which accorded it a potential for coercion and social control generally greater than in those societies that institutionalize at least some economic independence of the state. To the extent that the Front proceeds with its announced intention to marketize the economy and create more room for private enterprise (as has begun to occur, if cautiously and contradictorily), even this distinguishing feature will cease to characterize it.[17] Therefore, it is unclear what is gained by speaking of "neocommunism," except—and this may be a significant benefit—to remind one of the specific *trajectory* of what could prove to be just another authoritarian regime. In consequence, our general answer to the question posed in our title is No.

This said, we might point to features of the Front's governance to date

17. See Celestin Bohlen, "Romanians Brace for Hard Lessons in Free Market," *New York Times,* October 30, 1990, p. A7, which announced price reforms set for November 1, 1990.

that nonetheless indicate continuities with the practices and structures of the Ceauşescu era. As with the cautions we raised in discussing Front obstruction of the elections, we recognize that there may be other explanations for some of these practices, which may be "ordered from above" less than generated from below. It is certain, however, that continuity of personnel in many positions of bureaucratic authority will play a major role.

One structure of the Ceauşescu regime that seems to have remained in place is the Securitate (its independence reportedly somewhat compromised, however).[18] Many of our friends said they had seen the old *securist* of their workplace back in circulation after a period of absence and not, evidently, employed in a new calling. We also heard considerable speculation as to whether the mails and telephones have remained under surveillance. This lack of a public dismantling of the Securitate, beyond the pensioning of some of its most senior and most notorious members, can be explained only if a significant fraction of the Securitate was indeed instrumental in overthrowing Ceauşescu and in putting Iliescu and the Front in office. This would put the Front's leaders in debt to the Securitate and preclude their decimating it, as the East Germans did with the Stasi. That so powerfully organized and numerous a body, accustomed to considerably greater privilege than most citizens, remained more or less untransformed is a major reason for expecting some practices of the former regime to persist; what is not yet clear is whether they are carried out by the organization on its own (or some of its members) or on orders from the Front (or in conjunction with certain Front leaders).[19]

Second, there is the question of access to high position. In some areas— such as many institutions of intellectual and cultural life—there was extensive turnover of leading personnel. The Writers' Union, the universities, research institutes in some (but not all) fields, numerous important

18. While most of the Securitate has been subordinated to the army, a section of it, known as the Romanian Information Service, remains separate as an organization of state intelligence. Published reports of the continued operation of the Securitate periodically appear; see, for example, Capt. Adrian Ionescu, "Scrisoare deschisă adresată Parlamentului României," *România liberă*, February 1991, p. 14.

19. We do not accept Defense Minister Stănculescu's statement that the Securitate numbered only 8,400 people, nor even Iliescu's modest reckoning of 15,000 (see "Preşedintele Ion Iliescu," p. 14), which would average slightly more than one *securist* per settlement, clearly unrealistic. Given that most enterprises, including schools, hotels, hospitals, restaurants, collective farms, factories, research institutes, and so on, had at least one *securist* to whom persons were to report their contact with foreigners, for example, the number would seem more likely to run toward 100,000 (including persons whose wages were not drawn solely from police work but excluding those who "merely" reported on coworkers, family, and friends).

cultural publications, and the major publishing houses ceased to be run predominantly by old apparatchiks. Whether they and others like them will hold out, however, and whether they will be given the resources necessary to success, remains to be seen—presses publishing critical books, for example, still sometimes find themselves shut off from typesetting technology or paper, both in very short supply, and it is possible that the interference could be centrally directed. In many quarters, it is precisely the formerly privileged who have pooled their capital to buy or lease public property, in so-called "nomenklatura buy-outs." The great majority of those holding high position in December 1990 were also in elite positions in 1989, and some former party bureaucrats were promoted; only a handful of Ceauşescu's advisers seemed to be headed for punishment. Yet more troubling, the Front appointed new prefects for the counties, who then appointed all local mayors—a far cry from the promised "local elections." Villagers complained to us that the same people were still in charge locally and access to power was as constricted as before. Female factory workers in a largely female work force complained similarly that they had no representation and that most top positions were again held by nonelected males.

These judgments show that many Romanians perceive a structure of privilege little different from that under Ceauşescu. Yet the question is a complicated one: the maintenance of former party members in their posts cannot simply be seen as part of a sinister plan, for there were limited options for replacing them. This is nicely illustrated by reports that in some enterprises, workers requested, several months after the revolution, the reinstatement of their former directors, who had been removed. In Romania perhaps more than in many of its neighbors, few outside the party bureaucracy have had sufficient political or organizational experience to run things effectively.

To take a third example, the Ceauşescu regime was a classic case of one in which slogans and ideas, constantly repeated in public discourse were not supported by concrete political measures enabling those ideas to be implemented. It is possible that new ideas like "democracy" and privatization" may share the fate of "socialist democracy," "socialist equity," "the multilaterally developed society," and any number of other Ceauşescu slogans never realized in practice. Although we recognize that there are no easy formulas for managing the transition from centralized to market systems, some of the dilemmas of this transition produce continuities with the Communist period. To speak of "privatization" while creating very high risk for private firms, via severe price differentials between the private and state sectors, could prove analogous to "self-financing" under Ceauşescu, which purported to give enterprises reformist material incentives while denying their directors the capacity to make autonomous decisions. Both paper and printing costs for state presses, for example, are lower than those for independent ones. Private taxi drivers lament their higher gasoline prices and annual licensing fees, relative to state-sector taxis. Peasants fear that taxes on land will be too high to make independent cultivation feasible. These differentials have their economic rationale but also clearly inhibit "entrepreneurship." In addition, they encourage widespread personalism, as people use personal relations to obtain stock from the state sector at state prices and sell the items at a huge markup to the private sector. This perpetuates the systemic "corruption" associated with the former regime, although under new conditions. Also problematic is the current practice of freeing prices while enterprises remain predominantly state owned and property law is not clarified. Such developments do not inspire the population with confidence.

As with "privatization," so—possibly—with "democracy." Iliescu's government has found it difficult to accept criticism and opposition as part of the political process. Iliescu is not a Stalinist; he is a reformer, for whom opposition is, nonetheless, "counterrevolutionary" and conservative.[20] Upset that intellectuals were opposing the government rather than assisting it, he aggravated the division between them and workers by calling upon workers to suppress oppositional intellectuals—among whom were December's heroes, the students. (After a film clip was aired that showed the resulting melée, one of us heard many peasants comment: "Iliescu is worse than Ceauşescu! Not even Ceauşescu turned Romanians against each other. Miners beating Romanian students? This is the verge of civil war!") We recognize that the opposition has made tactical errors—like all groups in Romania since December 1989—but we fear that as under Ceauşescu, "democracy" will remain a slogan unless the Front learns to tolerate criticism.

How, given such continuities in practices, can we maintain that Romania is not "neo-Communist"—especially since so many members of the Communist Party apparatus still control so many of the organs of rule? First, because they achieved power thanks partly to a popular revolution

20. See "Preşedintele Ion Iliescu," pp. 12, 15. As Iliescu's one-time ally Silviu Brucan noted, "President Iliescu has today abandoned communist ideology, but for a time he was a party activist and that's a habit you don't shed overnight" (*Guardian Weekly*, September 9, 1990, p. 16).

that formed a new environment, one in which parliamentary representatives are elected and in which citizens assume, however tentatively, their right to express opinions. Second, because the Romanian press has become if anything *too* free, publishing without concern for veracity or slander. New conditions such as these militate against a full recreation of the Communist past; the environment is simply not propitious to "communism." Third, because the chief interest of the new leaders is not communism but power. If some of communism's structures remain, it is not because the leaders still want Marxism-Leninism but because those structures were eminently suited to concentrating political power and reproducing it.[21] This does not, in our view, make a neo-Communist regime.

Of "Demonstrators," "Miners," and the "Front"

Our purpose in the present section is to undermine still further a simplistic notion of the Front's "post-Communist communism" by showing that the power struggle at its center obstructs its ability to govern, and this intersects with the fact that release from forty-five years of Communist Party rule has made the population of Romania almost ungovernable. To make this point we describe events that took place on June 13–15, 1990, when first the police and then groups of miners beat up antigovernment demonstrators in Bucharest. We select this rather than some other problematic episode—such as the interethnic violence in Tîrgu Mureş in March 1990—because one of us was present for it, because it was heatedly discussed throughout our visits, and because unlike the March events, it occurred *after* the elections, when the Front could be confident of its popular mandate and ought, therefore, to have been capable of governing responsibly. That it found governing difficult, as we believe this episode shows, further reveals the confusion Ceauşescu's abrupt departure produced.

As with the events of December 1989, it is impossible to say what "really happened" in mid-June 1990. The episode actually began on April 23, when a group of students at Bucharest University started a demonstration against the Front, accusing it of neocommunism. They established a "Communist-free zone" in the city center, called for dialogue

21. For one of many arguments to this effect, see Katherine Verdery, *National Ideology under Socialism: Identity and Cultural Politics in Ceauşescu's Romania* (Berkeley, Calif., 1991), chap. 2.

with Iliescu, demanded that former members of the apparatus be barred from campaigning, insisted on the establishment of an independent television station, and so on. To register their concerns with the public, they barricaded a principal section of Bucharest's main thoroughfare and set up tents on the nearby grass; this obstructed the flow of traffic through the city center for nearly two months and aroused many citizens' ire. Demonstrators called repeatedly for a meeting with government representatives. Although Iliescu agreed several times to such a meeting, he was unwilling to have it televised as was demanded; hence, little dialogue took place.[22]

As the demonstration continued, augmented now by a number of persons on a hunger strike, other sorts of activities became attached to the margins—for example, hawkers selling drinks and sausages, cigarettes, newspapers, and trinkets. This petty commerce—called *bişniţă* (pronounced *bizhnitsa*, from "business") in Romanian, the people engaged in it being called *bişniţari*—became a major element in publicity about the demonstration. Several newspapers, television, and other sources presented the demonstrators as *bişniţari*, also alleging that their tents were sites of prostitution and drug use. Significantly, Gypsies formed a high percentage of the *bişniţari*, which meant that what became a public condemnation of "petty commerce" in the demonstration was also a public condemnation of Gypsies. This issue ran deeper than the demonstration, for many Romanians see Gypsies as the principal villains in the ongoing shortages in Romanian society—attributed to heavy Gypsy traffic in goods from the state sector. The unfolding events thus conjoined racism, uncertainty about the consequences of marketization, and government-sanctioned opposition to intellectuals.

Following the elections, in which many former party activists won office, most of the student demonstrators withdrew.[23] The demonstration, however, did not end, University Square remaining occupied by other opponents of the government and by *bişniţari*. At 4 A.M. on June 13, police awakened and arrested them in a manner that eyewitnesses and

22. We have Iliescu's agreement on the authority of a government minister; some of those who sympathized with the demonstrators, however, wrote or spoke as if Iliescu had refused a meeting. In his interview, Iliescu suggested that repeated efforts to achieve a dialogue had failed and implied that the reasons were on the other side ("Preşedintele Ion Iliescu," p. 13). We note that the demonstrators demanded meetings specifically with Iliescu, apparently not considering parliament a suitable recourse for their grievances. This strikes us as a legacy of older "paternalistic" politics. In few of the world's democracies would the head of state meet with demonstrators in a comparable situation.

23. See "Preşedintele Ion Iliescu," p. 14, where Iliescu acknowledges this.

demonstrators found gratuitously violent (contrary to Iliescu's description of the arrests as "relatively peaceful").[24] Taken to headquarters for questioning, they were grilled as to whom they had voted for and whether the Peasant party candidate Ion Raţiu or other opposition candidates had paid them to occupy the square. The square—emptied of demonstrators by late morning—was barricaded with buses and police vans.

By early afternoon, a number of persons dressed in civilian clothes had gathered nearby, including local citizens upset at the manner of the morning arrests. Fighting broke out among them and soon escalated: by mid-afternoon, the crowd—consisting of all social categories and ages—was throwing rocks and Molotov cocktails at the buses and vans barricading the square. With the center of Bucharest ablaze, the rioters then headed for the central police station, where they demanded the release of those arrested earlier and threatened to set the building on fire. Some people also headed for the Ministry of the Interior, damaging property and setting fire to vehicles in the street.

We underscore that as the violence escalated, uniformed police retreated: by late afternoon, despite the chaos in the square, no representatives of the state's forces of civic order—police and fire department—were to be seen (nor was the army present, though maintaining internal order is not its normal role). The reason for this absence remain wholly unelucidated. The consequence, however, was that in mid-afternoon President Iliescu made the first of two televised speeches, in which he called upon citizens to defend the government.

Late in the afternoon, the crowd marched toward the Foreign Ministry

---

24. This formed a subject of much disagreement, the government declaring that the demonstrators had violently resisted arrest by the police and the demonstrators declaring the opposite. The issue was a bone of contention between Iliescu and his interviewer, Nicolae Manolescu ("Preşedintele Ion Iliescu," pp. 13–14). Iliescu's description should be contrasted with those of several demonstrators and eyewitnesses, whose accounts were published in various magazines critical of the Front. See, for example, the entire issue of *Expres* for June 22–28, 1990; "13 iunie—violenţa putea fi evitată printr-un dialog onest," *Nu* 1, no. 10 (1990): 2–5; "13-14-15 iuniei 1990: violenţa pune stăpînire pe Bucureşti," *Zig-Zag,* June 19–26, 1990, pp. 4–5; "Extemporal," 22, June 22, 1990, p. 7; "Strada ca o pradă," 22, June 22, 1990, pp. 8–9; "Golanii şi minerii," *Democraţia,* August 20–26, 1990, pp. 4–5; "Ultima noapte în Golania," 22, July 27, 1990, p. 11. These include first-person accounts by workers who had been among the student demonstrators from early on. As with any "eyewitness" accounts, none of these should be taken as definitive. We also recommend H. da Costa, "Roumanie: Le temps des complots. Entretien avec Victor Stănculescu," *Politique internationale,* no. 50 (1990–91): 259–80; Group for Social Dialogue, *Raport asupra evenimentelor din 13–15 iunie 1990* (Bucharest, 1990); and the report of the parliamentary opposition, "O dramă naţională din nou în actualitate," *România liberă,* January 30, 1991, pp. 3–6. Our summary in the text is based on the above-cited and other published reports, combined with Kligman's notes from those days.

building and the television station; people entered the station, vandalized some rooms, and occupied the first floor.[25] Television viewers throughout the country were appalled as the broadcast went off the air for approximately an hour. Since this had not happened even at the height of the December uprising, when the station had been under artillery fire, interruption of the broadcast from the actions of a largely unarmed rabble raised questions later on about the possibility that this blackout had been intended—by someone high up, not by the crowd—to create an atmosphere of panic and instability, in support of the idea that a coup was in progress.[26] When the broadcast resumed, a visibly shaken Iliescu appeared and addressed the country as follows: "In the course of the afternoon, violent actions by extremist elements of a Fascist nature intensified.[27] We address ourselves to all democratic forces of the country with a call to support actions to liquidate this Fascist rebellion, to work together with the forces of order and the army to reestablish order, to isolate and arrest the extremist elements that must be brought to justice to account for their deeds."[28] It was to this appeal that people subsequently referred in saying Iliescu had called the miners to Bucharest, since everyone knew that when miners had come to "restore order" in the capital in January and February, they had promised to return if order were again threatened. What is most significant about this apparent attack on the television station was that it touched the central symbol of the December revolution. For most Romanians, it was on television that Romania's "fledgling democracy" had been born, and Iliescu was now calling people to defend this "sacred space" from a threat to their hard-won liberty.

In the early hours of June 14, thousands of miners began to arrive in Bucharest. They were directed to various strategic places in the city, including the headquarters or offices of prominent opposition groups. Among those visited were the headquarters of the Liberal and Peasant parties (which were devastated), the office of *România liberă*, an indepen-

25. Reports on this moment, like others, are mixed. Some claim that two "crowds" arrived, the first more or less unarmed and the next group well organized, armed, and brought in trucks. The Hungarian television studio, which filmed the crowd's arrival from the upper floor, later showed a video of it on the Cluj television station, during the Hungarian broadcast, which meant that few others in the country saw it. See also Alin Alexandru, "In 13 iunie, emisia a fost oprită fără nici un motiv," *Expres*, July 4–11, 1990, p. 2, who claims that when he arrived at the TV station, a crowd was milling around the corridors but not committing acts of violence.
26. See, for example, Alexandru, "In 13 iunie," pp. 2, 6.
27. The expression Iliescu used is *de tip legionar*, referring to the interwar Fascist formation, the Legion of the Archangel Michael.
28. *Nu* 1, no. 17 (1990): 1.

dent paper (which was ransacked), and the oppositionist Group for Social Dialogue (not damaged, but stridently attacked in Front newspapers thereafter). Dressed in workclothes and blackened from the chutes, the miners carried with them (or, according to some reports, were given when they arrived at the train station) the instruments necessary to impose order: iron crowbars, cudgels, clubs, rubber hoses with metal tips, and woodsman's axes. With these they viciously attacked the people who were once again filling the square. Eyewitnesses reported that when miners beat a demonstrator in the presence of the police, the latter rarely intervened but stood by, watching and sometimes even encouraging the miners to new acts of violence (as did other bystanders). During the rampage, the student leader Marian Munteanu was badly beaten and then arrested. Using Iliescu's language, the miners accused their victims of being "Fascists," as they relentlessly clubbed students whom they found in the university preparing end-of-year papers and exams. The extreme brutality resulted in at least six reported deaths. The university also suffered extensive damage as miners devastated the architecture and geology departments, in particular. Valuable collections and projects were gratuitously demolished.

As the citizens of Bucharest headed for work, they encountered columns of miners marching through central streets and shouting slogans in support of Iliescu and against *bişniţari*. The area around the university was filled with miners waiting and watching. In a lengthy discussion with six to eight miners milling about near the university around 9 A.M., one of us was respectfully told, "Ma'am, you can't imagine what we found there in the basement of the university! Counterfeit money, drugs . . ." Questioned about the type of drugs, they could give no answer. One of them added with some embarrassment that they had also found women's panties scattered about.[29] This morning lull in the action did not last long. Seemingly arbitrary violence continued throughout the day and, though with lessening ferocity, into the next morning. Newspapers reported that miners had also beaten Gypsies, and that when Gypsies organized to

29. These comments fully recapitulate what the Ceauşescu regime so often and so violently castigated as the evils of the West: money, drugs, and sex. The opposition parties had been accused throughout the campaign of trying to buy support, using both foreign currency and Romanian money, some of it counterfeit. Public comment had claimed that the demonstrators were involved in drug use and prostitution. (The Front newspaper carried a blurred picture of the "drugs" found at the demonstration site on June 13: unidentified pills, wholly unconvincing to a foreigner used to life on the border of a crack zone.) We wonder why groups accused of trafficking in such goods would leave them in visible places; we must then ask how they got there, and in whose interests.

protest this, the police came and fired on them.[30] There were also reports of Gypsies being beaten in their own apartment buildings by their neighbors.

Some innocent bystanders who fell victim to the miners' clubs were outraged by these events, but many Bucharest residents expressed gratitude and satisfaction that the miners had finally cleared the thoroughfare and brought order. Another who expressed his gratitude—and far more publicly—was President Iliescu, who appeared with the miners on television and thanked them for helping to restore democracy to Romania. After this they were escorted out of Bucharest by a convoy in a carnivalesque atmosphere.

This episode polarized supporters and opponents of the Front, as the latter raised distressing questions about the government's role in the affair and the former became angry at these attacks upon the credibility of elected officials with so broad a popular mandate. Interpretations of the event were rife, but no one could offer an account that was persuasive to all. As the newspaper *Expres* observed after listing a number of unanswered questions about June 13–15, "In this issue of our newspaper you will not find a single answer to these questions. No one has answers."[31]

The most succinct summary of these events offered three alternative interpretations.[32] First, the official account: a Fascist conspiracy had tried to overthrow the government, and the attacks on the police headquarters and Ministry of the Interior had been supported "from abroad," making clever use of the demonstration in University Square. (Note the "plot" mentality, discussed earlier.) Since the police had proved themselves incapable of managing the situation, miners had been called to the capital. Such an interpretation presupposes both a political motive and an internal force sufficiently well organized and armed to take power in the wake of a coup—both absent. Second, the chief account given by government critics: the Front itself had organized both the devastations of June 13 and the repression of June 14–15 so as to discredit the main opposition parties, the independent press, and critical intellectuals. (Again, a plot.) The ultimate aim was the restoration of one-party rule of the neo-Communist type. This view, like the other, lacks a convincing political rationale: no governing party that has just received an electoral landslide

30. See Clementina Filip, "Romii se bat şi ei," *Zig-Zag*, June 19–26, 1990, p. 5.

31. *Expres*, June 22–28, 1990, p. 1.

32. This summary is from Nicolae Manolescu, "Trei zile care au zguduit ţara," *România literară*, June 21, 1990, p. 2.

would have anything to gain by mounting such a massive repression of so small an opposition,[33] especially inasmuch as to do this would clearly create an international scandal highly damaging to the Front.

A third interpretation mixes elements of these two, focusing attention on a fragmented and restive Securitate that had infiltrated all groups involved in the episode. The infiltrators had the dual objective of (1) avenging themselves upon that fraction of their own organization that had obtained power and not brought others along, and (2) forcing the government to take a harder line with internal disturbances (thereby assuring the organs of repression a more constant role than they would have in a truly democratic Romania). This "Securitate" thesis numbered several adherents, including Prime Minister Petre Roman, who—in an interview with the Spanish radio and press—voiced the idea (he later changed his mind), while claiming that these elements of the Securitate were *not* under the Front's control. Even President Iliescu hesitantly assented to it, in part.[34]

On this reading, Securitate agents actively contributed both to the violence on June 13, supposedly wrought by "demonstrators," and to the devastation of university buildings and Peasant and Liberal party headquarters the next day, actions attributed to "miners."[35] The professionalism of some acts on the thirteenth outstripped the capacity of student demonstrators—particularly the attack on the television station, which brought the crowd directly into the most sensitive points of that building as if it knew the floor plan perfectly, not hesitating at doors that led nowhere important.[36] There were, in any case, few students among that crowd. As for the "miners," newspapers ran stories of known Securitate who were recognized among them.[37] Eyewitnesses (including one of us) heard miners say, "We know what we have to do here, we were precisely

---

33. Iliescu also expressed this judgment in combating the view that the Front had organized the miners' arrival and the beating of demonstrators. See "Preşedintele Ion Iliescu," p. 12.

34. Ibid.

35. Some claimed that the fire at police headquarters had broken out on the *top floor, before* people had entered the courtyard, which makes it likely that instigators within the crowd were in league with police in the building. (See Nicolae Manolescu, "Post-scriptum: reparaţia morală necesară," *România literară*, June 28, 1990, p. 2. He gives no source for this affirmation.) As for the devastation of university buildings, many people believed those "miners" came from Băneasa, the Securitate school on the outskirts of Bucharest.

36. This was reported by the head of the TV station himself. See Manolescu, "Trei zile."

37. See, for example, "In Bucureşti, minerii au fost aduşi de un căpitan al Securităţii," *Expres*, June 22–28, 1990, p. 1, and Victor Niţă, "Fiecare fabrică a avut un Nicolae Cămărăşescu," *Expres*, July 4–11, 1990, p. 1.

informed . . ."[38] or, when asked why they had come to Bucharest, "Orders." "From whom?" "Don't know, just orders." "Why aren't you letting anyone pass through here?" "Those are our orders." Precisely from whom was not clarified; however, since miners from the provinces could not have had the names and home addresses of intellectuals critical of the Front, it is clear that someone had to furnish them. And how else to explain, we would add, that after Gail Kligman had filmed the events of June 13–15, the film from her camera disappeared—from a locked suitcase in a hotel room?

Amid these conflicting reports and interpretations it is difficult to draw definitive conclusions. It seems certain to us that the "miners" included both *real* miners, genuinely aggravated that a handful of demonstrators was disrupting their elected government, and also Securitate, of at least two kinds: those from the Securitate school near Bucharest, and those from the mining centers. One should remember that after the riots and strikes among miners in 1977, the mining centers in the Jiu Valley were infiltrated by Securitate, many of them working as functionaries in the trade union (whence it would have been easy for them to organize the miners to go to Bucharest).[39] The "demonstrators," too, may well have contained not only idealistic students and others upset with the Front's undemocratic behavior but, with them, various other groups—*bişniţari* (and agents posing as *bişniţari?*), and provocateurs of some kind (also Securitate?) who radicalized the actions of the crowd on June 13 into a destructive melée. The reasons for such action include rivalry both among factions of the Securitate and between it and the army, especially in view of the precipitous decline in the fortunes of the formerly all-powerful Securitate after December 1989. If indeed Securitate were mixed up in all these groups, it is impossible to say whether they represented sections of a single organized group or (more likely) different Securitate factions, and under whose orders.

In short, the episode raises more questions than can be answered. The most difficult questions are: why would a government that had been

38. George Crişan, "Instigatorii infiltraţi în rîndul minerilor," *Zig-Zag*, June 19–26, 1990, p. 5.

39. See "Cei ce erau în haine civile au fost trimişi după haine," *Expres*, July 4–11, 1990, p. 3, which claims that "miners from father to son" were not the ones who left for Bucharest and that the Securitate-run trade union organized miners to head for the capital. There is further evidence of central coordination of the miners' movements in the report of the parliamentary opposition, "O dramă naţională din nou." Not all of the region's mining complexes agreed to be "organized" to go; those that chose not to were later reprimanded. See Dan Pavel, "Ziua minerului la Valea Vinului," *22*, August 24, 1990, p. 5.

overwhelmingly elected jeopardize its situation by participating in these events? To what extent did Front leaders order these actions—better said, *which* Front leaders were involved, and why?[40] Who may have given tacit consent, and who was caught off guard? What relation of forces do the events suggest? What part did the army play? The Securitate? It is, in any case, noteworthy that Defense Minister Stănculescu was conspicuously out of the country on June 13. Why was the government patently unable to use and control its repressive forces on June 13, as any legitimately constituted public power ought to be able to do? Also incomprehensible, why did the newly elected parliament not call an emergency session on June 13, 14, or 15? Instead, a scheduled meeting was postponed. Why did this representative body—in a classic gesture of paternalistic deference—give Iliescu virtually full authority to manage what was obviously a social crisis?

In our view, the "Front," despite its landslide, proved incapable of stabilizing governance over a population whom decades of repression and discontent had made at least temporarily ungovernable. The situation was exploited by groups struggling for fuller access to power, relative to the Front and to each other: groups in the army and the former Securitate. That Iliescu was unable to bring in a suitable force of civil police to create order in University Square shows great uncertainty as to *who* is to maintain order in public spaces.[41] Persons with whom we spoke suggested that some of the police forces sent in to maintain order were indeed hesitant, given the very bad image that the symbolic struggle around the "revolution" had created for the organizations of repression: everyone was now scrambling to avoid being labeled villains and to pin such labels on others. In the end, on June 14–15 public order was restored by a civilian "police" using illegal violence.

The image presented to us is of a "ruling Front" divided against itself, its component segments split among warring factions both within and outside the government and contending with each other intragovernmentally as well. Inside each institutional center—army, police, council of state, and so on—is ongoing contention to consolidate power, as people struggle to edge one another out. Each center of influence—individuals or small groups—works behind the scenes to strengthen its power base with

40. Many indications of involvement by members of the Front are documented in the report of the parliamentary opposition, "O dramă națională din nou." Indeed, this report openly accuses the prime minister, president, minister of the interior, and other public officials of active or de facto complicity in the affair.

41. See the interview with the defense minister, Victor Stănculescu, in Da Costa, "Roumanie: Le temps des complots," esp. pp. 260–61.

other segments. Because no one's allegiance is certain (a legacy of the atomization produced under Ceauşescu's rule), coalitions shift. We find it quite possible that *some* groups in the Front were implicated in organizing the miners, supporting other factions in the Securitate or army who had a grudge to work off; we do not find it plausible that the Front itself was sufficiently unified to accomplish this.[42]

Indeed, we question the coherence and unity of *all* groups named in one or another interpretation—the "Army," the "Securitate," the "Front," and so on. Such unifying labels are unsuited to describing groups with fuzzy boundaries, internal conflicts and fissures, and constantly changing coalitions—the consequence of the disestablishment of the Communist Party, the one organization that had produced the appearance of unity and monolithic control. Instead of seeing in this episode Iliescu's inadequacy as a leader, as some do, we see in it the extent to which all the contending forces to which he owed his position intersected in him.[43] When these forces locked, canceling one another out, he was immobilized as a result. This is not to absolve his government of responsibility for its handling of the crisis, which was reprehensible, but only to suggest caution in interpreting both its "neocommunism" and its singleness of purpose.[44] The episode shows with great clarity that the fall of the Romanian Communist Party repeats the story of Humpty-Dumpty, with the government of the National Salvation Front assigned the hopeless task of putting the pieces together again.

June 13–15 was a crucial moment in both the reconfiguration of Romanian politics and our understanding of those politics. It was a moment in which none among the contending forces had achieved clear superiority, no coalition among factions had cemented itself; the linkages being

42. Our picture of the Front as disorganized and incoherent agrees with the similar view expressed by the minister of culture, Andrei Pleşu: "It is absurd to present the Front as a body that is compact, monolithic, coherent. On the contrary, everything is confused, polychrome. It contains former Communists and rightists, professional revolutionaries and also reactionaries, idiots and hotheads. A meeting of the Front is a permanent quarrel," interview published in *Le Monde* and summarized in *România liberă*, February 18, 1990.

43. See Ion Buducă, "Analiza unei ipoteze," *România liberă*, July 8–9, 1990, p. 2.

44. A number of Front supporters had trouble understanding why the miners episode was so upsetting to Westerners, asking us, "why you Americans don't like us any more." When we replied that no president of a democratic country would applaud the vigilante actions of a group that has taken into its own hands the state's function of maintaining order, our interlocutors found this difficult to follow; they concentrated instead on Iliescu's reasons for having thought the government was in peril, which justified all his subsequent behavior. We fully agree that he had to do something about the demonstrators' ongoing disruption of central Bucharest, but we cannot condone the methods used, and we unequivocally condemn the one certainty of the event—that Iliescu thanked the miners, before a large public, for their help.

forged in that moment had fateful consequences, helping to consolidate institutionally the advantage of some over others. If, as seemed likely by the spring of 1991 (when this essay went to press), the Front's "unity" and rule depended more on the organs of force than was true elsewhere in Eastern Europe, it was from the June events that this emerged as the outcome, and not, as some would have it, from a simple "neo-Communist" continuity with the past.

Whither State and Society? Problems and Prospects

We suggested above that the situation in Romania is more complex than may appear. Similarly, the difficulties confronting the country are too numerous for full review. In this final section we briefly mention certain problems tied to the legacy of Ceauşescu and then focus on the difficulties of constructing a better relation between the organs of rule and the population to be governed, which we call the "state-society relation."[45] We see changing this relation as vital to a genuine transformation in Romania.

In our discussion of "democracy" and "privatization" we made the point that government policies have been confused, the provisional consequence being continuity with prior practices. The confusion is understandable. Not only does there exist no blueprint for the sort of transition Romania and the other Eastern European societies are attempting; the very question of the proper path for Romania is hotly debated, as are the models it should follow and the desired content of the notions employed ("democracy," "market," "privatization")—all much discussed, with little agreement. By no means is everyone convinced that free markets and private property are what they want. In these debates, powerful groups oppose alterations in their position of privilege, complicating the emergence of a consensus on the process of change. Contradictory tendencies abound. The Front puts forth an economic program calling for more markets yet punishes "speculation," rather than using this petty commerce to define an "entrepreneurial spirit" that would support marketization. Ordinary citizens, in turn, express similar ambivalence and uncertainty by attacking *bişniţă* and the Gypsies they see as its carriers.

Genuine and deep differences exist on the desirability of the changes

---

45. We do not employ the concept of "civil society," a concept that in our view is more interesting as an object of research and critical reflection than as an explanatory notion.

some see as necessary. In the sphere of agriculture, for example, it was widely assumed that the end of Communist Party rule would automatically mean decollectivization. Not all collectivized villages, however, *wanted* to decollectivize, and within each village opinion was seriously divided.[46] Elderly farmworkers not only feared loss of their pensions but could not imagine how, lacking all but rudimentary tools, they would work more land than the half hectare they already farmed.[47] Elsewhere, by contrast, whole villages voted to decollectivize and then went even further, destroying all the buildings of the collective farm and allotting the land they stood on to young and poor couples who lacked housing plots. Former landowners sought to reclaim their holdings, often in flagrant disregard for the dislocations this might bring others. Conflicts arose that revealed deep grievances rooted in a given collective farm's past. Many peasants spoke of the need to form their own unions, to ensure representation of their interests (which are regionally differentiated), as existing parties do not. Numerous subtle local differences affect the desirability of decollectivization, and much discussion will be necessary to resolve this problem wisely.

If in its first year the Front did not arrive at a consensus on these questions, it also did not arrive at an understanding of "political pluralism" or democratic processes that would satisfy the average Westerner (or, for that matter, the average Romanian). Years of Ceauşescu-inspired distrust, suspicion, fear, and social atomization—by now deeply ingrained in people's habits—stand in the way of developing tolerance for other opinions, which is essential to a functioning democracy. Here, we can do no more than emphasize the necessity and the difficulty of altering these habits, not just for Romanians but for others in the region.

Problems of tolerance refer not only to the formation of political opinions but to issues of both nationality and religion. Conflicts between Romanians and Hungarians have received much international publicity; ameliorating these conflicts will require not just a clearer sense of their place in the confusing environment of Romanian politics but also the

---

46. See, for example, David Kideckel, "The Politics of Decollectivization in Romania after Ceauşescu," manuscript, Central Connecticut State University, New Britain, Conn.

47. In some collectivized villages, decollectivization has been associated with struggles against personalism and involves long-standing kinship and local class conflicts. The most extreme case is that of Săpînţa village, in Maramureş, where conflict precipitated the intervention of local, regional, and state authorities, including the army, and resulted in a trial that was held out of the district. The Săpînţa affair is representative of the daily conflicts between past and future. See 22, October 5, 1990, pp. 8–10.

development of greater tolerance between members of both groups.[48] In addition, the racism everyone practices against Gypsies cannot continue to be ignored. A less well publicized difficulty concerns religious freedom—more specifically, access to the means to practice freedoms supposedly guaranteed by the state. Although the post-Ceauşescu government decreed freedom of religious belief, it has done little to enable persons of the Greek Catholic, or Uniate, faith to practice their religion. When the Communists forcibly joined the Uniate church with the Romanian Orthodox church in 1948, they left Uniates with none of the paraphernalia necessary for worship—including, of course, church buildings. In Transylvania, where this issue is hottest, tolerance is in very short supply on all sides of the question.

Many of the problems to be addressed have been fought in the idiom of a generational struggle—a form of wording that often obscures politicking over other issues. The "generation gap" encapsulates many contradictions between past and present, focusing tensions that are well captured in concerns over the "betrayal of the revolution" in which young people gave their lives to change a system that older ones could not escape. Generational differences are manifest within the Front in the apparent division between its older members and the younger technocrats (who form the majority of government ministers). Generational conflicts in the Liberal and National Peasant parties came to a boil in June 1990 (not connected with the miners). Similar struggles began in the army in February; the demands of younger officers led ultimately to the dismissal of Defense Minister Militaru, who was replaced by General Victor Stănculescu. This solution does not, however, satisfy all younger officers.

Following Ceauşescu's overthrow it became clear that the most crucial obstacle to Romania's "transition" was a crisis in the relation between state and society: the organs of governance were disrupted by infighting and power struggles, while the populace showed itself relatively ungovernable. To improve this relation will require a long process of mutual accommodation. Romanians must gradually learn that even in a "free" society, certain limits must be agreed to, and their rulers must learn to accept limits that are more flexible than those to which party bureaucrats

48. For example, "what really happened" when Romanians and Hungarians clashed in Tîrgu Mureş in March is another of those impossible questions similar to the ones we have addressed in this paper. Did the Securitate provoke the whole thing, as some claim? Was the government of Hungary behind it?

like Iliescu were accustomed under party rule. It will be a process in which rulers and ruled acquire different conceptions of one another and of the behavior suited to their new conceptions. For example, Romanian politicians are used to dichotomizing the world into an inner circle of people with "correct" views and everyone else, assumed to be ignorant or misguided. This dichotomy is linked with one in which anyone who disagrees is a "traitor"—those who aren't with us are against us. Most Romanians, for their part, are equally used to thinking in terms of "us" and "them"—"them" being the rulers, seen as monolithic, monologic entity, uniformly oppressive. Such views do not lead to political nuance, to compromise seen as honorable, or to either subjects' or rulers' taking responsibility to educate and tolerate the other.

There is, in fact, a glaring contradiction in how most Romanians think of the "state." On the one hand, it is seen as an instrument of totalizing intrusiveness, all too unpleasantly experienced under Ceauşescu. Many Romanians understand the state as negative in and of itself, and they resist anything that resembles the construction of state power. Simultaneously, they live with internalized expectations of a state that is paternalistic, that frees them of the necessity to take initiative or worry about their pay checks, hospital bills, pensions, and the like. They simultaneously blame the state for everything and expect the state to resolve everything. Both elements of this amalgam of accusation and expectation will have to be modified, in order to achieve a state-society relation that is workable. One cannot dispense with a functioning state, which is the repository of laws safeguarding citizens' rights and of institutions that encourage and protect democratic practices (including an effective police force). Nor can one expect to enjoy benefits without having to do any work, as many Romanians appear to believe. These aspects of the "ungovernability" of the Romanian populace are every bit as much in need of socialization as are the clumsy and self-defeating tactics of the forces of rule, discussed at such length in this essay.

There have been some signs of a process of reciprocal learning about the nature and the limits of state authority. When authorities charged the student leader Marian Munteanu with incitement to violence, arrested him in the emergency hospital bed in which he was immobilized from a vicious beating, and then moved him in this condition to a prison hospital ward, they were seen as having gone too far. Members of the political opposition showed that they had learned from the organizational mistakes of the University Square events: they coordinated in major Romanian cities several peaceful demonstrations that included disciplined marches of as many as sixty thousand people. These actions, supplemented by international attention to Munteanu's plight, gradually forced the government to concede, setting him free. Although others remained unjustly imprisoned even as this symbol of opposition was released, we see this as a major step in which citizens had learned to take responsible initiative and government had learned that it might have to listen to them.

The process of mutual socialization will be lengthy and difficult, but it is necessary to breaking reciprocally reinforced patterns of paternalism. Some of the measures that we believe will help to bring about a democratic public sphere and an improved state-society relation include the following:[49]

(1) The Romanian state must respect human rights and formulate legal provisions for protecting democratic principles. It must exercise its repressive authority responsibly, not only ceasing to abuse repressive power but obstructing the use of such power by other groups in society, particularly former Securitate.[50]

(2) Independent associations and institutions—long absent in Romania—must be formed and expanded, to mediate state-society relations and broaden civic experience. Their development will help to prevent a return to the totalizing state power that characterized the Ceauşescu period.

(3) Independent media must be created. State-controlled television is the most blatant violation of this requirement—particularly grave given how deeply dependent the population is for its civic education on a medium so readily manipulated by the ruling party. During the June events, television showed nothing of the violence miners had visited upon people. When a late-night student program showed some of the footage six weeks later, viewers were outraged, taking this revelation as yet another instance of deliberate government disinformation. Access to television time is biased against those critical of the Front. Nor will the televi-

---

49. See Gail Kligman, "Reclaiming the Public: A Reflection on Creating Civil Society in Romania," *East European Politics and Societies* 4, no. 3 (1990): 393–439.

50. Attention to human rights has gained momentum since their flagrant disregard in June 1990. The Social Democratic Party called for coordination of the country's democratic forces to draw up legal statutes for "the protection of freedoms and not their limitation, for social justice rather than the preservation of privilege, for social solidarity rather than the estrangement of society's diverse segments" (Sergiu Cunescu, "O propunere a PSDR: Convenţia Naţională pentru Democraţie," *România liberă*, September 20, 1990, p. 2a).

sion problem be resolved by permitting one more station to be set up, if that one is not committed to democratic values.[51]

Although the press (unlike television) has become free, it is not independent. The state's differential pricing policy affects it and can be used as a form of "censorship," as can the dependence of the press on the state for access to supplies of paper. The ongoing "paper shortage," a possible form of controlling the opposition, must be clarified as part of institutionalizing a "free press" and of improving relations between the government and its critics.[52] This applies equally to access to printing presses, mostly state owned. During the events of June 13–15, printers refused to typeset four independent papers; they later relented, but dissociated themselves explicitly from the content of what was printed. The conditions permitting this and comparable attempts at censorship must be altered.

(4) The university system should be made as independent as possible of state control, even if state funding remains its principal source of funds, and academic freedom should be more firmly institutionalized.[53] The creation of a university system capable of braking the incursions of state power would also be enhanced by programs that give more academics access to international scholarship, something most of them were denied in the decades of party rule.

(5) Last, there must develop an "opposition"—potentially several, having their own political agendas and creating their own social bases.[54]

51. The reference is to right-wing émigré Iosif Constantin Dragan, rumored to have been authorized to broadcast in Romania. The gross anti-Semitism and chauvinism of newspapers already published under his subsidy does not make one confident of the quality of his television programming.

52. On September 19, 1990, *România liberă* issued a truncated publication of a single sheet, in solidarity with another paper (*Tineretul liber*), which the "paper shortage" had forced to reduce its pages. Papers of the Front do not seem to suffer such shortages.

53. An independent university system is particularly important given that research has been centralized (and thus made even more vulnerable than before to central control) under the Romanian Academy.

54. While we find the term "opposition" misleading and problematic, it is commonly used to refer to those who are not supporters of the Front. This continues old habits that need changing. The opposition is discursively homogenized but internally diverse, united chiefly by anti-Communist convictions. In November 1990 a broad-based, extraparliamentary, "nonpolitical" alliance was formed that was nationwide and called itself the Civic Alliance. It consists of a varied array of opposition groups including the Group for Social Dialogue, Independent Group for Democracy, Braşov's 15 November Group, the Timişoara Society, and others, and it enjoys the support of many independent unions and the officers' group working for democratization of the army. (We take exception to the self-designation "non-political," which is nonetheless eloquent testimony to how dirty a word "politics" had become under Communist Party rule.)

Without these elements of pluralist politics, we can expect more victories
by the ruling group in future elections. The opposition constituted to date
is still responding to the center, rather than developing initiatives of its
own and constituting viable alternatives, and it sometimes ignores the
wider population that should be brought into the process.[55]

How much of this is feasible, given Romania's historical and more
recent legacy, is difficult to say. An alternative path could, unfortunately,
emerge from growing everyday hardships, provoked by economic policy
and further aggravated by international events such as the Persian Gulf
crisis, which might increase social instability and lead to government
paralysis. In this case, we would anticipate a military takeover (perhaps in
conjunction with the return of the exiled King Michael).[56] Indeed, we
heard Romanians say, "We need a military dictatorship for a while; there
is no other way out of this chaos." Although we sympathize with the
sentiment and with the difficulties people are (and will be) experiencing,
we prefer to emphasize what we would see as a more benign and hopeful
outcome.

The Ceaușescu regime has undoubtedly left its mark on Romania.
Whether that mark will prove indelible depends in part on Romanians'
having both the chance and the ability to shape for themselves a new
future consciously different from the past, which they also took part in
shaping.[57] This future, we submit, cannot be simply one of "post-Communist communism," an option that has ceased to be supported in either
the internal or the global environment. A start has been made—even if
shakily—toward the future by the fundamental changes that have already
taken place: Romanians can express political views openly in public, they
are able to travel, their parliament is elected and has begun to learn how

55. We recognize that our recommendations are "culture-bound." Our joint experience
with Romania is such that we are convinced that something like the values of pluralist
democracy must be more fully institutionalized in that country, where an overly powerful
state and the erosion of civil liberties have a history longer than that of party rule.

56. The Civic Alliance actively supports an initiative to hold a referendum on the return
of the exiled king, who (at the time of this writing) enjoyed the support of Defense Minister
Stănculescu, himself replaced in April 1991. One should not rule out the possibility of the
king's return, even should there be a military takeover, for he represents a source of legitimacy lacking in the rule of the Front and equally important to any military government that
might hope for continued backing from European states.

57. In his speech on Germany's unification, the patrician president Richard von
Weizsäcker openly pointed to the relation between the "burdens of history" and the "responsibilities of the future." He noted what is true throughout the region: "The power of the
system has been broken, but the trauma is still alive" (*New York Times*, October 4, 1990, p.
8A). See also, for example, "Raport al GDS şi al Comitetului Helsinki din România asupra
evenimentelor din 13–15 iunie 1990," 22, September 21, 1990, pp. 8–10.

to behave like a body for political debate, multiple parties exist, independent unions have been formed, and the press, while not independent, is free. Despite the obstacles still to be overcome, these are enormous changes, and we must not overlook the achievement they represent. A democratizing process has begun, even if it is disruptive and painful; we hope it will continue.

Improbable Maverick or Typical Conformist? Seven Thoughts on the New Bulgaria

Maria N. Todorova

The best thing about one of Timothy Garton Ash's latest pieces, his "Ten Thoughts on the New Europe," was his ending, that is, his Tenth Thought: "We should keep things in proportion. Most of the rest of humankind will (rightly) say: 'If only we had your problems.'"[1]

Although Garton Ash had not envisaged Bulgaria, this key phrase of multiethnic East European origin certainly sums up the attitude Bulgarians have vis-à-vis Europe. Now that I have borrowed his conclusion (itself borrowed from East European everyday jargon), which rightly or wrongly reflects Bulgarians' perceptions of their own and Europe's problems, it might not be thought too immodest to propose only seven thoughts on the new Bulgaria.

What follows is an attempt to convey the general feeling about developments in Bulgaria immediately before and after the autumn of 1989 from a Bulgarian perspective (or, rather, from one possible Bulgarian perspective). I would wish to believe that my approach is essentially Weberian, that is, multifactoral, and does not necessarily reflect a hierarchy of priorities, especially now that it is not bon ton to sound *marxisante,* let alone outright Marxist. Still, it must be the Freudian curse of a long-term brainwashing that has conditioned the order of problems to be outlined, beginning with the economy.[2]

1. Timothy Garton Ash. "Ten Thoughts on the New Europe," *New York Review of Books,* June 14, 1990, p. 22.
2. There is justification for that starting point in the fact that, for all the euphoria over democratization, intellectuals' revolution, and the rest, economic problems have dominated the public discourse throughout.

The Economy

> *Question to Radio Erevan:* "Can shock-therapy help
> us accomplish in a shorter time what Sweden has
> achieved in 200 years?"
> *Answer:* "Certainly. It can be done in only 199."

Bulgaria was a relative latecomer to the East European economic crisis. The year 1984 has been pointed to as the last in a nearly fifteen-year period of comparatively stable foreign-trade relations, although the deficit had been steadily rising from the beginning of the 1980s.[3] What happened in the second half of the 1980s was that Bulgaria lost all the elements that stabilized the economy of the country and, with a foreign debt of over $10.3 billion, steadily crept from a profound economic crisis into an even deeper one.

Throughout its postwar existence Bulgaria's exports were linked to the economies of the Soviet Union and the other Eastern bloc countries, that is, to the non-hard currency markets, with over 80 percent (a proportion higher than any of its COMECON counterparts) going in that direction. The rest went primarily to the oil-producing countries of the Near and Middle East. It has to be kept in mind that Bulgaria is one of the states most dependent on oil imports in all of Europe.

The fall of oil prices in 1985–86 was followed by the practical loss of Bulgaria's main dollar markets, with the result that those countries are over $2.3 billion in debt to Bulgaria. Such debts can hardly be expected to be paid soon, especially with the Middle East crisis.[4] At the same time, the cheap flow of Soviet oil drastically diminished; as of 1991 even the small amount that remains goes on a dollar basis.

The disintegration of the traditional East European and Soviet markets, which had been Bulgaria's only export possibility for the produce of its heavy, electronic, chemical, and light industries became a major problem for the effectiveness and, indeed, the very existence of these industries.[5] On the other hand, if one considers the structure of the foreign debt, the extreme dependence of Bulgarian industries on foreign imports is indi-

---

3. *Demokratsiia*, February 22, 1990. The deficit in millions of U.S. dollars has been: 919 (1982), 1,125 (1983), 2,111 (1984), 1,456 (1985), 1,727 (1986), 1,947 (1987), 2,003 (1988).

4. The debt falls mostly on Iraq, Libya, Nicaragua, Algeria, Syria, Ethiopia, Mozambique, Angola: *Duma*, July 23 and 24, 1990.

5. Over 70 percent of its COMECON exports are machinery and electronics: *Financial Times, Newsletter*, May 4, 1990. It goes without saying that most Bulgarian produce, like most East European produce, cannot compete on Western markets despite the cheap labor force, because the goods are of lower quality and are based on antiquated technologies.

cated by the fact that over 60 percent of the hard-currency expenditures during the last five years went for the import of raw and other materials.[6] There is practically no industrial branch whose hard-currency return is bigger than its hard-currency expenditure. The continuous devaluations of the dollar were an additional blow. On the whole, the country exports for dollars but imports for deutsche marks, yens, and schillings.[7]

All of the above is meant not to explain the *reasons* for the economic crisis at the end of the 1980s but solely to explain its *timing*. What is important here is that by the end of the 1980s Bulgaria's economy faced a profound structural crisis, the result of the disintegration of its traditional foreign markets.[8] The reasons for the specific market orientation of Bulgaria in the postwar period fall outside the framework of this analysis; besides, they are the outcome of a primarily political agenda (the Moscow-Yalta-Potsdam arrangements and the creation of the Stalinist "world order") rather than of an economic choice.

A lot has been written on the absurdity of the "socialist" economies, which can be characterized not as developed or underdeveloped but as erroneously developed economies. This *systemic* characteristic has also been accordingly applied to Bulgaria in the latest flood of overall verdicts on the crumbling Bulgarian economy. Tempting but simple explanations based on the irrationality of the system, however, obscure a finer, nuanced, and concrete historical analysis.

Stalinism has been described as, among other things, a modernizing revolution, contradictory and even counterproductive, and highly inappropriate for Eastern Europe.[9] Yet, for Bulgaria, the verdict of an "ill-conceived attempt at modernization" is not so unambiguous. In many respects, at least in the first two decades, the effect was to boost the economy of a backward agricultural country.

To a great extent the development of "socialism" in Bulgaria immediately after 1944 and until the 1960s can be, and has been, seen in the light of modernization theory as a gigantic and drastic attempt at industrialization through the rupture of the ties of the petty individual producer with his immediate economic basis: private property, both in the rural and in the urban milieu. It has been repeatedly shown that the extensive develop-

---

6. *Duma,* August 3, 1990.

7. The biggest debts are to Germany ($1.8 billion), Japan ($1.4 billion), and Austria and England (about $1 billion each) (*Duma,* July 23, 1990).

8. Bulgarian economic development has been characterized by a larger commitment to foreign trade than any other East European country or the USSR. See John R. Lampe, *The Bulgarian Economy in the Twentieth Century* (London, 1986), p. 156.

9. George Schöpflin, "The Stalinist Experience in Eastern Europe," *Survey* 30, no. 3 (130) (October 1988): 126.

ment of the planned economy within the framework of an overcentralized administrative structure, with an emphasis on heavy industry at the expense of all other sectors of the economy, and regardless of efficiency criteria, to a high degree achieved its goal. By the early 1960s the country "had firmly established the basis of modern economic growth and structural change."[10]

The period from the 1960s witnessed a gradual transition from extensive to intensive growth; that is, greater attention was paid to productivity per input than to increased inputs. A series of reform measures, which fluctuated with the political developments in the Soviet bloc, were enacted to realize the transition. On the whole, the aim of the reforms was greater efficiency, to preclude a switch to a market economy, although introduction of market mechanisms and decentralization of ministerial controls were spelled out as its essence.

The most important pressures for reform in Bulgaria, aside from the ones typical for the whole "socialist" system with its widening technological gap from the West, especially after the 1970s, were the growing importance of foreign trade and the shortage of labor. The latter was the result of the sweeping economic shifts of the previous decades and the specific demographic development of the country.[11] The disintegration of the first and the impasse reached by the second by the end of the 1980s contributed largely to, though by no means determined, the course of events in 1989.

The Communist episode in Bulgarian history is bound to be seen in terms of a specific response to the challenge of integrating peripheral and backward economies into the European mainstream. It has had some achievements to its credit and many more inadequacies, but the basic challenge of *longue durée* is looming large over Bulgaria just as it has been looming ever since the nineteenth century.

Demography and Social Structure

> Are we striving for the road to Europe, or for the road
> to the old people's home?
>
> *Trud*—(newspaper), June 18, 1990

The industrial revolution of the 1950s and 1960s was accompanied by demographic and social shifts, some with expected, others with un-

10. Lampe, *The Bulgarian Economy*, p. 9.
11. Ibid., p. 199.

foreseeable results. The dramatic flow of the labor force from the countryside to the cities was a common characteristic for all East European countries, yet nowhere else did it reach the dimensions and the quick pace that it did in Bulgaria. The combined effects of the extremely rapid industrialization and the miserable overpopulation in the countryside in the interwar period, alongside the administrative pushing through of the collectivization program, resulted in a drastic change in the rural/urban ratio of the country: from 24.7 percent in 1946 the urban population almost doubled by 1965 (46.5 percent), to reach 66.4 percent in 1987.[12] This depletion of the number of agricultural workers resulted in an automatic swelling of the ranks of industrial, construction, and transportation workers.[13]

From a sociological-psychological viewpoint the adjustment of a first generation of urbanites and a first generation of industrial workers to the life-style of the city was accompanied by inevitable and deep-reaching frustrations and partial lumpenization. Yet however deep, these frustrations were not enough to counterweigh an even deeper aversion to rural life as remembered from the interwar period; thus all hopes of a subsequent population shift to the villages, based simply on nostalgia and a minimum of economic incentives, turned out to be utopian dreams. On the other hand, the strong town/village opposition typical of the interwar period was transformed into an intercity opposition between "citizens" and "peasants," groups with rather undefined social bases, given the fluidity of the Bulgarian social structure. For a country with one of the stablest and most respected peasant traditions in Europe, the extent to which the sobriquet "peasant" has acquired a pejorative meaning is amazing.

Yet, despite the undoubted narrowing of the seemingly unbreachable gap between village and city in the last four decades, the traditional conflict between town and village has been translated and exacerbated into another conflict: between the capital, Sofia (population about 1.2 million), and the countryside, the "province."[14] This became especially evident at the time of the free elections in June 1990.

12. Robert N. Taafe, "Population Structure," in K.-D. Grothusen, ed., *Bulgaria: Handbook on Southeastern Europe,* vol. 6 (Göttingen, 1990), p. 445 (hereafter this handbook cited as *Bulgaria*).

13. Roger Whitaker, "Social Structure," *Bulgaria,* pp. 463–64.

14. The resentment against the real or perceived privileges of the capital found apt reflection in one of the popular anecdotes: "The Bulgarians consist of one million Sofioters and eight million vegetarians." On the other hand, the cities in general remain dependant on food supplies from the village, especially on the family level.

The second major transformation during the postwar period concerned population growth. Bulgaria had entered its period of demographic transition by the turn of the century, and from the 1920s on there was an significant decline in both mortality and fertility, with the lowest level of natural increase occurring in the 1980s (1.3 per thousand for 1985), a level second only to that in the German Democratic Republic (GDR) and Hungary.[15] In fact, the Bulgarian population had stopped reproducing itself.

The massive dislocations accompanied by the continuing and intensifying change in the birth and death rates drastically affected the age structure of the population. At present, the Bulgarian citizenry is demographically the oldest in the Balkans and close to the age level in Hungary and the GDR. This is to say that only about 42 percent of the population is under thirty years of age, whereas 31 percent is over fifty, a classical example of a regressive population.[16] The retired labor force is over 2.3 million, out of a total population of just over 9 million and, of every one hundred people of the active laboring population, forty-two have reached the age of retirement, a share twice as large as that in the developed industrial countries.[17] This fact has had, and for some time will have, a not insignificant effect on the political spectrum.

The third major change in postwar Bulgarian society affected the educational level of the population. The introduction of universal, compulsory education in relatively backward societies is one of the incontestable achievements of the East European regimes.[18] The number of people with higher education active in the labor force has increased from less than 10,000 in 1939 to more than 340,000 in 1989, of which about 120,000 are engineers.[19] Here, however, I would like to stress only two aspects: on the one hand, the creation of a relatively well educated work force and, on the other, the relative overproduction of an "intelligentsia" looking for white-collar jobs. The latter aspect, alongside the rapid formation of a first-generation intelligentsia and a first generation of rural people in an urban setting, has left an indelible mark on the character and quality of the intellectual climate.

15. Taafe, "Population Structure," p. 443.
16. Ibid., p. 435.
17. *Duma*, May 29, 1990. The usual retirement age is sixty for men and fifty-five for women, though it is lower for some sectors of the economy (e.g., mining, nuclear energy), and for the military.
18. See Peter Bachmeier, "Schulsystem," and Milan Benes, "Hochschulen und Wissenschaft," both published in *Bulgaria*.
19. *Duma*, May 30, 1990.

There is one exception to the above outlined demographic and social structure. An examination of the ethnic and religious backgrounds of those who went from village to city attests that, as a whole, the Muslim population remained primarily agricultural.[20] As for the ethnic Turks, they are heavily concentrated (over 80 percent) in the northeastern and the southeastern parts of the country, they engage especially in the time-consuming and specialized field of tobacco farming. A growing number of Turks work in different industrial enterprises. There is also a crust of educated Turks in the urban centers (doctors, teachers, engineers) that has been formed in the last forty years and, though comparatively not numerous, is highly influential. As is to be expected, among them are to be found the most ardent exponents of a distinct ethnic consciousness.

The demographic development of the Turkish population in Bulgaria until 1965 followed a double trend: on the one hand, a gradual decrease of their relative proportion in the overall ethnic structure of the Bulgarian population; on the other, an increase in their absolute numbers. Although 1965 was the last census that specified ethnic origin, in the next two decades there was an obvious increase in both aspects, given the age structure of the Turkish population and its consequently much higher birth rate. This increase in number, as well as other factors, seems to have had a decisive effect on the events of 1984/85, unleashing a problem which came to be known, rightly or wrongly, as the "ethnic conflict."

The Ethnic Conflict

No matter how you turn, your past is always behind you.

—Proverb

In the winter of 1984/85 the Bulgarian authorities launched a massive campaign to change the names of the Turkish population to Slavic Bul-

20. About 69 percent of the Turks and 64 percent of the Pomaks live in villages: *Kultura*, no. 33, August 17, 1990. The Muslim population comprises Turks, Bulgarian-speaking Muslims (Pomaks), Muslim Gypsies, Tatars, and Muslim Albanians, the latter two numbering only several thousand people. There are no reliable statistics on ethnic and religious background, but the Turks by the mid-1980s were estimated to number about 900,000 (between 830,000 and 960,000), that is, over 10 percent of the total population. The number of Pomaks was about 150,000, and that of Gypsies, of whom 75 percent were Muslim and 25 percent Orthodox Christians, was about 450,000. See Stefan Troebst, "Nationale Minderheiten," *Bulgaria*, pp. 474–89; Hugh Poulton, with MLIHRC (Minnesota Lawyers International Human Rights Committee), *Minorities in the Balkans* Minority Rights Group (London), Report 82, October 1989.

garian names. This was certainly not the first mass renaming of Muslims in Bulgaria (there had been previous ones in 1912–13, 1941–44, and 1971), but it was the first one launched explicitly at the Turkish-speaking Muslims. The move was not preceded by any propaganda campaign and was reported in official statements only after the fact. Even its ideological legitimization (the "restoration" of the original Bulgarian names and national consciousness to descendants of Islamicized Bulgarians who, through forceful or voluntary conversion, had lost their language and religion) was not original.[21] It was, however, the first time such a campaign had been aimed at ethnic Turks.

During the renaming campaign there were reports of attempts to resist it met by violence.[22] Interestingly, the renaming, although an obvious violation of human rights and strongly opposed by the majority of the Turkish population, did not by itself become the center of the mounting resentment in the years to come.[23] It was rather the accompanying brutal measures against Islamic rituals and customs, as well as against the use of the Turkish language, that radically mobilized the minority public opinion and led to the protests of 1989.

In the four years following the renaming there was practically no organized opposition on the part of the Turkish population. As a whole, with the exception of people directly implicated in the so-called revival process and some outright nationalists, the Bulgarian population empathized with the plight of their co-citizens. There was certainly international pressure on Bulgaria, especially from the Muslim countries, but on the whole it seemed as if the question was subsiding, until, in the spring and summer of 1989, a special confluence of factors triggered the mass exodus of Turks from the country.

It still remains to be carefully weighed how much of the exodus was a spontaneous act, the result of mass psychosis, and how much it was induced by the security apparatus and Turkish propaganda.[24] In the course of just over two months, more than 300,000 Turks left Bulgaria,

21. This ideology had been promoted in the interwar period by patriotically minded Bulgarian Muslims who were looking for ways to integrate the Pomaks in the Bulgarian mainstream.
22. Estimates of victims rest on rumors (between 300 and 1,500). Amnesty International gives the number of just over 100 ethnic Turks killed by the security forces. Many more were detained in prison or labor camps.
23. Part of the more educated urban dwellers saw in the change of the names a means to obliterate the difference between itself and the Bulgarian "ruling" majority, and to be naturally integrated into it.
24. See the report of Helsinki Watch from October 1989: Ted Zang, *Destroying Ethnic Identity: The Expulsion of the Bulgarian Turks* (New York, 1989).

although the interesting figures are obviously the next two: by the end of 1989, that is, even before the reversal of the anti-Turkish policies, over 130,000 Turks had returned to Bulgaria, and by the second half of 1990 this figure reached close to 160,000.

What was indicative, however, from a psychological point of view, was the change from the Bulgarian population's initially sympathetic attitude after the mass exodus to a growing resentment of the Turks, which reached its culmination in the winter of 1990. The variety of motivation and expression is considerable. There is no doubt that the general frustration of the Bulgarian population, caused by the overall social, economic, political, and moral crisis, can be, and in many instances is being, manipulated into easily inflammable nationalist feelings.

It must be stressed, however, that there has not been a long-standing *organic* ethnic conflict between the Turkish and Bulgarian populations (compared, for example, with the Serbian-Albanian or the Hungarian-Romanian controversies). Despite the latest manifestations of nationalism and the overblown attention they received in the mass media, the conflict, essentially designed and created by the political authorities, has better prospects to be safely contained.

The so-called Turkish problem in Bulgaria dates from the last decades of the nineteenth century and is essentially a phenomenon of the same order as any other minority problem created by the disintegration of a huge multinational empire, in this case the Ottoman Empire. With minor exceptions the minority problems in the Balkans have been solved through assimilation or emigration. The specific situation of the Turks in Bulgaria (the most backward social stratum, and geographically, linguistically, and religiously isolated) coupled with intensive emigration propaganda from the Ottoman Empire, and after 1923 from Turkey, precluded the possibility of successful integration or assimilation. At the same time Turkey, despite its strong emigration propaganda, was always careful to limit the flow of immigrants, thus, no matter what its motivation, perpetuating an explosive issue.

The events of 1984–85 have been seen as the logical outcome and culmination of a three-decades-long policy of pressure in Bulgaria against the Turkish population. Immediately after the ascendancy of Todor Zhivkov in 1956, a new national policy was modeled that deviated to a great extent from, or even reversed, the policy pursued in the first postwar decade. This latter policy had been based on the full recognition of national minorities and was, in fact, an adaptation of the Soviet model, exported and imposed first via the Comintern, and later through the Cominform.

The new policy postulated that Bulgaria was not a multinational state (which ipso facto forestalled a potential federative structure on the Yugoslav or Soviet model), that the Bulgarian Turks were an inextricable part of the Bulgarian socialist nation (that is, that citizenship took priority over ethnic consciousness), and that a strong distinction should be drawn between confession and nationality. In 1956 a long-term policy began of gradual and uneven encroachments on the cultural autonomy of the Turkish minority.[25]

Although retrospectively the interpretation of the events of 1984 as the corollary of a long-term policy seems flawless, the neatness of this evolutionary construct can be challenged. First, nationalistic though Bulgarian policies during the Zhivkov administration might have been, culminating in the esoteric and messianic patriotic frenzies of his irrational daughter in the early 1980s just before her early death, they did not inevitably lead to the forceful, and often violent, mass renaming of the Turkish Muslim population.[26] Throughout the 1960s and the 1970s different political alternatives, all aiming at the gradual and peaceful integration of the Turkish Muslim population, had been discussed at the top government and party levels.

Second, the whole operation of the renaming disclosed important frictions between three different echelons of power: the local party and administrative apparatus; the army; and, last, the Ministry of the Interior. This became especially evident during the second act of the drama, during the summer of 1989.

The exact history of the 1984 decision is still awaiting its meticulous historian; however, there is no doubt that it was not discussed (or accepted) at any party or government level but was a manifestation of personal

25. For example, the government closed the separate Turkish schools; relegated the study of Turkish to the status of foreign-language education, until it finally disappeared altogether from the school curricula; and harassed Muslim religious institutions. See Stefan Troebst, "Zum Verhältnis von Partei, Staat und türkischer Minderheit in Bulgarien 1956–1986," in Roland Schönfeld, ed., *Untersuchungen zur Gegenwartskunde Südosteuropas*, vol. 25, *Nationalitätenprobleme in Südsoteuropa* (Munich, 1987).

26. Ironically, though not surprisingly, given the Ceauşescu precedent, the career of Zhivkov's daughter Liudmila as head of Bulgarian cultural policies has been almost unanimously hailed in the West as a manifestation of independence and a window to the West. See, among others, her assessment in Richard Crampton, *A Short History of Bulgaria* (Cambridge, 1987), and Joseph Rothschild, *Return to Diversity: A Political History of East Central Europe since World War II* (New York, 1989).

politics (of Todor Zhivkov and his immediate entourage). Behind the
decision in part were the specific demographic developments of the Turkish community, and its implementation was hastened by the forthcoming
national census scheduled for December 1985. Additional explanations
were spelled out or hinted at in the subsequent period: the fear of the
Cyprus precedent, the Albanian Kosovo problem, the rise of Islamic fun-
damentalism, the influence of the Iranian revolution, the example of
Lebanon—all countries quite close to Bulgaria. Doubtlessly, the relative
economic stability until 1984 also gave the decision makers the self-
confidence to embark on an adventurist ethnic policy.

All these considerations are important insofar as they help assess the
relative influence of the "ethnic conflict" factor in the subsequent events,
and especially the initial change of November 10.[27]

The International Dimension

> What the U.S. can put aside, will go to Israel, to
> Turkey, to Pakistan, and a small part to the Catholic
> Lech Wałęsa.
>
> —*Kultura* (newspaper) June 8, 1990

It has been rather pompously suggested that the exodus of the Turks did
to Bulgaria what the buoyant march of the East Germans to the West did
to the Berlin Wall. This comparison is tempting because of the coincidence of dates and the neatness of a simple explanation.[28] As has already
been pointed out, the very number of returnees from Turkey even before
November 10 attests to the presumptuousness of such a contention. Still,
the international isolation of Bulgaria after 1985, which added to its
image as the bogeyman of Eastern Europe, certainly was greatly responsible for the coup that ousted Zhivkov on November 10.[29]

27. An interesting, though hardly founded contention, based on 1984 as the first year of
the economic crisis and the beginning of the anti-Turkish campaign, was advanced by the
Movement for Rights and Freedoms (commonly known as "the Turkish party"): namely,
that it was the "Turkish" question that brought about the loss of Islamic markets and thus
became the cause of the enormous accumulation of foreign debt. If nothing else, it is at least
a proof of how much the economic argument dominates the present political discourse in the
country.

28. The Berlin Wall fell on November 9, and Zhivkov the next day.

29. The reformist president Petŭr Mladenov, who succeeded Zhivkov, had been his long-
term foreign minister, and had to bear all the consequences of the international isolation of
Bulgaria.

Two other elements, however, deserve mention in this analysis of how far the international climate contributed to the Bulgarian autumn of 1989 and the subsequent developments. The first element is the reverberations of the global crisis affecting the system of modern communism, and first and foremost among them is what has come to be called "the Gorbachev syndrome." The crucial influence of the new foreign policy of the Soviet Union on the events in Eastern Europe has been recognized, openly or reluctantly, by practically all participants in the drama. In the Bulgarian case, too, the influence of *perestroika* has been of immediate consequence, much more than the example with reform experimentation in Poland or Hungary.[30]

The unique standing of Bulgaria among the Soviet satellites as the most faithful and compliant ally has attracted attention and has been more or less adequately explained in terms of the effects of a deeply internalized historical tradition alongside "a real complimentarity of economic interests and developmental strategies."[31] This standing, among other factors, precluded the attempt, so eloquently and melodramatically spelled out in other East European countries, to depict the decades leading to 1989 as nothing short of a national liberation struggle against an alien ideology and Soviet imperialism.

The second element concerns the precarious geopolitical position of Bulgaria compounded by a nineteenth- and twentieth-century foreign political experience summarized in the notion of national catastrophes. The Balkan countries have for so long been pawns in the geopolitical game of the great powers that the feelings of resignation in "this wretched Bulgaria," as Winston Churchill acridly put it, concerning foreign political developments, are hardly surprising.[32]

Resignation, of course, does not imply complete passivity, and it often breeds commendable realism. In the global euphoria over events in Eastern Europe, Bulgaria has voiced strong concern that the deconcentration of armaments in Central Europe might bring about a concentration in the

30. Even so, the speculation that Gorbachev gave the green light for the ousting of Zhivkov, while worth looking into, seems more to be the result of a conditioned spasmatic reflex on the part of old-fashioned Sovietologists to look to the Kremlin for all explanations.

31. Rothschild, *Return to Diversity*, p. 212. The "historical tradition" has to be understood primarily in terms of the role Russia has played in the liberation struggles of the Bulgarians against the Ottoman Empire. It must be added, next to the sentimental dimension, that Bulgaria has never had a common border with Russia and that, after the Second World war, Soviet troops were never stationed in the country.

32. An unfounded but quite indicative slogan emerged immediately after the Bush-Gorbachev Mediterranean meeting in December 1989: "Yalta—Malta."

flanks—in a word, that the receding of the tensions from the center would be at the expense of rising tensions in the periphery.[33] It must be remembered that, no matter how reluctantly, the Soviet Union and the Warsaw Pact have come to be seen as the sole guarantors of national sovereignty.[34]

The Intellectual Climate

> There have been worse times, but there haven't been meaner times.
>
> —N.A. Nekrasov
>
> And bad times set in: nobody reads, and everybody writes.
>
> —From an ancient Sanskrit manuscript

Inevitably, as the dominant discourse on East European intellectual developments has been shaped and conceptualized in the framework of the Polish, the Hungarian, and the Czech paradigms, the respective evolution in the other East European countries tends to assume the character of a predictable aberration. The emancipatory character of the Central European myth is widely recognized even by those who do not necessarily buy it; however, its discriminatory aspects vis-à-vis the ones stigmatized as outside the privileged club have yet to be assessed.

One of the results is that those who try to explain the Bulgarian case, instead of analyzing the concrete historical and social circumstances, are reduced to the (lack of) paraphernalia set up to objectify the Central European idea. Thus, the non-Europeanness of the country, and the Balkans as a whole, is explained by such historical stereotypes as the alleged character of Byzantine Orthodoxy, the lengthy "Asiatic" presence of the Ottomans with all ensuing economic, social, and cultural repercussions, and so on.[35]

---

33. *Rabotnichesko delo*, March 8, 1990.

34. Inflated though it may be, Bulgaria is really concerned about the often aggressive standing of a strong (50 million), highly militarized Turkey, which has U.S. support. (A recent poll indicates that close to 40 percent of the Bulgarian population sees Turkey as a national threat.) The concern is further fed on the Cyprus precedent and the character of the Greek-Turkish relations.

35. It is imperative to point out (although I do so regretfully) that even the most sophisticated exponents of the Central European idea, many of them historians, display an unashamed but self-confident (and therefore aggressive and conducive to overgeneralizations) ignorance of the history of the Balkans. Strangely enough, this ignorance is even more profound than that concerning Russia. For attempts to objectify the Central European idea not by literary but by historical arguments, see Jenő Szűcs, "Three Historical Regions of

The issue would be inconsequential if it had not been internalized by a significant part of the Bulgarian intelligentsia itself, producing a much more serious result: a severe and paralyzing case of a double inferiority complex. One aspect of this complex is common to all the intellectuals of Eastern Europe, and stems from their relative isolation from the Western mainstream of intellectual developments and their incomparably lower material possibilities (their social status, however, is often superior to that of Western intellectuals). The other aspect is internal, further marginalizing Bulgaria and the Balkans within the East European periphery. As with the first, it is based on an even greater isolation, compounded, however, by a quasi-ghettoization. Thus, Bulgaria's objective isolation (based on geography, geopolitical factors, the practical absence of an intellectual emigration) is intensified by feelings of being overlooked and forsaken. In the Bulgarian context, even the illusion of the Hungarian writer György Konrád's pretentious appeal to the "international intellectual aristocracy" of Europe and the West is inconceivable.[36]

Isolation, naturally, breeds parochialism; but even where intellectual achievement is outstanding, a certain incestuousness in the intellectual climate forewarns of the intelligentsia's ability to participate only in internal exchange, not in the international dialogue.

On the other hand, because of the specific historical context in nation and state formation, the Bulgarian intelligentsia is still in the process of being made. It does not have traditions common to Poland, Hungary, Czechoslovakia, and Russia, where it developed in rather differentiated societies. In Bulgaria not only the postwar but also the prewar intelligentsia was mostly of the first generation, with strong roots to its previous social background. Only in the 1970s, and especially in the 1980s, could one speak of the formation of a *Klasse für sich,* with separately articulated interests.

Also, given the specific characteristics of the Bulgarian political scene, the intelligentsia had a peculiar standing. In the proliferation of labels about the East European regimes before the events of 1989 (totalitarianism, Stalinism, authoritarianism, Communist dictatorship, imposition of alien ideological models, Soviet imperialism, and so on), the one

Europe," in J. Keane, ed., *Civil Society and the State* (New York, 1988); G. Schöpflin, "Cultural Identity, Political Identity, National Identity," in G. Schöpflin and N. Wood, eds., *In Search of Central Europe* (Cambridge, Eng., 1989). For an important critique of the notion, see F. Fehér, "On Making Central Europe," *Eastern European Politics and Societies* 3, no. 3, (1989).

36. Cited in Timothy Garton Ash, "Does Central Europe Exist?" in *The Uses of Adversity* (New York, 1989), p. 202.

that best fitted the Bulgarian political and intellectual landscape seems to have been paternalism.

The party's paternalistic attitude toward the intelligentsia is a common phenomenon in Eastern Europe: it was partly the result of ideology, partly of the social background of the party leadership, which shared the traditional anti-intellectual suspicions of peasants and workers. In Bulgaria, where the ideas of socialism and communism had strong indigenous roots, unlike in many of its East European counterparts, the Communist Party had lost its predominantly intellectual character by the mid-1920s. Still, in the peculiarly paternalistic scene of Bulgarian political life, Zhivkov managed to implement a successful policy of dividing or corrupting the intelligentsia while not creating martyrs and saints.[37]

This paternalism had at least two side effects. First, no tradition of a "culture of protest" was created despite single manifestations.[38] As a result the intellectuals either lapsed into the posture of what E. P. Thompson has called attentism (that is, the wait-and-see policy), or acted on the premise that compromise was to be preferred over passivity. Also, the use of the "periphrastic" was kept to the end, unlike in the countries which developed a normal language in the samizdat.[39] The second side effect of paternalism, repercussions of which are being felt at the present moment, was its foreshadowing of what was in many ways the proper and predictable response: an infantile reaction against it, compounding the effect of the almost total lack of political culture in the country.

In the present euphoria over words, the effects of a belated *glasnost'*, there is passionate discussion about the manifestations of a perceived cultural crisis.[40] It seems, however, that the strongest negative legacy of the past few decades is the deep demoralization of very significant societal strata.

Outside of the problems of the intelligentsia, but important for the overall intellectual climate, is the coming into the open of generational conflict. Although undoubtedly an eternal conflict, at the moment it is exacerbated by the overall crisis and often assumes overt political dimensions.

Finally, a word on the church and religion, especially in view of the

37. Based on nepotism and regionalism, Zhivkov's regime, however, did not reach the excesses of the clan dictatorship of Ceaușescu, with whom he is usually compared.

38. The first organized activities can be traced back to 1988.

39. "Periphrastic" is "the intellectual version of getting around the system rather than confronting it" (Timothy Garton Ash, "A Hungarian Lesson," in *The Uses of Adversity*, p. 147).

40. Mostly in the weekly papers *Kultura* and *Literaturen front*.

central role they played in Poland and the influential place they have in other East European societies, Russia included. The church in Bulgaria has had an eminent and respected history, primarily as an educational and national organization. Although its activities have nowadays intensified and it has the appeal of a traditional institution at a time of total reassessment and nationalist upsurge, it is unlikely that it will seek a role different from that it has played in the past.[41] On the other hand, there is a proliferation, not entirely unexpected, of esoteric groups dealing with occult and extrasensory activities, a usual and predictable side effect in times of crises and in times of chaos.

From the Coup d'État to the Elections

> We resign from Bulgaria: let the cowards live there.
> —Opposition leader

> All decent people are cowards.
> —Dostoyevsky

The Bulgarian *perestroika* (the attempt at reform from above in the continuum of the Communist Party domination) has been aptly described as having lasted from November 10 to December 14, 1990, that is, from the downfall of Zhivkov to the first openly voiced anti-Communist demonstrations.

In the confluence of different crises "the crisis of the ruling elite" has an important place. In the light of developments that led to the coup of November 10, 1989, the suggested cleavage between the triangle of authorities (party bureaucracy, army, and security apparatus) proved to be instrumental. The tension between these centers of power had apparently existed for some time, intensifying with the impending economic crisis, the ecological problems, the activation of the traditionally passive intelligentsia, the exacerbation of the Turkish problem, and the overall international climate.

Sofia in the fall of 1989 was for a short period reminiscent of Prague in 1968 (in overall atmosphere, in the initiative for changes coming from within the party, in one of the dominant discourses centered on democrat-

---

41. In a recent poll 43 percent of the interviewed described themselves as believing in God (but not religiously active); in another poll the percentage is 50. This might be a substantial number in view of the recent past, but compared with the numbers in other East European countries (the USSR included), it is rather modest.

ic socialism, and so on). But there were fundamental differences: a radically transformed international conjuncture, and the hectic but steady formation of real opposition outside the party.

In the futile debate on whether November 10 should be seen as a revolution or a coup, one thing at least is clear: what followed was the legalization of alternative political thinking, expressed in the Round Table talks and the proliferation of political parties, associations, movements, and clubs that quickly saturated the deficient political market.[42] In the several months from the fall of 1989 to June 10, 1990, the date of the first election for a Grand National Assembly, the political spectrum was polarized between "Mister Democrat" versus "Comrade Reformer."

Psychologically, this was the time of the great catharsis: accumulated frustrations had to be, and were, finally articulated. The year 1989 has already received the striking epithet of the Year of Truth.[43] But in a country where there had been an *absolute* suppression of alternative truths, what followed was the intolerant proclamation of alternative *absolute* truths.

In the heated pre-election campaign the two basic opponents (the recently renamed Socialist Party [SP], the former Communist Party, and the Union of Democratic Forces [UDF], a coalition of sixteen political parties and organizations) came out with practically identical programs, despite differences in wording and passionate claims for basic ideological incompatibility on both sides. Thus, a power struggle had already transpired before the elections, although it became obvious only in the postelection period.

The results of the first elections on June 10 (for 200 seats by proportional representation) and June 17 (for another 200 by a simple majority) were a shared surprise, posing the question of the improbable maverick or the typical conformist. The SP received a 52.75 percent electoral victory (211 deputies); the UDF followed with 36 percent of the votes (144 deputies); the Movement for Rights and Freedoms (MRF) carried the Muslim vote and won 5.75 percent (23 deputies), and the Agrarian National Union received 4 percent (16 deputies). The remaining 1.5 percent was carried by four tiny parties with six representatives.[44]

42. On the proliferation of political organizations, well outnumbering fifty, see *Biuletin na BTA*, February 1990.

43. Timothy Garton Ash, "The Year of Truth," *New York Review of Books*, February 15, 1990.

44. The MRF was founded on January 4, 1990, at the height of the nationalist demonstrations organized against the government's decision to revoke the assimilation policies at

Despite the pre-election local and international polls forecasting a Socialist victory, the SP was surprised (it had not hoped to get such a vote); the opposition, hastily formed only after the events of November 10, hoped that events would follow the by then common East European paradigm (and was disillusioned). The world at large (that is, vocal West European and American media), despite some occasional profound analysis, as a rule tried to find a predictable and trivial explanation, based usually on the side effects of the now internalized Central European myth: That is, that the Orthodox Balkans were immanently conformist, not freedom-loving, nondemocratic, and so on. The internal explanations of the electoral outcome have been manifold and often contradictory: manipulation and intimidation (these accusations proved unfounded);[45] social and political inertia due to the aging electorate and an overall fear of abrupt change; a series of grave tactical mistakes on the part of the young and inexperienced opposition, which staked its future heavily on a negative campaign; and the absence of a figure of unabated innocence and uncontested intellectual appeal like Andrei Sakharov or Václav Havel.

It is important to keep in mind that in Bulgaria the Communists were not directly (or not to any great extent) identified with foreign political domination; moreover, rightly or not, the period of Communist rule has been historically associated with rising living standards; despite the important role of the opposition in providing a political alternative it is an undisputed fact that the changes were initiated by the Communist Party; in the ensuing internal shifts, the new Socialist Party leadership came to be associated with several reformers with genuine social standing; finally, in the emphatically egalitarian social traditions of Bulgaria, socialist discourse still holds appeal for a significant part of the population.

In the end, in a climate of extreme polarization between two political monsters, with no immediate hope for the formation of a political center, the population achieved what the parties could not. It secured the necessary and only hopeful outcome: a *balance* between the political forces, in which no power (party or leader) would be able to dictate.

---

the end of December 1989. It claims to be a supraparty organization dedicated to human and ethnoreligious rights, and not to be confined to any given minority, despite its mostly Muslim electorate. The Agrarian National Union, a centrist party, is the heir to the former satellite Agrarian Union, to be distinguished from the BANU "Nikola Petkov," which is a member of the UDF, although the union of the two is expected. Altogether 91 percent of the electorate (6,976,602 people) voted.

45. Aside from the positive verdict of international observers, these are the first Bulgarian elections without a single political murder.

The First Steps

> Bad politicians promise a lot, and do nothing; good
> politicians likewise do nothing, but at least promise
> less.
>   —The Talmud

> The trouble with making love in public is not the
> embarrassment, it's that everyone gives you advice.
>   —Prime Minister Andrei Lukanov

The new Grand National Assembly convened in July and, after a serious impasse, managed to reach a compromise on August 2, electing as president Zheliu Zhelev. A figure of undoubted high moral standing, Zhelev was a dissident philosopher who after November 10 became the leader of the young opposition movement.

By mid-September Andrei Lukanov, who had headed the post-November 10 government, was appointed prime minister. An economist and politician of experience, he came up at the beginning of October with an all-Socialist cabinet, despite his commitment and prolonged attempts at coalition.[46] Understandably, the opposition did not want to share the responsibility for the unavoidable unpopular measures.

Ironically, the Socialist government's program of quick and fundamental change is more radical than the program of the opposition: "Now," said Lukanov, "neither the platform of the BSP nor of the UDF is applicable. As prime minister I will not follow any party line but the logic of life and the market."[47] Given his disastrous legacy in industry, agriculture, finance, and the ecology, the pragmatic approach prioritizing economic issues seems to be the most commendable.

It is estimated that the restructuring of the economy in the next five to six years will cost ten to fifteen billion dollars.[48] Accepted as a member of the International Monetary Fund since the end of September 1990, Bulgaria shares few illusions of help coming from the West, although it is clear that the extremely complex task of the East European transition is hardly possible without a kind of Marshall Plan.[49]

Albeit slowly and with great difficulty, a political dialogue is taking shape in parliament among the intolerant monologues. The parliamen-

---

46. Some cabinet members have no party allegiance.
47. *Duma*, October 12, 1990.
48. Ibid.
49. See John Kenneth Galbraith, "The Rush to Capitalism," *New York Review of Books*, October 25, 1990.

tary commissions are preparing new laws on practically all issues, with a strong priority on the privatization program, which are expected to be passed in the immediate future.

With the practical measures to follow it still is to be seen whether 1989 will not be assessed in the future as the year in which the technocracy that was, in fact, established and strengthened throughout the two preceding decades was legitimized and emancipated from bureaucratic and ideological control.

Conclusion

Is it necessary to be crazy in order to be a pessimist?

This question tortured the minds of high school students in Tŭrnovo on the eve of the Balkan wars in 1913. Eighty years later the question has spilled over from adolescent to adult minds. There are enough reasons for pessimism: the economic situation is catastrophic. Looming food and fuel shortages could easily inflame the polarized and explosive political scene, to which the manipulable ethnic conflict, although it has subsided for the moment, can be added.

The only obvious reason for optimism is that the process of change (though not its direction) is now clearly recognized by everybody as irreversible. Still, despite the extreme and frequently uncivilized polarization, parliamentary life is a fact. In the long run, several factors support an activist (and implicitly optimistic) position against an equally understandable posture of passive resignation.

Possible scenarios are being spelled out by hyperactive and attention-starved political scientists and politicians: from rosy utopias of a quick integration with the European Community, or even a Balkan federation, to apocalyptic visions of a social explosion (the "Romanian syndrome"), of the spilling over of the ethnic conflict (the "Yugoslav syndrome"), of a military takeover, of quick pauperization in the orbit of a Germanized Europe, and so on. In the rapidly changing political climate the borderline between inconceivable and plausible scenarios is feverishly shifting.

For a historian, however, science fiction (that is, future scenarios) is as unacceptable as counterfactual history (the euphemism for the "what if" taboo). Therefore, to come back to the dominant psychological climate of the present: the high school students in Tŭrnovo on the eve of the Balkan wars in 1913 concluded that one need not be crazy in order to be *temporarily* desperate.

Post-Communism as Post-Yugoslavism: The Yugoslav Non-Revolutions of 1989–1990

Ivo Banac

> It happens from time to time in human societies that hate and anger burst their banks, that they destroy everything, overshadow reason, and silence all better human instincts. While they rage it seems as if it were Doomsday and that instead of everything that stands, lives, shines, moves, and speaks, only a dead ocean of hate and anger will remain—as reason unto itself. But a deeper and better considered view shows that it is not so, and that hate and anger do not destroy life—they only transform it. This world is fashioned in such a way that love and reason lead to the construction of better order, but hate and anger remove evil and injustice. Only hate and anger can erase the frontiers of rotten empires, move the foundations of crumbling institutions, and bring down wrongs, in a swift and pure way; wrongs that threaten to reign supremely and lastingly. Because hate gives strength and anger provokes movement. Afterward, hate quenches and anger abates, but the fruits of strength and movement remain. That is why the contemporaries, living in such historical circumstances, see only hate and anger, as if they were apocalyptic beasts, and the posterity, on the contrary, only the fruits of strength and movement.
>
> —Ivo Andrić

Andrić did not have to spell it out. In Yugoslavia, hate and anger have to do with nationhood. Their troubling face is evident in their inclusiveness. Even the brightest spirits of Yugoslavia have not been spared. There is a poem among the posthumously published papers of Danilo Kiš titled "The Poet of Revolution on the Presidential Ship," in which Kiš, the most cosmopolitan of Serbian writers, assumes the persona of Tito's Croat protocol officer. The cynical and affectedly dainty Croat lectures his Serbian ward on the etiquette of entertaining the Great Leader, taking all along unpleasant potshots at Serb attitudes ("by the way, they say, you do not love the Croats too much"), Serbian language ("surely, over there in Šumadija and Srem, you do not say it as . . ."), and Serbian provincialism ("how do you say in the environs of Čačak").[1] Kiš was angry at what he imagined to be Tito's Croat retinue. The unspoken point was that access and power were used to humiliate *les autres*.

That much was right. Despite the high-sounding words about the "trinominal people" (under the Karadjordjevićes) and "brotherhood and unity" (under the Communists), the essence of Yugoslav politics has been the national question. Stripped of all the nonessentials, this has meant the clash of conflicting national ideologies that have evolved in each of Yugoslavia's numerous national and confessional communities, reflecting the historical experiences of the Serbs, Croats, Slovenes, and other constituent nationalities. For most of its duration, certainly until 1939, the first Yugoslav state (1918–41) represented a compromise between Yugoslavist unitarism and Serbian supremacy. All the institutions of the prewar Serbian state, most especially the monarchy, the army, the central administrative apparatus, the church (or more correctly, the privileged position of the reconstituted Serbian Orthodox patriarchate) were preserved and extended in the South Slavic lands of the former Habsburg Monarchy (Slovenia, Croatia, Bosnia-Hercegovina), as well as in Kosovo and Macedonia (acquired by Serbia in the Balkan wars of 1912–13), and in Montenegro (united to Serbia under the conditions of military occupation in 1918). Serbia's predominance, sometimes brutal, sometimes merely clumsy, was justified by two different, frequently competing, but oftentimes complementary ideologies. The first of these—easy to understand but unappealing to the non-Serbs—was the ideology of Great Serbian nationalism: the idea that all Serbs, however defined (linguistically, religiously), should be gathered within one state. The second, a far more complicated system of allegiance, was that of Yugoslavist unitarism. This ideology claimed that the Serbs, Croats, and Slovenes constituted a single Yugoslav people. Hence, those who insisted on absolute equality among the interchangeable "tribes" were either small-minded or prompted by

1. Danilo Kiš, "Pesnik revolucije na predsedničkom brodu (Iz rukopisne zaostavštine)," *Književne novine*, November 1, 1989, pp. 1, 8.

foreigners. Besides, the industrial northwest (Slovenia and northern Croatia) was richer and bound to get through without scathe. Hence, contrary to the wishes of many high-minded unitarists (numerically insignificant, but politically influential among the Croat and Slovene intellectuals, less so among the Serbs), integral unitarism came to be regarded as an implement of Serbian hegemony and therefore increasingly discredited.[2]

Throughout the interwar period, the resistance of the non-Serbs and the intransigence of the Belgrade authorities precluded the search for an early solution of the Yugoslav national question. The Cvetković-Maček agreement of 1939, which established an autonomous Croatian banate and brought the Croat leaders into a semblance of power, could have augured the beginning of Yugoslavia's restructuring. The prospects were indeed conditional, since the nationalist opposition among the Serbs considered the "concessions" excessive, whereas the nationalist opposition (among the Croats and the other non-Serbs) viewed the "agreement" as trifling. The Second World War interrupted the new management of the national question with singular ferocity. The occupying powers (Germany, Italy, Hungary, Bulgaria) went after the Serbs, and encouraged the anti-Serb excesses among the other nationalities. Serbia itself was reduced to a special German zone of occupation, which was increasingly garrisoned by Bulgarians. The marginalization of Serbia meant the aggrandizement of Croatia, which, organized as an "independent" ally of the Axis, and ruled through the Ustašas (Insurgents), a minuscule Croat Fascist organization, was independent mainly in the scale and folly of both institutionalized and "irregular" anti-Serb violence. At the same time, the predominantly Serb guerrillas, or Chetniks, initiated anti-Croat and anti-Muslim violence, which was necessarily smaller in scale, being the handiwork not of a state, but of armed bands, themselves increasingly drawn into the Axis web.[3]

The Chetniks, however, were ostensibly the army of the Yugoslav government-in-exile. Their leader, General Draža Mihailović, officially was the minister of the army in the Allied-recognized, London-based cabinet of King Petar II. Hence the inability of the government-in-exile to project

2. On the interwar phase of Yugoslavia's nationality relations, see Ivo Banac, *The National Question in Yugoslavia: Origins, History, Politics* (Ithaca, N.Y., 1984).

3. For the best and handiest overview of the wartime developments in Yugoslavia, see Jozo Tomasevich, "Yugoslavia during the Second World War," in Wayne S. Vucinich, ed., *Contemporary Yugoslavia: Twenty Years of Socialist Experiment* (Berkeley, Calif., 1969), pp. 59–118, 363–77. The same author has also provided the best researched and most comprehensive monograph on the Chetniks. See Jozo Tomasevich, *War and Revolution in Yugoslavia, 1941–1945: The Chetniks* (Stanford, Calif., 1975).

a broader-based Yugoslav—rather than Serb—image, and the unwillingness of the non-Serbs to acknowledge this government as their own. The principal beneficiary of these troubles, which were seemingly intractable to diplomacy, were the Communists. Although the Communist Party of Yugoslavia (KPJ) had only 6,600 members in October 1940 and some 17,800 additional members in its youth organization, it could boast of a tightly reined leadership under Josip Broz Tito, mobility and militancy among its predominantly youthful and artless cadre, significant influence among the intellectuals in all areas of Yugoslavia, and, perhaps most important, an attractive program for the solution of the national question. The liberation of Yugoslavia, according to Tito, could only be accomplished as the liberation of all of its peoples as separate individualities. Hence the decided—though arguably uneven—emphasis on the "liberation of Croats, Slovenes, Serbs, Macedonians, Albanians, Muslims, etc." within a Soviet-styled federal state.[4] The Communist program, in short, was the negation of two ideological strains of interwar order. In stressing the equality of nations (not just some nondescript nationalities or ethnicities) the Communists were overturning Serbian hegemony. In stressing the individuality of nations they appeared to be toppling Yugoslavist unitarism. The military expression of this negation was the defeat of the Chetniks and the dethronement of the king. Though the Ustašas and other antiunionists, too, were defeated, their defeat was of a different order. They lost as Axis allies, not as an alternative to the Communist program for the solution of the national question.[5]

Without communism there would not have been a postwar Yugoslav state. Tito's domestic policy was determined by the Soviet federal model, which not only was more apparent than real but actually put a premium on the power of the center. As a result, the Yugoslav national question initially was transformed from the prewar conflict of opposing national ideologies into the conflict over the structure and composition of the Yugoslav federation, played out mainly within the constitutional-political frame. Initially, at least, Tito had need to stroke Serb national sensitivities. Himself a Croat, his support was thinnest in Serbia, where the Chetniks had their base, and strongest among the Croats, the Serbs of Croatia and Bosnia-Hercegovina, and in Montenegro. From 1944, Tito increasingly restrained the federalist expectations of the non-Serb segments

4. Josip Broz Tito, "Nacionalno pitanje u Jugoslaviji u svjetlosti narodnooslobodilačke borbe," *Sabrana djela* (Belgrade, 1982), 13:99.

5. The following sections are a condensation of parts of an earlier article. See Ivo Banac, "Political Change and National Diversity," *Daedalus* 119, no. 1 (1990): 141–59.

of the KPJ. He could not agree with those of his non-Serb comrades who insisted on preserving the proclaimed rights of nations and federal units (republics since 1945). Nor did he wish to lend immunity to formal axiomatic constructions that protected the republic-based Communist parties or prompted the growth of separate national institutions. Such approaches might carry weight with the non-Communists, but the running of Yugoslavia would in no way differ from the running of the KPJ.

Tito's conflict with the Croat and Macedonian national Communists (Andrija Hebrang, Metodi Andonov-Ćento) pointed to the slow drift, not just toward centralism, which is immanent in Communist dictatorships, but toward the revival of Yugoslavist unitarism and the policy of amalgamating the South Slavic nationalities into a single Yugoslav supranation. The unitarist revival accompanied the break with Stalin in 1948, and was thereby an aspect of the country's bureaucratic transformation, but on an anti-Stalin platform. Edvard Kardelj, the second man of the Yugoslav Politburo and the topmost Slovene Communist and party reformer, was the first notable personage to resist the new unitarism. In 1957 he warned that "bureaucratic centralism," connected with its "ideational-political manifestation of great state hegemonism," was still vibrant in Yugoslavia. Moreover, based on bureaucratic-centralistic tendencies, there appeared new attempts at the revival of "old chauvinistic 'integral Yugoslavism,' as a tendency of negating the existing South Slavic peoples and aimed at affirming some sort of a new 'Yugoslav nation.'" Kardelj denounced the "absurdities of such tendencies," which "necessarily undermine the genuine fraternal relations among the independent peoples of Yugoslavia" and warned that the "remnants of old Great Serbian nationalism" were seeking contact with unitarism under the cloak of Yugoslav unity.[6] After several reversals typical of Tito's pragmatic course, Tito himself joined Kardelj's reform faction in July 1962. The reasons for Tito's shift are complex but essentially had to do with the realization that his federal system was in danger of being devoured by creeping Serbian hegemonism after the passing of the Partisan generation.

The removal of Aleksandar Ranković in 1966 signaled Tito's victory over "domestic conservative-centralist forces" that were entrenched in Serbia. There followed a series of moves that restricted the prerogatives of Ranković's machine and legitimized greater national liberties for the Croats, the Bosnian Muslims, and the Albanian minority. In fact, Tito's

6. Edvard Kardelj (Sperans), *Razvoj slovenačkog nacionalnog pitanja*, trans. Zvonko Tkalec, 3d ed. (Belgrade, 1973), p. xxxvii.

unstudied way of handling the national question led him in the 1960s and the 1970s to espouse the same formal axiomatic constructions (rotating party and state presidency, exact proportionality in party and state organs by republic and province of origin, limited tenure of office, formal harmonization of interests among the federal units in legislation) that he eschewed in the 1940s. Decentralization was enshrined in the constitution of 1974, which shifted considerable power to the republics and autonomous provinces, encouraged the growth of regional bureaucracies, and placed great emphasis on the management of state affairs by consensus. Nevertheless, this constitution retained the majority of power for the federal center and the ruling party, and was, hence, by no means the code for a confederacy. In fact, the constitution of 1974 was Tito's answer to the intraparty opposition of national and modernizing provenance. Tito countered the Croat Communist leaders Savka Dabčević-Kučar, Miko Tripalo, and many others, who were purged in December 1971 after a biennium of Croat national communism, with an ostensibly antiunitarist device predicated on the "national statehood" of the republics. He countered Serbian Communist leaders Marko Nikezić and Latinka Perović, who were purged in October 1972, with an ostensibly unitary device predicated on the "socialist self-managerial" status of the republics and party monopoly.[7]

Tito's death in May 1980 did not unlock the door of Yugoslav chaos. Yet retrospectively it seems that Tito died in the last ditch of Communist federalism. The constitution of 1974 was meant to reaffirm national equality but also to impose party control over the growing national movements. Its provisions lifted Serbia's autonomous provinces of Vojvodina and Kosovo to a level almost identical to that of the republics, but it also strengthened party controls. Tito's legacy was really mortification by grievance. To the Serbs, the country was "parcelized" (that is, they themselves were parceled out among the strengthened republics and autonomous provinces) and without a legitimate center. To the non-Serbs, the country was still built on the vestiges of prewar unitarism and centralism, and governed by more-or-less endurable national "partiocracies," which always fell short of pursuing genuine national interests. In this respect, the

---

7. On the political developments from the fall of Ranković to the constitution of 1974, see Dušan Bilandžić, *Historija Socijalističke Federativne Republike Jugoslavije: Glavni procesi, 1918–1985* (Zagreb, 1985), pp. 320–457. For a recent reappraisal of the Croat national movement of 1971 by its surviving principals, see Milovan Baletić, ed., *Ljudi iz 1971: Prekinuta šutnja* (Zagreb, 1990). On the purge of the Serbian leadership, see Slavoljub Djukić, *Slom srpskih liberala: Tehnologija političkih obračuna Josipa Broza* (Belgrade, 1990).

situation of the Croats was particularly untenable, as the legitimacy of Croatia's post-1971 party leadership rested solidly on relentless extirpation of Croat nationalism, which was always defined as quasi-fascistic. The great "Croat silence," marked by fear and accompanied by repression and censorship, made Croatia an extra in the storm that was building in the vacuum created by Tito's death. The smug slogan of "after Tito, also Tito" was ruptured by the Kosovo street protests of 1981 and provided the opening for Serbia's campaign against the system Tito had built.

The cancer that has eaten at the entrails of Yugoslavia since Tito's death can be recognized—without a great margin of error—as having Kosovo for its locus. In 1981 the Socialist Autonomous Province of Kosovo was governed by the League of Communists of Yugoslavia (SKJ), as the ruling Communists had called themselves since 1952, in the person of several old-line Albanian leaders, as well as a few of their juniors, both Albanian and Serb. Kosovo had 1,584,441 inhabitants, an increase of 117.7 percent since 1948. Of that number 1,226,736 (77.4 percent) were Albanians, a vast increase of 146.2 percent since 1948. Serbs and Montenegrins counted 236,526 (14.9 percent), an increase of 18.3 percent since 1948. In fact, the percentage of Serbs and Montenegrins in the population of Kosovo had declined from 27.5 percent in 1948. The Slavic element, dominant and growing in Serbia itself, was almost halved in this autonomous province of Serbia, the province in which the historical memory of the Serbs invested the greatest emotional energy. To the Serbs, Kosovo is not just a piece of land, it is *the* sacred land, where they lost their terrestial empire, having been defeated by the Ottoman Turks on the Field of Kosovo in 1389 after their ruler, Prince Lazar, abjured earthly victory in favor of celestial empire. In the words of Matija Bećković, the bard of contemporary Serbian nationalism, "The battle of Kosovo was never finished. It is as if the Serbian people have waged only one battle— by widening the Kosovo charnel-house, by adding wailing upon wailing, by counting new martyrs to the martyrs of Kosovo. . . . Kosovo is the costliest Serbian word. It was paid by the blood of the whole people. . . . Kosovo is the equator of the Serbian planet. The ceiling of the lower and the foundation of the upper world. Here the conscience of the Serb people was split into the period before and after Kosovo. Kosovo is the Serbianized story of the Flood—the Serbian New Testament."[8]

Bećković's words could not have been written in 1981, and not just

8. Matija Bećković, "Kosovo je najskuplja srpska reč," *Glas Crkve* 17/V, no. 3 (1989): 19.

because the vigilant party in Serbia would have censored them as "nationalistic." More important, it would have taken a great leap of imagination in 1981 to view the student demonstrations in which the slogan "Kosovo—Republic" was raised (incidentally, not for the first time) as a declaration of intention to martyr Serbs. The Albanian youth simply wanted the privilege of first-class citizenship ("We are Albanians, not Yugoslavs!"), the release of political prisoners ("We want our imprisoned comrades!"), and social justice in impoverished Kosovo ("Some are in armchairs, some are without bread!"). At first the party leaders, including the Kosovo Albanians, made obvious and stodgy attacks against the "counterrevolutionary" demands of the demonstrators.[9] In April 1981 Mahmut Bakalli, the secretary of the Kosovo party organization who would soon be purged, noted that the demonstrations had "exclusively hostile motives."[10] During the same period Azem Vllasi, the most docile of Albanian leaders, stressed the restraint of the police and minimal losses of human life.[11] By May 1981 Serbian leaders started using the Kosovo issue as a pretext for attacks against the "tendencies that favor the 'statehood' [of federal units] and underestimate the class character of the national question."[12] But as the campaign got into gear the Albanians started being charged with "irredentist" ambitions, "genocidal" plans, "overproduction" of intellectuals and national euphoria, misappropriation of "alien" (Albanian) colors, and the overuse of their native non-Slavic language. Under circumstances of extreme repression and an anti-Albanian campaign, it became the case of a self-fulfilling prophecy.

Some 3,344 Albanians were jailed between 1981 and 1985 for "nationalistic" offenses. The Belgrade press increasingly excoriated the federal agencies (the central government and its media managers) for opportunism, news blackouts, and the encouragement of the provinces' "branching off" from Serbia. The first attacks against the constitution of 1974 were launched in 1981, notably in the theses of the Central Committee of the League of Communists of Serbia (SKS), which included claims that Serbia was the only republic not constituted as a state due to the disruptive role of the autonomous provinces.[13] The first claims that the Kosovar Communists failed to resist the emigration of Serbs and Mon-

9. Fadil Hoxha, "To je delo kontrarevolucije," *Politika*, April 4, 1981, pp. 1–2.
10. "Svim snagama onemogućiti neprijateljsko djelovanje," *Vjesnik*, April 8, 1981, p. 4.
11. Azem Vllasi, "Neprijatelj nije niti će uspjeti u svojim namjerama," *Vjesnik*, April 14, 1981, p. 5.
12. Tihomir Vlaškalić, "Pokušaj organizovanja otvorene pobune," *Politika*, May 7, 1981, p. 5.
13. Dušan Bilandžić, *Jugoslavija poslije Tita (1980–1985)* (Zagreb, 1986), pp. 83–94.

tenegrins from Kosovo were raised in 1982.[14] And then in 1985 came the
bizarre case of Djordje Martinović, who was (or was not) impaled (or
abused himself) with a broken bottle (or a bottle that broke in his anus)
by two Albanians (or by Albanians of his own invention). At stake was
the veracity of Kosovar authorities (who argued that Martinović was in
effect a pervert) and the Serbian authorities and public opinion (who were
convinced that Martinović was a victim of violence and a crude cover-
up).[15] At stake, too, was the autonomy of Kosovo, since it appeared that
even the purged ranks of Albanian Communists were unreliable, while the
Serbian investigatory agencies were constitutionally prevented from acting in the province.[16]

The issue of Kosovo afforded the pretext for the revision of Tito's constitution, which was caricatured as following in essence the slogan "Weak
Serbia = Strong Yugoslavia." The challenge was picked up by the Serbian
elite and was expressed most completely in the "Memorandum of the
Serbian Academy of Sciences" (1986). This document, which was first
repudiated and later openly embraced by its authors, alleged that Serbia
had been discriminated against within Yugoslavia, both politically and
economically. The concerted activity of a Slovene- and Croat-led "anti-
Serb coalition," the document claimed, continued the traditional "Ser-
bophobia" of the international Communist movement. Under the circumstances Serbia, and the Serbs as a nation, had a right to determine their
own national interest.[17] This position increasingly became the program of
Serbia's Communists after May 1986, when Slobodan Milošević, the
diminutive Sloba of populist parlance, a relatively unknown apparatchik,
became the head of the SKS.

It has been said that Milošević's career can be divided into the period
before and after his speech to some fifteen thousand Serbs and Montenegrins on the Field of Kosovo, in the night of April 24 and the early
morning of April 25, 1987, after their protest meeting was attacked by
Kosovo's then predominantly Albanian police. Milošević took the side of
the demonstrators and charted a clear policy that favored Kosovo's Serbs
and Montenegrins. He told them, "The first thing that I wish to tell you,
comrades, is that you must remain here. This is your land, your houses
are here, your fields and gardens, your memories. . . . It was never charac-

14. Z. Šuvaković, "O iseljavanju—konkretno," *Politika*, March 11, 1982, p. 4.
15. For contrasts in the initial reports of this case, see "Smišljen neprijateljski akt," *Politika*, May 6, 1985, p. 8, and "Sam sebe povredio," *Politika*, May 8, 1985, p. 10.
16. Dušan Dražić, "Tko je nadležan," *Borba*, June 27, 1985, p. 2.
17. "Memorandum SANU," *Duga*, June 1989, pp. 34–47.

teristic of the spirit of the Serb and Montenegrin people to knuckle under to difficulties, to demobilize itself when it must fight, to become demoralized when the going is tough. You must remain here on account of your ancestors and descendants. Otherwise, we would be shaming the ancestors and disillusioning the descendants."[18]

Milošević, in effect, overturned the whole policy of the party, whose approach was to make a show of curbing all nationalisms, though some more so than others. By September 1987 he succeeded in purging the SKS of established Titoists (Dragiša Pavlović, Ivan Stambolić) who were opposed to the "lightly promised haste" with which he offered to solve all Serbian frustrations over Kosovo. Once in power, his authority in Serbia was largely uncontested and his power limited only by political expediency. Milošević's takeover came on the wings of a growing cult of personality ("Serbia is only asking, when will Sloba replace Tito"; "Sloba, Serbian, Serbia is with you"; "Slobodan, say when, we shall fly like bullets"), media manipulation, and a campaign to brutalize the Albanians. In Kosovo, Milošević pursued a policy of permanent military occupation, police repression, and party purge. His men succeeded in wresting the control of the Kosovo party organization from Titoist Albanians, who were purged in droves (Azem Vllasi, Kaqusha Jashari, Fadil Hoxha, Veli Deva, Ymer Pula) and replaced by Serbs and other non-Albanians. In February 1989, after the sit-down strikes of Albanian miners at Trepča, which triggered a general strike in Kosovo, Milošević announced the arrest of Azem Vllasi at a mass rally in Belgrade.[19] Vllasi, subsequently arrested, tried, and quietly released, has noted that his efforts at defusing the Kosovo time bomb did not agree with Milošević, who "wanted to build his career precisely on Kosovo by stirring up constant tensions and anti-Albanian sentiments."[20]

Milošević did not just ally the SKS with an unrealistic Serbian nationalist project of keeping Albanians permanently subjugated in Kosovo. His innovation was in turning the Serbian party organization into *the* party of Serbian nationalism. He reawakened the old Serbian nationalist myths (dynasty, army, Chetniks) and dreams of establishing a Great Serbia that would include most of present Yugoslavia, dreams that had been kept repressed under Tito. He turned Communist policy and ideology into instruments of a pan-Serb nationalist movement, sometimes with unexpected results, as in the demagogic claim that the Vatican and the

18. Slobodan Milošević, *Godine raspleta* (Belgrade, 1989), pp. 143–44.
19. Milenko Vučetić, *Vllasi* (Zagreb, 1989), pp. 224–25.
20. Azem Vllasi, *Majstori mraka: Zatvorski zapisi* (Zagreb, 1990), p. 9.

Comintern had conspired against Serbia. He permitted the denigration of Tito not because of Tito's dictatorial record but because Tito was a Croat and a federalist. He put the party-state of Serbia, with its media, cultural and educational institutions, armed power and federal influence, and even the usually disloyal intelligentsia, in the service of Serbian national homogenization and supremacy. The Serbian Orthodox church and the bulk of the Serbian anti-Communist emigration, sensing Milošević's devotion to the objective of Great Serbia, hailed him as their leader.

The foot soldiers of Milošević's "anti-bureaucratic revolution" were bands of toughs assembled by various Serbian nationalist organizations, including the revived Chetniks, and ultimately by Milošević's police. With the aid of these *squadristi,* who accomplished destabilization through extralegal violence, Milošević brought down the autonomist leadership in Vojvodina in October 1988 and the Titoist leadership of Montenegro in January 1989. Unobstructed by the Yugoslav People's Army (JNA) and other pillars of Titoist order, he virtually abolished the autonomy of Kosovo and Vojvodina in March 1989, when he octroyed the Serbian (and Yugoslav) constitution by extending the direct authority of the republic to the autonomous provinces. He took the final step in the total destruction of Kosovo's autonomy in July 1990 when he dismissed Kosovo's provincial parliament, banned most of the Albanian-language press, and shut down the Albanian-language program of TV Priština. (These measures, in turn, provoked the clandestine gathering of Albanian deputies at Kačanik, in September 1990, where they proclaimed the constitution of the phantom Republic of Kosovo.)

Milošević's destabilization of Yugoslavia was weakly resisted by the Communists of Slovenia and Croatia, and practically not at all by the Communists of Bosnia-Hercegovina and Macedonia. In a similar vein, the federal government of the prime ministers Branko Mikulić and Ante Marković (the former from Bosnia-Hercegovina, the latter from Croatia, both Croats by nationality) did virtually nothing to defend Yugoslavia's Titoist foundations from Milošević's assault. It was as if Milošević's box, too, released Delusive Hope. The Serbian Communists demanded a blank check for any and all measures taken against the autonomy of Kosovo, including approval of their campaign to demonize Albanians. Dark hints were made about the covert complicity between the "northwest" (Slovenia and Croatia) and Albanian "irredentists." For all the timidity of the Communists from the "northwest," the cynicism of Milošević's policy in Kosovo and the fear it engendered elsewhere provoked growing resistance, both inside and outside the party organizations. The Slovene democratic opposition led the way with the criticism of Milošević's policy (Taras Kermauner, Dimitrij Rupel), the confrontation with the JNA and its total-itarian practices (muckraking policy of the weekly *Mladina*, the military's prosecution of Janez Janša), and the construction of its own political alternative program (demands for the establishment of a depoliticized "civil society," the Slovene national program of *Nova revija*). The Slovene Communists, led by extremely liberal Milan Kučan, did not stand in the way of opposition. The same was true in Croatia, where the growing strength of the liberal wing of the party pushed back the dogmatist faction of Stipe Šuvar, the principal theorist of the SKJ Left in the 1980s and arguably the most detested politician of postwar Croatia, and opened the floodgates to the long-repressed national opposition. By the spring and summer of 1989, both Slovenia and Croatia could boast of a plethora of political parties. By the end of the year these parties were legalized by the Communists, who, moreover, promised free elections in early 1990.

Political pluralism was Milošević's unintended contribution to Yugoslav politics. The result was that Yugoslavia's Communist Party was split between the Serbian party organization headed by Milošević and the vacillating and discredited party organizations of the other republics. Milošević united Serbia (and the Serbs), but at the same time destroyed Tito's party. This probably would have happened in any case, as a result of the collapse of communism throughout Eastern Europe in the fall of 1989. It happened, however, under the imprint of Milošević's threat at the Fourteenth Extraordinary Congress of the SKJ in January 1990. Milošević's voting machine was readied for a confrontation with liberal Slovene Communists, whose leadership Milošević actually attempted to overthrow by a putsch disguised as a "meeting of truth" about Kosovo. When the Slovenes sensibly banned the meeting, scheduled for 1 De-cember 1989, the anniversary of Yugoslavia's unification in 1918, pre-venting the arrival of Serb demonstrators to Slovenia's capital of Ljub-ljana, Milošević declared the break in relations with Slovenia and the boycott of all Slovene goods. In the brawl that ensued on the floor of the SKJ congress, the Slovenes walked out and the Croats, refusing to proceed in the rump session as Milošević insisted, pulled down the curtain on what was the last party congress. Both left with a sigh of relief. In the words of a Croat Communist intellectual, "Personally, I see no way of remaining in the same party with Milošević. And I no longer have to."[21]

Multiparty elections in Slovenia and Croatia (respectively in April and

---

21. Dag Strpić, "Zbogom, Miloševiću," *Danas,* January 30, 1990, p. 13.

May 1990) were won not by reform Communists, without whom the elections could not have taken place, but by Slovene and Croat national parties committed to a confederal solution of the Yugoslav state crisis. Slovenia's DEMOS, an acronym for the Democratic Opposition of Slovenia, a coalition of Christian Democrats, Slovene Democrats, Social Democrats, and the Peasant Alliance, dominated the new Slovene government, although the electorate chose Milan Kučan, the former Communist leader as the president of Slovenia. In Croatia, the winner-take-all electoral law favored the Croat National Union (HDZ), a nationalist party cum movement seeking to reconcile distinct strains of Croat national ideologies, including the contributions of national Communists. Its leader, Franjo Tudjman, a former general of the JNA and a prominent dissident, was elected the president of Croatia by the HDZ-dominated parliament (Sabor). In both republics initial steps were taken toward the establishment of democratic institutions and market economy. Moreover, both Slovenia and Croatia embraced the West in its totality, something that Milošević necessarily eschews. Unfortunately, the amateurishness of the new administrations, their preoccupation with symbols and trivial matters, as well as their populist politics, all notable especially in Croatia, have hampered a more determined transition to democracy. Nevertheless, greater results surely would have been accomplished had not both republics been subjected to increased pressures by Milošević and the JNA. Croatia, especially, has been the target of a vicious campaign, designed to portray its leaders as latter-day Ustašas.

Franjo Tudjman is decidedly not an Ustaša. A Partisan commissar who won his general's epaulets under Ivan Gošnjak, Tito's longtime defense chief, he has been trying to effect a historic Croat reconciliation, but on the traditions of the Left. The programmatic attributes of his HDZ included the recognition that the "modern Croat national consciousness was built upon—and must continue to be based upon—the freedom-loving revivalist traditions of [Ante] Starčević's Croat historical state right, [Stjepan] Radić's all-human democratic republicanism, as well as on the visions, but also the experiences, of the Croat Left—Marxist and Communist—from the common struggle with the Serb and other peoples for a socialist self-managed society, a free homeland of Croatia, and an equal community of peoples founded [on wartime Partisan political consultations]."[22] This leftist and—under conditions of Communist rule—

22. "Prednacrt programske osnove Hrvatske demokratske zajednice," *Hrvatska demokratska zajednica. Bilten za članstvo,* no. 1 (June 1989): 5.

legalist aspect of the HDZ sought to bridge the radical and Jacobin late-nineteenth-century Croat nationalism of Ante Starčević, the pacifist peasantism of Stjepan Radić—Croatia's paramount leader and national martyr of the interwar period, and the traditions of the Partisan Forest, redefined as a state-building program.[23] But the success of the HDZ would not have been as notable had Tudjman's party been perceived as a party of the national Left. This "most Croat of parties" won precisely because it championed unambiguous Croat aspirations ("uncontested, nontransferable, nonsuperannuated, and indivisible sovereignty of the Croat people").[24] Like the DEMOS, Tudjman's HDZ won because it promised to cut no deals with Milošević and because it hinted at virtual—and quite possibly full—independence as a way out of Milošević's cauldron.

The contention between the "northwest" and Milošević necessarily was intensified after Croatia and Slovenia agreed to cosponsor a draft confederal constitution, which proposed to establish a loose confederation among Yugoslavia's six republics in an arrangement portrayed as similar to that of the European Community. Tudjman and the Slovenes came out in favor of a minimalist confederal center, with jurisdiction over commerce, customs, mails, railroads, and agricultural policy. Each republic would have its own armed forces and would "designate" contingents to serve under a joint confederal command. Nevertheless, the sentiment for complete independence, too, has been on the rise in Slovenia and Croatia, as is clear from Slovenia's plebiscite of December 1990 in which 89 percent of the electorate (turnout was 94 percent) voted for a sovereign and independent Slovenia. In sharp contrast, Milošević, fully sovereign in his own initiatives, is totally opposed to any confederation, much less Slovenian or Croatian independence. Speaking to the Serbian parliament on 25 June 1990, he said that "Serbia must clearly and in good time say that it connects its current administrative borders only with federally organized Yugoslavia. Should there be any changes in the organization of Yugoslavia, should it be confederalized, all constitutional questions will be open. Confederation is not a state but an alliance of states; therefore, there can be no confederation, even if all political subjects of Yugoslavia wanted it, within the framework of existing, administratively determined borders among the republics. In such a case the question of Serbia's

23. On Tudjman's intellectual evolution as seen through his historical writings, see Ivo Banac, "Svršimo s odiljanjem od Hrvatske na ljevici," *Globus*, January 10, 1991, p. 4. The text contains a misleading title, which was imposed by the editors, and numerous typographical errors.

24. Hrvatska demokratska zajednica, "Izborni proglas stanovništvu Hrvatske i cijelomu hrvatskom narodu," March 21, 1990, p. 1.

borders is an open political question."[25] As far as Milošević is concerned, for Serbia the only acceptable alternative to a federal Yugoslavia is a much enlarged, independent Serbia that would embrace the areas where the substantial Serb minorities live in Croatia and Bosnia-Hercegovina. A survey published in August 1990 by the Belgrade oppositional journal *Samouprava* shows that the Serbian political opposition shares Milošević's view, whereby the western borders of Serbia ought to be drawn slightly east of Zagreb and Rijeka, making much of present-day Croatia a part of emerging Great Serbia.[26] These ambitions—not the occasional clumsy snubbing of Serbs by the HDZ leaders, much less the alleged revival of wartime anti-Serb outrages committed by the Ustašas— are behind the current Serb demands for political autonomy in Croatia.

Just as Serbia's political establishment at the beginning of the century initiated a series of military actions aimed at grabbing the remnants of Ottoman holdings in the Balkans, Milošević's party (renamed the Socialist Party of Serbia in July 1990) and its allies have charted an adventure of unforeseeable consequences aimed at grabbing as much territory as possible from the disintegrating Yugoslav state. The stirring up of the Serbs in Croatia, especially at Knin, a commune in Croatia's Adriatic hinterland, where 79 percent of 44,000 inhabitants are Serbs, was symptomatic. Since August 1990 the Serbs of Knin have been holding Croatia hostage in two ways. First, they have humiliated the Tudjman administration, paralyzed rail communication, blocked highway traffic with timber beams, roughed up journalists and travelers, scared off foreign tourists vacationing along Croatia's Adriatic coast, raided the police stations for arms and ammunition, killed several Croatian policemen (some of Serb nationality), carried out a bogus referendum on the autonomy of Croatia's Serbs, established their self-appointed Serb National Council, and proclaimed the Autonomous District of Krajina (Frontier), unofficially Western Serbia. Second, they sent a signal that the Yugoslav state crisis will be solved not by elections and negotiations but by violence and armed strife.

The "timber revolution" by the Serbs of Knin (whose militants are eager to inflame Lika, Kordun, Banija, and eastern Slavonia) is significant not only because it is backed by Milošević. The object of the Serb insurgents in Croatia is to seize all territories that can be claimed for the emerging Great Serbian state. They aim to hold these territories at all

25. Slobodan Milošević, "Neka gradjani Srbije odluče o Ustavu," *Politika*, June 26, 1990, p. 1.
26. "O granicama Jugoslavije u slučaju otcepljenja neke od njenih republika," *Samouprava*, August 1990, pp. 3–6.

costs, stir up trouble, provoke the Croatian authorities to use force, and prompt federal military intervention. In essence it is the struggle for the control of the Yugoslav army. The JNA is still a Titoist institution; in fact, it is virtually the last bastion of Tito's party, where the basic organizations of the defunct SKJ operated until the end of 1990. Clearly an ideological army cannot survive as the fist of a phantom party. Nor can it survive as a participant in the contention among the republics. To survive, if that is at all possible, it must depoliticize itself, assume a purely defensive posture, and stay above the political fray. That will prove nearly impossible. The JNA, dominated by a predominantly Serb officer cadre, has already become the tool of Milošević's policy in Kosovo. Since the fall of 1990 it has obstructed the Croatian authorities in various ways, most notably by challenging their right to arm their police and territorial defense units (national guard). In October 1990, defense secretary General Veljko Kadijević succeeded in having the federal presidency nullify the amendments to Slovenia's constitution, whereby the republic's parliament would command Slovenia's territorial defense units in peacetime. In early December he issued grave threats against those who would establish "purely national armies," which he promised to disarm. His harsh words were notable because of their ideological tilt. Kadijević indirectly accused the West of destabilizing the cold-war order: "Forces which dominate today are imposing entirely new rules of behavior. In an attempt to establish their supremacy as comprehensive and definitive, they avail themselves of various types of force. That increases the possibility of local and regional conflicts, including war." He declared himself, too, an unreconstructed Communist: "Historically speaking, the future belongs to the idea of socialism. The experiences of the developed countries also confirm that [socialism] belongs among the highest civilizational accomplishments of the contemporary epoch."[27]

The position of the JNA commanders is evident from a remarkable document titled "Information on the Current International and Domestic Situation and the Forthcoming Tasks of the JNA," which was prepared by the political administration of the Ministry of Defense and released in January 1991. Official Yugoslav agencies have not produced a more anti-Western document since Tito's honeymoon with Khrushchev in the early 1960s. Briefly, the Yugoslav army planners were cheered by the growing strength of Soviet conservatives at the end of 1990, whereby the "disintegration of that great country [the USSR] has been slowed." As a result,

27. "Jugoslavija neće biti Libanon," *Danas*, December 4, 1990, pp. 10–12.

the prospects of "socialism," whose systemic reversals were apparently the handiwork of the West alone, not of internal weaknesses, have increased. But not everywhere. "Socialism" will survive in the countries of "autochthonous revolution," notably Yugoslavia:

> As far as our country is concerned, in the West they have understood that the idea of Yugoslavism and the commitment to socialism have far deeper roots than they have estimated, and that the destruction of socialism in Yugoslavia is not the same as in some other countries. That is why it can be expected that they will change their methods somewhat and initiate a still stronger attack. It would be highly important for them to succeed in Yugoslavia. They would thereby begin to break a country where an autochthonous revolution had won. Forthcoming activities will manifest themselves on two fronts and with two basic aims. First, they will seek to overthrow the Communists who have maintained themselves in power, either in individual republics or on the level of the [Yugoslav] federation. With that aim in mind, they will attempt to place obstacles in the path of economic reform, or will seek to incite social disturbances in reaction to the ways in which the reform is being conducted, and then, on the model of Bulgaria and Romania, they will constantly seek to repeat the elections, until their protégés gain power. Second, they will continue to split Yugoslavia, while simultaneously blaming the Communists for this situation.

The document directed harsh attacks at the CIA and the State Department for their attempts "to destroy socialism in Yugoslavia, even at the price of the country's destruction," while these agencies at the same time tried to prevent the army from "stemming this process": "The pleas of certain Western circles on behalf of democracy is transparent demagoguery, since for them democracy is only that which corresponds to their aims and interests. Under the label of democracy, in our conditions, they understand, first of all, everything that is anti-socialist."[28]

The army's reaffirmed Communist allegiance is manifested in another important way. The organization of the SKJ in the JNA was ostensibly dissolved at the end of 1990, but, in fact, it collectively joined the "purified" version of Tito's party, the League of Communists–Movement for Yugoslavia (SKPJ), which was established in November as the unofficial "party of generals." Present at its constituent session were Kadijević; his

---

28. Politička uprava SSNO, "'Rušenje komunizma nije uspelo': Informacija o aktuelnoj situaciji u svetu i našoj zemlji i neposrednim zadacima JNA," *Vjesnik*, January 31, 1991, p. 5.

deputy, Admiral Stane Brovet; the head of the general staff, Blagoje Adžić; the president of the SKJ committee in the JNA, General Božidar Grubišić; former defense secretaries Nikola Ljubičić and Branko Mamula; the minister of the interior, General Petar Gračanin; and numerous other generals. Among the members of the new party's initiation committee were Momir Bulatović, the head of the ruling SKJ in Montenegro, various ancien régime dogmatists, and Mirjana Marković, the wife of Slobodan Milošević. The party is of two minds on social questions. One of its founders protested that "our aim is not socialism, but communism. That must be corrected in our program, because socialism is a phase leading toward communism, that is, a phase in which the multiparty organization is still existing." But the party's president, a hard-liner from Macedonia, noted, "We do not declare ourselves the vanguard of the working class, nor as a workers' party. We are a party of all citizens of Yugoslavia who are well disposed to our program." In fact, the glue that holds the party together is not the vague systemic aspect of Titoism. Rather, this is the party of the 1950s—of Tito's unitarist phase, which remains attractive to those representatives of the old order who would postpone a jump into Milošević's national crucible. As a result, the SKPJ will be centrally directed. "Our way of organizing ourselves will avoid the possibility of confederalizing the SKPJ, which was one of the main reasons for the breakup of the SKJ."[29]

What are the links between Milošević and the JNA? They share common enemies, but they are not the same. Milošević is primarily a Serbian supremacist, who wishes to rule over those areas of Yugoslavia in which Serbs are or should be found. In his roster of opponents Croatia holds a high place, but not necessarily Slovenia, where there are no Serb enclaves. The Serbian leader would welcome the JNA's support in toppling Tudjman, or for that matter any strong opponent of Serbian tutelage, but he is not necessarily nostalgic for the army's dream of the "socialist" restoration. As for the army commanders, though certainly split in the degree of their admiration for Milošević, they as a whole probably admire him a lot less than they would care to admit. Key figures among the top army brass in the last several decades have been Serbs from Croatia (Miloš Šumonja, Djoko Jovanić, Branko Mamula, Veljko Kadijević), who are hostile enough toward Croat nationalism, but prefer that Serbian nationalism be kept in check, as well. Titoism of the unitarist phase was their preferred

29. "Komunisti u vremeplovu," *Vreme*, November 26, 1990, pp. 18–19; Aleksandar Ćirić, "Uskrsli komunisti," *Vreme*, December 31, 1990, pp. 14–15; Petar Ignja, "Bunde nismo predvideli," *NIN*, January 4, 1991, p. 20.

solution because it tabooed discussion of individual national interests and thereby obscured the real national inequalities of the system. They are painfully aware that democracy is inimical to the frozen "stability" of Titoist socialism. They therefore recognize Milošević as an ally against Tudjman, and perhaps especially against the Slovenes. But they probably harbor a notion of not needing him once the Yugoslav West is pacified. Their goal is the "socialist" restoration.

The plans for the restoration are encountering problems. Multiparty politics have spilled over the central and eastern portions of Yugoslavia, with varying results. The elections in Bosnia-Hercegovina and Macedonia, in November 1990, demonstrated the strength of the national parties in these former hubs of Communist dogmatism. The new administration of Bosnia-Hercegovina was a coalition of principal Muslim, Serb, and Croat parties, pointing to the possibilities of at least uncertain accord. Although the elections in Serbia and Montenegro, in December 1990, proved quite disappointing to the non-Communists (and thereby provided a democratic cover to Milošević and his Montenegrin allies), they nevertheless showed the weaknesses in Milošević's armor. Apart from Kosovo, where the Albanians boycotted the elections in protest against the authorities' refusal to register their parties, the elections in Serbia pointed to Milošević's relative weakness in nationally mixed areas (Vojvodina, the Sandžak), as well as his unpopularity in Belgrade and other urban centers. For all that, Milošević's reckless moves—such as the December 1990 secret ordinance requiring Serbia's national bank to issue $1.8 billion worth of new money without any backing by the government or the federal national bank—mean that the confrontation among the republics is likely to escalate, particularly along the cleavage between Serbia and Croatia. The possibility of a restored quasi-unitarist—but essentially Great Serbian—dictatorship or civil war is great. The most sensible alternative is peaceful, internationally supervised, negotiated dissolution, leading to at most a loose confederal arrangement.

Unlike some of its Central European neighbors Yugoslavia has not yet entered a clear post-Communist phase. This is because postwar Yugoslavia itself is the product of Communist rule. In Yugoslavia, post-communism also means post-Yugoslavism. Andrei Amalrik's well-known essay *Will the Soviet Union Survive until 1984?* written in 1969, contains the following apt thought, "Just as the adoption of Christianity postponed the fall of the Roman Empire but did not prevent its inevitable end, so Marxist doctrine has delayed the break-up of the Russian Empire—the third Rome—but it does not possess the power to prevent it."[30] Amalrik was wrong about the agency of the breakup (there has been no war with China), but he did not underestimate the fragility of the Soviet state—the fragility of a state brittle with national contention. Analogous rules obtain in Yugoslavia. Some will protest that the overemphasis on national conflicts obscures other factors, not least of all the power of various social forces and economic changes. Perhaps. Yet, in Yugoslavia today, one can see only the apocalyptic beasts of hate and anger. Luckier observers, living in post-Yugoslav times, will be able to study the fruits of strength and movement.

30. Andrei Amalrik, *Will the Soviet Union Survive until 1984?* (New York, 1970), p. 65.

Albania: The Last Domino

Elez Biberaj

On the eve of the violent overthrow and the execution of Romanian dictator Nicolae Ceauşescu in December 1989, the president of Albania and first secretary of the ruling Party of Labor (APL), Ramiz Alia, assured the world that his country was immune to the dramatic developments that were reshaping the political landscape of Eastern Europe. Addressing a meeting of the Communist-controlled Trade Unions Council on December 11, 1989, Alia confidently declared: "There are people abroad who ask: Will processes like those taking place in Eastern Europe also occur in Albania? We answer firmly and categorically: No, they will not occur in Albania." The Albanian leader said that after the break with the Soviet bloc in 1961 and alliance with Mao Zedong's China, Albania had embarked on a totally different political and economic road from its former allies. He added that his country was not faced with the same problems as other East European states. "The crisis that is sweeping the countries in the East is the crisis of a definite community, the crisis of what used to be called the socialist community, but not the crisis of socialism as a theory and practice. Consequently, the events taking place there have nothing to do with us."[1]

One year later to the day, on December 11, 1990, Alia accepted demands by Tirana University student demonstrators and permitted the

1. Tirana Domestic Service, December 12, 1989, trans. in Foreign Broadcasting Information Service, Washington, D.C., *Daily Report: East Europe* (hereafter FBIS-EEU), 89-239, December 14, 1989, pp. 1–4.

creation of independent political parties. On March 31, 1991, less than four months after the legalization of the opposition, Albania, long considered the odd man out in the international Communist system and the last bastion of Stalinism in Europe, held its first multiparty elections since the early 1920s. With this momentous event, Albania, for decades self-styled as the only socialist state in the world, joined other East European countries in moving from a one-party to a multiparty system. This remarkable development was influenced by several interrelated factors, the most important of them being the devastating failure of APL's policies, the impact of the East European revolution, and the emergence of non-Communist political parties in the Albanian-inhabited province of Kosovo (Kosova) in neighboring Yugoslavia.

Albania and Eastern Europe: Different yet Similar

The Albanians followed with great concern economic and political changes in the Soviet Union and Eastern Europe in the wake of Mikhail Gorbachev's rise to power, which coincided with Alia's own accession to power following Enver Hoxha's death in April 1985. Gorbachev and Alia inherited remarkably similar problems: a political system insensitive to the population's needs and demands and a stagnating economy, most dramatically reflected by pervasive food shortages. The Albanian leader, however, was less daring than his Soviet counterpart in efforts to reinvigorate his society. Alia stressed continuity with Hoxha's policy, and before the East European revolution he carried out only cosmetic reforms, which aimed at improving the functioning of the Communist system rather than changing it. Although many people apparently hoped he would become "Albania's Gorbachev," during the first five years of his rule Alia did not act as a decisive and determined leader. Although under his leadership Albania became a more permissive society and there was a breakdown of many ideological barriers inherited from Hoxha, his vacillation, compromise, and procrastination only deepened the country's political and economic crisis. The regime's failure to implement reforms had brought the country's command-style economy practically to a standstill. The Albanians saw their standard of living, already the lowest in Europe, plummet further. Profound economic hardships led to the disaffection of large sectors of the population.[2]

2. For background see Elez Biberaj, *Albania: A Socialist Maverick* (Boulder, 1990), and J. F. Brown, *Surge to Freedom: The End of Communist Rule in Eastern Europe* (Durham, N.C., 1991), Chap. 9, passim.

Exercising a tight grip over the society, at a time when Communist parties in other East European countries were relaxing their control, the APL attempted desperately to discourage the population from coveting the democratic reforms under way in the Soviet bloc. It linked Eastern Europe's internal problems with the implementation of what it termed "revisionist" policies and betrayal of socialism. The official media insisted that the Communists in Albania enjoyed legitimacy, since they had come to power on their own, in contrast to Communists in the Warsaw Pact countries who were installed in power by the Red Army. Alia rejected not only the notion of giving up the APL's constitutionally guaranteed monopoly of power but also failed to change the most damaging aspects of Hoxha's policy, which were leading the country into deep political and economic turmoil. He did not reject the self-reliance policy, honoring constitutional prohibitions on acceptance of foreign aid and investments, with disastrous effect on economic performance. The economy continued to be plagued by overcentralization, persistent interference from the center, perverse incentives, tremendous waste of resources, distorted prices, inefficient enterprises, widespread corruption, and rampant shortages of basic goods. Similarly, there was no appreciable improvement in the human-rights situation, which had given the country a bad image abroad, and the regime continued to insulate the population from "alien" influences through severe travel restrictions on the Albanians and by limiting the number of foreigners permitted to visit Albania. Political and economic interactions with other countries were kept low, although a slight expansion of ties with Western and East European countries was evident, particularly with West Germany.

Despite the almost total lack of official contacts with the Soviet Union, the Albanian ruling elite perceived Gorbachev's economic reforms as potentially destabilizing for their own regime. Albanian officials, including Alia, and the state-controlled media described the Soviet leader as just another Khrushchev and his *perestroika* as a "revisionist" policy that would lead to the total restoration of capitalism in the Soviet Union. But perhaps of more concern to the Albanians was Gorbachev's *glasnost'* policy, which coincided with increasing internal demands in Albania for an end to taboos and for a more objective media treatment of both domestic and foreign developments. In March 1989, at a conference devoted to Soviet reforms and sponsored by the Institute for Marxist-Leninist Studies, Foto Çami, reputedly the most liberal member of the APL Politburo, accused Gorbachev of having launched a "general onslaught" against socialism. Çami argued that Soviet "revisionist" reforms were adversely affecting the implementation of reforms in Albania by strengthening conservative forces who insisted that changes would eventually lead to the decline of APL's leading role in the society.[3] A hard-line party theoretician denounced the emerging political pluralism in the Soviet Union, claiming that the toleration of "pluralist ideas" was incompatible with socialist ideology.[4]

Subsequent developments in Eastern Europe did not take the Albanian regime or population by surprise. Despite the country's isolation, the Albanian population was well informed about developments in the region. Many followed developments in Eastern Europe by tuning in to foreign radio and television. In addition, the Albanian state media provided wide and surprisingly objective coverage. No event in Eastern Europe had a greater impact on Albania than the revolution in Romania. The symbolism of the execution of Ceauşescu, whose brutal methods of rule paled in comparison with those used by Hoxha, could not escape either the Albanian nomenklatura nor the population. In contrast to its negative stand on previous developments in Poland, Hungary, East Germany, Czechoslovakia, and Bulgaria, the Albanian regime was quick to distance itself from any identification with Ceauşescu. The Albanian media launched a fierce attack on the Romanian dictator, and Albania became one of the first countries to recognize the post-Ceauşescu government.

Following events in Romania, the Albanian government came under increased foreign and domestic pressures to initiate long-overdue systemic changes. Amid persistent reports of anti-government demonstrations, especially in the northern city of Shkodër and a rapidly deteriorating economy, many observers predicted that Alia and his regime would meet the same fate as their counterparts in Romania. Moreover, developments in Kosovo had a direct bearing on the political situation in Albania. With the accession to power in Serbia of Slobodan Milošević in 1987, ethnic Albanians gradually lost their political autonomy and became the object of an unprecedented repressive policy.[5] Serbia's policy reduced the Albanian majority in Kosovo to a position of subordination, and throughout 1989 and early 1990 there were violent demonstrations in the province. Under such inauspicious conditions, Kosovo witnessed the emergence of several

3. *Zëri i Popullit*, March 17, 1989, pp. 1–3.
4. Ismail Lleshi, "Pluralizmi ideologjik, 'Gllasnosti'—degjenerim i mëtejshëm i jetës shpirtërore në Bashkimin Sovjetik," *Studime Politiko Shoqerore* 16, no. 1 (1989): 44.
5. Elez Biberaj, "Yugoslavia: A Continuing Crisis?" *Conflict Studies*, no. 225 (October 1989): 6–12.

non-Communist political parties, which, in addition to advocating full autonomy and republican status for Kosovo, demanded the establishment of a multiparty system and a free market economy—anathema to the Tirana regime. The fact that the ethnic Albanians, under virtual Serbian military occupation, demanded political pluralism could not but encourage similar demands by their brethren in Albania.

Alia's Response

It was against the background of increased pressure for change and with the country in the throes of an economic crisis that in late January 1990 Alia convened a Central Committee meeting to assess the impact of developments in Eastern Europe on Albanian domestic politics. Alia rejected the possibility of political pluralism and again struck an optimistic note, saying: "The calls that are being made abroad for changes in our country, for departure from the road that we are following, do not find support in our country and are not in tune with the opinion and will of the broad strata of the working people." Claiming there was "a solid" domestic situation, he specifically linked his opposition to the creation of other political parties to a broad concern that a multiparty system would undermine Albania's independence and stability. In an attempt to enhance his regime's legitimacy and ensure political stability, Alia resorted to an old Communist tactic of putting heightened emphasis on nationalist themes and linking the APL and socialism with the preservation of the country's independence.

At the same time, Alia announced a cautious program of reforms. The Central Committee plenum decided that henceforth basic party organizations would hold open meetings, workers would play a greater role in the selection of cadres, competition would be introduced in the election of cadres, and terms of elected officials would be limited. In the economic field, the plenum approved a decentralization of the decision-making process, giving local authorities and enterprises greater autonomy. For the first time since the Communist takeover in 1944, the authorities recognized the importance that market forces played in regulating production. And in order to stimulate agricultural production and deal with growing shortages in the cities, cooperatives were permitted to sell their surplus products freely.[6]

6. Tirana Domestic Service, February 3, 1990, trans. in FBIS-EEU, 90-026, February 7, 1990, pp. 3–8.

But despite Alia's optimistic tone, the leadership was unable to ameliorate the situation. The announced changes were too little and too late. With growing antigovernment demonstrations and labor unrest, the APL showed signs of declining control over the domestic political scene. In April 1990, at the tenth plenum of the Central Committee, Alia announced further changes, formally approved by the People's Assembly in May, which aimed at bettering Albania's abysmal human-rights record. Albanians were given the right to travel abroad, the ban on "religious propaganda" was lifted, and the death penalty for defectors was abolished. The Ministry of Justice, eliminated in the 1960s during the Cultural Revolution, was reinstituted.

In a dramatic break with Hoxha's ideological legacy, Alia reversed the government's long-standing policy on several major issues. Although only two months earlier a senior Foreign Ministry official had reiterated Tirana's opposition to the restoration of ties with the two superpowers and acceptance of foreign credits and investments,[7] Alia expressed his country's desire to normalize ties with Washington and Moscow, and indicated that new laws would be promulgated to permit the government to accept foreign investments. Albania also requested admission as a full member to the Conference on Security and Cooperation in Europe (CSCE), which it had shunned for fifteen years. Western powers, however, refused to grant Albania full membership because of its record of human-rights violations and failure to abandon the one-party system, although at the Copenhagen CSCE meeting it was granted observer status. Echoing Alia's stand on political pluralism, an Albanian delegate at the Copenhagen meeting, Sazan Bejo, told journalists there was no opposition in Albania because everybody supported the government. Bejo said, "If there is full approval by the people for the government, there is no need to artificially create opposition to [the Communist] government."[8]

In view of developments in other East European countries, Alia's policies did not go far enough and indeed amounted to little more than a mild relaxation of an authoritarian regime. But in the context of Albania, with its long self-imposed isolation, more than four decades of rule by one of Europe's most repressive regimes, and no conspicuous signs of active or organized opposition, these were significant changes. Foreign journalists who visited Albania in spring 1990 reported that Alia enjoyed considerable popular support as he toned down the APL's harsh rhetoric

---

7. Interview with Muhamet Kapllani, then deputy foreign minister, *Yomiuri Shimbun* (Tokyo), February 5, 1990, p. 5, trans. in FBIS-EEU, 90-027, February 8, 1990, pp. 1–2.

8. *Financial Times*, June 7, 1990, p. 16.

on ideological issues and raised widespread hopes that finally Albania was on the way to rejoining Europe.[9] The most ardent advocates of reform appeared to be some of the country's leading intellectuals and young technocrats, including Albania's best-known living writer, Ismail Kadare, the cardiologist Sali Berisha, the prominent scientist Ylli Popa, the economist Gramoz Pashko, and the writers and journalists Neshat Tozaj and Besnik Mustafaj. Although not operating as an organized group, these intellectuals, members of the APL, expressed independent views that earned them the wrath of conservative forces lamenting Alia's alleged straying from Hoxha's policies. The literary weekly *Drita* (Light) and the youth newspaper *Zëri i Rinisë* (Voice of youth), served as platforms for reformist intellectuals who advocated sweeping political and economic changes.

Kadare, taking advantage of his reputation at home and abroad, had made increasingly vocal statements on the necessity of immediate changes, especially in the field of human rights. In a review of Neshat Tozaj's bold novel *Thikat* (Knives), which denounced the flagrant violation of human rights by the secret police (Sigurimi), Kadare said that only by admitting and correcting past mistakes would Albania be able to forge ahead.[10] In February 1990 Kadare had requested a meeting with Alia in which he urged the president to put an end to human-rights violations, implement democratic reforms, take immediate measures to improve the precarious economic situation, and open up the country to the outside world.[11] Disappointed with Alia's slow reaction, Kadare publicly raised some of these issues in an interview with the youth newspaper.[12]

Other intellectuals followed in Kadare's footsteps. Sali Berisha, who later would emerge as leader of the first opposition party, the Democratic Party, called for a rapid expansion of Albania's relations with the outside world, adding that isolation had damaged the nation's interests. In a veiled attack against Alia's chief foreign policy adviser, Sofokli Lazri, head of the Institute of International Affairs and reportedly an opponent of the expansion of ties with the West, Berisha said continued isolation would only protect the privileges of those in power. In a clear attack on the officially held view, Berisha urged the authorities to tolerate the ex-

9. See David Binder's reports in the *New York Times,* May 14, 15, 25, and 27, 1990; and the *Times* (London), April 30, 1990.

10. Neshat Tozaj, *Thikat* (Tirana, 1989); Ismail Kadare, "'Thikat': Një roman me rëndësi në letërsinë shqiptare," *Drita,* October 15, 1989, p. 11

11. Ismail Kadare, *Nga një dhjetor në tjetrin* (Paris, 1991), pp. 29–41.

12. See *Zëri i Rinisë,* March 21, 1990, pp. 3–4.

pression of diverse opinions.[13] Diana Çuli, a member of the Writers' Union, emphasized the need for an objective assessment of the state of affairs in Albania. "Identifying the causes of detrimental phenomena and attempting to eliminate them does not 'sully reality,' but confronts reality with the attitude of a citizen who is honest in his relations with his country and state." Çuli said Albania had to free itself of what she termed a prevalent "bureaucratic" mentality. "This mentality," she wrote, had "created undeserved honors and privileges for itself and for incompetent people, for economists who destroyed the economy, architects and engineers of projects that caused losses for the state budget, incompetent doctors, untalented writers and artists, and so forth."[14]

Despite increasing pressures for change, Alia botched the chance to take a dramatic leap toward instituting genuine democratic reforms and taking radical economic measures that Albania's truly untenable conditions required. Measures permitting travel abroad were implemented slowly and on a selective basis. The secret police intensified the campaign against regime opponents, including outspoken intellectuals. Kadare writes that the Sigurimi had allegedly compiled a list of more than one hundred intellectuals to be arrested at an appropriate time.[15] Many people apparently concluded that the measures Alia had announced were intended mainly to impress foreign public opinion.

Popular support for Alia eroded quickly after some five thousand Albanians entered foreign embassies and missions in Tirana. The incident, which marshaled unprecedented international public opinion against Albania, reflected a serious lack of trust in the government and represented a dramatic indication of the wide gulf separating the nomenklatura from the masses. Faced with its most severe crisis to date, the government permitted the refugees to emigrate. Denounced by Alia as "hooligans and vagabonds," the refugees represented all strata of the Albanian society. Most of them said they had decided to emigrate because they had lost all hope of reform in their country. A special Central Committee meeting dismissed several hard-line senior officials, including the minister of the interior, Simon Stefani. Alia delivered a conciliatory speech, but remained steadfast in his demand that reforms be gradual:

> Changes cannot be made within a day, or by rushing, without being well thought out and well coordinated, without examining and analyz-

13. Interview with Sali Berisha, *Drita*, May 20, 1990, pp. 5–6.
14. Diana Çuli, "Mendimi krijues dhe mentaliteti burokratik," *Drita*, July 8, 1990, pp. 5, 12.
15. Kadare, *Nga një dhjetor në tjetrin*, p. 87.

ing objective conditions, without sounding the views of the people, and without preparing the technical base for their implementation. Those who demand the opposite, whether calling themselves super-democrats or super-radicals, do not want democracy, but its prevention and destruction.[16]

Alia announced additional measures aimed at arresting the decline of the economy and placating the despondent populace.[17]

But the importance of these measures was mitigated by the fact that the newly appointed member of the Politburo, the arch-conservative Xhelil Gjoni, immediately emerged as the number-two man in the Albanian hierarchy. A highly unpopular figure who at one time had served as first party secretary in Tirana, Gjoni overshadowed the more reformist members of the Politburo, including Çami, who had been blamed by the conservatives for the decline of the party's control over the media. Under Gjoni's direct supervision, a fierce campaign was launched against families and relatives of refugees, many of whom were expelled from the party and fired from their jobs. At the same time, reports persisted that during the embassy incident security forces had killed hundreds of people and buried them in mass graves at the Dajti mountain, near Tirana. These reports were denied by the authorities.[18]

With Gjoni's appointment, Alia sent mixed signals regarding his future course. Some observers speculated that he favored swift changes but was being blocked by conservative forces within the Politburo and Hoxha's widow, Nexhmije, who was seen as being at loggerheads with the president. While this possibility cannot be excluded, it is more likely that Alia, whose legitimacy was based on Hoxha's legacy, himself opposed rapid change and needed an iron hand like Gjoni to prevent the situation from getting out of control. A product of Hoxha's system and well aware of the East European experience, Alia preferred the implementation of gradual changes under APL's guidance and full control. There is no evidence to indicate that Alia wanted to move more rapidly than in fact he did. As subsequent developments showed, Alia did not embrace democracy and made concessions only under pressure and when the alternative, using the army to crush peaceful demonstrators, was politically too risky and therefore unacceptable.

As the leadership struggled unsuccessfully to dispel the crisis atmo-

16. *Zëri i Popullit*, July 7, 1990, pp. 1–2.
17. Ibid., July 8, 1990, pp. 1–2.
18. Pirro Kondi, "Për nje qëndrim më aktiv e sulmues në propaganden e partisë," *Zëri i Popullit*, September 28, 1990, p. 2.

sphere, expressions of anxiety and criticism of APL's policy became increasingly prominent. In a meeting with intellectuals in August, Alia, with Gjoni standing by his side, was faced with open demands to abolish the one-party system and permit political pluralism.[19] Alia rejected these demands, but promised an increased role for elected bodies, including the People's Assembly, separating party and state, loosening up Communist control over mass organizations, and refining the approach of appointing managing cadres in economic and state sectors.[20]

But despite the regime's inflexible position, the media voiced views that were sharply at odds with those of the leadership on different issues, suggesting that some members of the top leadership were pushing for swift reforms. An editorial in the party's theoretical journal *Rruga e Partisë* (Path of the party), acknowledged that "some restrictions" existed but promised that in the future these restrictions would be narrowed and freedoms expanded. "Democratic processes" in Albania, the editorial emphasized, "are still in their initial stages." While *Rruga e Partisë* struck an optimistic tone, insisting that the democratic processes under way were the initiative of the APL and that "only the party can lead this great process through to the end,"[21] Sali Berisha, writing in *Bashkimi* (Union), the organ of the Democratic Front, the country's largest mass organization, said the country was in the throes of an acute crisis and time was running out. In a biting rebuttal to official statements that pluralism would divide the nation, Berisha launched a sweeping attack against what he termed "antidemocratic and conservative elements" that were opposing the democratization of Albania:

It is first of all bureaucratized cadres and employees who have created and allowed themselves unfair privileges who are conservatives and antidemocrats. Now that the time has come for them to surrender these things, these people, like those unfortunate persons who concoct a lie and end up believing it themselves, think that these privileges are fair—even that these privileges are their birthright.[22]

Berisha, who had clashed with Alia at the meeting the president held with the intellectuals in August, was about to be transferred from Tirana to a

19. Kadare, *Nga një dhjetor në tjetrin*, pp. 252–54.
20. Tirana Domestic Service, August 10, 1990, trans. in FBIS-EEU 90-156, August 13, 1990, p. 1.
21. "Demokratizimi i jetës—forca që çon përpara ekonominë, kulturën dhe qyteterimin shqiptar," *Rruga e Partisë* 8 (August 1990): 5–10.
22. *Bashkimi*, September 17, 1990, pp. 2–3.

provincial town because of his vocal political views. But with the publication of his article in *Bashkimi,* the authorities apparently concluded that his transfer could backfire, since by this time Berisha had attracted domestic and foreign attention.[23]

Echoing some of Berisha's ideas, an article in the APL daily *Zëri i Popullit* (Voice of the people) warned that continued restrictions on freedom of expression would have serious consequences. Drawing an analogy with the demise of Communist parties in Eastern Europe, the author wrote: "Nobody has a monopoly on the truth, neither apparatuses, the party, nor Communists. A monopoly on the truth and decision making sooner or later leads to a failure to heed the voice of the masses, and alienation from their aspirations and interests."[24]

Events were moving at a pace that was far outdistancing the regime's ability to keep up, and the crippled economy threatened to provoke a popular revolt. Production and exports declined, unemployment and inflation rose, and there were endemic shortages of many necessities. The APL agreed to give up its constitutionally guaranteed monopoly on power, and a new law provided for multicandidate elections. Mass organizations, such as the Democratic Front, the veterans' organization, the trade unions, and the youth organization, which had served as transmission belts for the party, were declared independent from the APL and granted the right to put forth their own candidates in the elections for the People's Assembly, then scheduled for February 10, 1991.

On October 25, 1990, as foreign ministers of the Balkan countries were concluding their two-day conference in Tirana, the highest regional meeting ever held in the Albanian capital, Ismail Kadare announced in Paris his defection to France, expressing deep disappointment over the slow pace of change. Kadare's defection represented a dramatic warning of Albania's acute crisis. Some intellectuals, at great personal risk, openly expressed support for Kadare, whom the authorities accused of having betrayed his country. Because of the writer's popularity, the government evidently could not marshal sufficient public opinion against him, and his books were not withdrawn. The reformers lost a strong supporter and potentially an influential leader.[25]

As 1990 approached its end, many Albanians, particularly in urban

23. Interview with Sali Berisha in March 1991.
24. Artan Fuga, "Pluralizmi i mendimeve—kusht i domosdoshëm për demokratizimin e mëtejshëm të shoqërisë," *Zëri i popullit,* October 3, 1990, pp. 2–3.
25. Elez Biberaj, "Helping Democracy from Afar," *The World and I* 4 (April 1991): 381–89.

areas, appeared to be in an unusually rebellious mood and expressed their diminishing confidence in the effectiveness of the Alia regime. With the economy in a shambles, the APL's inability to rectify the situation, and the dwindling legitimacy of existing political institutions, courageous intellectuals, radical students, and rebellious workers pushed for an overhaul of the political system. In one of the more extraordinary examples of criticism against official policy, the party daily published in mid-November excerpts of a debate in which Berisha openly called for the introduction of political pluralism.[26] Even members of the establishment, suggesting that the gloomy atmosphere was pervasive among the political elite, betrayed a loss of confidence in the system and expressed heightened concern that a failure to reverse the economic decline would lead to serious political and social unrest that could unravel the regime. But Alia continued to be less alarmist, claiming the party was capable of rectifying the situation.

The End of a One-Party System

On December 8, 1990, demonstrations began at the Student Center at Tirana University. Ostensibly caused by economic problems, the demonstrations soon took on political overtures. A police intervention on December 9 further exacerbated the situation. The students chose Sali Berisha as an intermediary to present Alia a list of demands, which included calls for the legalization of other political parties. Alia was faced with the most serious crisis of his career: either make basic concessions or order a military crackdown and face the possibility of mass civil disorders and bloodshed. Although only a month earlier he had maintained that political pluralism would lead to galloping localism and engender political and economic instability, Alia unexpectedly reversed his position. On December 11, in a meeting with student representatives, led by Azem Hajdari, a twenty-eight-year-old philosophy student at Tirana University, Alia accepted demands for the establishment of independent political parties. He also announced the expulsion of four Politburo members—Muho Asllani, Simon Stefani, Lenka Çuko, and Foto Çami—and two candidate members Qirjako Mihali and Pirro Kondi. The next day, the first opposition party—the Democratic Party—was founded, to be followed during the next four months by the Republican, Ecological, Agrar-

26. *Zëri i Popullit,* November 18, 1990, p. 3.

ian, National Unity, and Social Democratic parties as well as the Independent Trade Unions. With this action, the last bastion of communism in Europe surrendered its monopoly of political power. This momentous event, which signified the lifting of the pressure cooker's lid, was almost immediately followed by violent anti-Communist demonstrations in Kavajë, Shkodër, Elbasan, and Durrës, which were suppressed by the police and army troops backed by armored vehicles. Because of heightened political tensions and a pervasive sense of insecurity, during the next four weeks some fifteen thousand Albanians fled to Greece.

The APL, concerned about being politically outflanked by the emerging opposition and about losing control, moved to regain the initiative. It tried to shed its rigid Stalinist image by having the Soviet dictator's name removed from all institutions. Nexhmije Hoxha was replaced as head of the Democratic Front, but Hoxha's legacy was not repudiated. At an extraordinary national party conference in late December 1990, Alia, while defending the APL's "historic" achievements, acknowledged that "various mistakes had been made." But he said that Hoxha alone could not be blamed for past mistakes: "We all, the entire party, bear responsibility for everything."[27] He stopped short of denouncing his predecessor, despite mounting popular pressures to do so. The APL committed itself to implementing radical economic reforms and to replacing Albania's highly centralized system with market mechanisms.[28] With its new, reformist program, the APL apparently hoped to arrest the precipitous decline in its already dwindling political prestige. While ostensibly seeking a dialogue, Alia clearly regarded the opposition, particularly the Democratic Party, as a threat to the APL's political future.

From the outset, the odds against the Albanian opposition were probably far greater than anywhere else in Eastern Europe. The fledgling democratic movement lacked organizational experience and had little resources and no contact with the outside world. In spite of inauspicious circumstances, opposition parties moved rapidly to attract and retain a significant spectrum of proreform forces.

The Democratic Party, whose main support base was in the ranks of students, intellectuals, and workers, emerged as the most important opposition political force. Soon after its legalization, the Democratic Party, under the charismatic leadership of Sali Berisha, organized rallies

27. Tirana Domestic Service, December 1990, trans. in FBIS-EEU, 90-250, December 28, 1990, pp. 1–9.
28. Albanian Telegraphic Agency, January 4, 1991, in FBIS-EEU, 91-004, January 7, 1991, pp. 3–6.

throughout the country, which witnessed a passionate outpouring of pent-up emotion against more than four decades of Communist rule. Democratic Party leaders outlined specific proposals for radical reforms, which called for the creation of a Western-style political system based on the rule of law and respect for human rights, dismantling APL control of the media, a thoroughgoing privatization, and an infusion of foreign aid. They demanded a sharp division between state and party, including the total depoliticization of the military, the security forces, and foreign policy. Blaming Hoxha for the gross misallocation of resources, which had led to destructive industrial and disastrous agricultural policies, the democrats issued a comprehensive and far-reaching program of policies designed to transform Albania's centrally planned economy into a functioning market system. Gramoz Pashko, the author of the party's economic program, insisted it was imperative that Albania move rapidly toward a market economy through a total overhaul of the economic structure and a radical revision of existing legislation to attract foreign capital and technology to develop the country's abundant mineral resources. He advocated that collective and state farms be broken up and the land be given back to the peasants.[29]

In contrast to the Democratic Party's radical approach to economic reform, the Republican Party advocated a middle-of-the-road approach, the eventual goal being Albania's integration into the world economy. Other parties had less clearly defined goals and objectives, and, at least by spring 1991, failed to attract any significant support.

With the publication of opposition newspapers, especially *Rilindja Demokratike* (Democratic revival) and *Republika*, organs of, respectively, the Democratic and Republican parties, the media experienced significant changes and the APL's monopoly over the press eroded. Journalists who for more than four decades had been totally subservient to the APL and played the role of propagandists, now began to play the role of critic of the government and the society. They demanded constitutional guarantees of a free press. *Bashkimi*, the organ of the Democratic Front, took an increasingly independent position, and *Zëri i Rinisë*, although still carrying the youth organization's label, published articles that conflicted with the APL's views. Meanwhile, the newspaper of the Writers' Union, *Drita*, became a strong supporter of the democratic opposition. Still, the APL continued to exercise tight control of radio and television.

Following a miners' strike in Valias near Tirana, labor unrest in several

29. *Rilindja Demokratike,* January 5, 1991, pp. 3–5, and March 16, 1991, p. 5.

other cities in January 1991, the exodus of thousands of citizens to
Greece, and increasing foreign criticism, Alia, who was trying to orchestrate the reform process while desperately clinging to power, gave in to
opposition demands and agreed to postpone parliamentary elections until March 31. The opposition parties had demanded a delay until May
1991, contending that they needed more time to organize. Alia appealed
to the patriotism of Albanians, urging them to avoid paralyzing strikes
and help rescue the country's stagnant economy.

Although with the legalization of an opposition its influence had eroded, the APL continued to control the main levers of power, including the
military and the secret police. Recognizing that the army and Sigurimi
were highly politicized and likely to carry out APL leadership orders,
opposition leaders were careful not to provoke a backlash from conservative forces, which could lead to large-scale nationwide unrest. They
came under increasing pressure from more radical elements, however,
especially students and workers, who were unwilling to accept any outcome short of the total overthrow of the Communist system. In February,
students organized protests demanding the removal of Enver Hoxha's
name from Tirana University and the resignation of the government.
When the authorities refused, more than seven hundred students and
faculty members went on a hunger strike. On February 20, more than
100,000 people gathered in Tirana's central square and tore down Hoxha's statue. The army and security forces did not intervene. In a dramatic
reversal of his position, Alia accepted student demands. He set up a nine-
member presidential council, assuming personal control over the country,
and announced a new government, replacing Prime Minister Adil Çarçani
with Fatos Nano, a prominent thirty-nine-year-old economist.

The downing of Hoxha's statue in Tirana and in several other cities
caused an immediate Communist backlash, and according to Alia the
nation was on the verge of civil war. Conservative Communists in the
southern city of Berat set up the Union of Volunteers for Enver Hoxha,
which organized pro-Hoxha rallies all over the country, intimidated and
beat up opposition supporters, and restored Hoxha's statues in many
places. Members of this organization threatened to march on the capital
and re-erect the dictator's monument. In Tirana, amid rumors of a potential military coup, clashes broke out between supporters of the APL and
the Democratic Party at the military academy. Four people were killed and
dozens injured. The deepening political crisis caused another mass exodus: some twenty thousand Albanians fled to Italy.

Amid this tense political atmosphere the election campaign got under way. The ruling party enjoyed a clear advantage over opposition parties; it possessed a strong nationwide organization and enormous resources. After the removal of Hoxha's statue in Tirana, the APL reimposed its traditional censorship on radio and television, which slanted the coverage of the election campaign. The opposition, on the other hand, had at its disposal very few resources and insufficient time to build a viable national organization. While the APL controlled radio and television, Tirana's two dailies, *Zëri i Popullit* and *Bashkimi,* and newspapers in the country's twenty-six administrative districts, there were two main opposition papers, *Rilindja Demokratike* and *Republika,* published twice a week with an average circulation of sixty thousand copies. In the cities, the Democratic and Republican parties encountered little difficulty in publicizing their election platforms. In the countryside, however, where more than 60 percent of the population lived, they were unable to spread their message. Whereas in the urban centers the APL monopoly had been broken, in the rural areas Communist Party committees remained very powerful and intimidated opposition supporters. Moreover, there was a massive discrepancy in the size of voting districts. While in the urban areas a voting district could have as many as thirteen thousand registered voters, in the rural areas some had only five thousand. The APL used various means at its. disposal to mobilize the peasantry, which had been brutalized and isolated for decades and was least disposed to change. On the eve of the elections, the government expanded the peasants' private plots. The ruling party also attempted to score points by reportedly releasing all political prisoners and permitting the opening of mosques and churches, which had been closed down by Hoxha in 1967. As the election day approached, the Communist-controlled media launched a well-coordinated campaign against Democratic and Republican parties, portraying democratic candidates in an especially unflattering light.[30]

Election results confirmed a trend evident in other Balkan countries, Romania, Bulgaria, and Yugoslavia's Serbian and Montenegrin republics, in which the voters failed to make a clean break with their Communist past. The APL won 169 seats (67.6 percent) out of 250 seats in the People's Assembly. The Democratic Party won 75 seats (30 percent), while OMANIA, a group representing Albania's ethnic Greek community, won 5 seats (2 percent). The National Veterans' Committee, an organization of

30. Top officials of the Democratic Party, such as Gramoz Pashko, Azem Hajdari, Neritan Çeka, Besnik Mustafaj, Natasha Lako, and Napoleon Roshi, became the targets of a vicious character assassination campaign. See *Zëri i Popullit,* March 24, 27, 29, and 30, 1991.

Second World War veterans and closely allied with the APL, won one seat (0.4 percent). The APL swept the countryside, but did poorly in the major cities, particularly in Tirana. Alia and several other prominent APL officials, including the secretary of the party, Spiro Dede, and the foreign minister, Muhamet Kapllani, lost in their bids. Voter turnout was very high: 98.92 percent; 56.17 percent voted for APL candidates, while 38.71 percent voted for the Democratic Party.[31] The new parliament elected Alia president for a five-year term. He subsequently resigned as the APL's first secretary and as a member of the Central Committee and the Politburo. Fatos Nano was renamed prime minister. Meanwhile, the Democratic Party rejected an offer to join a coalition government.

Conclusion

Most Albanian political forces agreed that the condition of the country after the elections was truly precarious. On April 2, security forces in Shkodër killed four people and wounded fifty-eight others when Democratic Party supporters organized demonstrations protesting alleged vote fraud by the APL. The society was polarized between the cities, which were overwhelmingly anti-Communist, and the impoverished countryside. Leading economic indicators had plummeted, and there was a huge leap in unemployment and continued labor unrest. Worker morale was very low and pessimism pervasive. Albania will have to grapple with the social and economic legacy of close to five decades of Communist misrule, and the population will have to accept formidable hardships, difficulties, and challenges.

In contrast to the Democratic Party, which advocated a swift overhaul of the command system, Prime Minister Nano urged a gradual approach. Although he had a fairly liberal reputation on economic issues and had showed flexibility on ideological issues, Nano rejected the possibility of comprehensive economic reforms. But to stabilize its economy, Albania will need deep-seated reforms, including full privatization, the abandonment of price controls, and well-developed financial institutions as well as foreign investments. Despite the promulgation of liberal legislation on foreign investments, the government had limited success attracting them. No Western country was likely to provide economic assistance just to

31. *Bashkimi*, April 18, 1991, p. 1. See also Commission on Security and Cooperation in Europe, U.S. Congress, *The Elections in Albania March–April 1991* (Washington, D.C., April 1991).

prop up the Communist government. Foreign governments and companies tied their investments to further democratic changes and the restoration of political stability.

Despite its election victory, the APL appears badly split along ideological lines, with the conservatives desperately resisting pressures from the rank and file for the renovation of the party and the rejection of Hoxha's legacy. Unless it reforms itself, the party runs the risk of soon becoming a spent force. Already, many members have concluded they were better off without the party and are resigning in increasing numbers. It seemed highly unlikely that the APL would be able to retain sufficient control of the democratization process to ensure for long its continuation in power. While Nano's plan gradually to loosen up APL's grip over the economy will result in increased prosperity for some Albanians, decentralization will also lead to increased unemployment, galloping inflation, and rising expectations that the ruling party is in no position to meet. Moreover, the APL will have to reassess its past and grapple with questions of justice, rehabilitation, and issues connected with the building of a genuine pluralist system.

The transition from centrally planned communism to market-driven capitalism will be a complicated process. Albania has had a long tradition of authoritarian rule. With the exception of the short-lived experiment with a parliamentary system in the early 1920s, Albania has never had a genuine democratic government, with a system of checks and balances. The collapse of the population's fear and the sudden relaxation of the Communist dictatorship, in the absence of democratic institutions, could lead to increased political tensions and the revival of regional rivalries. Moreover, large segments of the population were affected by Communist repression and many people demand redress as well as revenge against the Communists. With increasing signs of unrest and sporadic clashes between opposition supporters and security forces, some observers have warned of the danger of a conservative Communist backlash and authoritarian regression. While such an eventuality cannot be ruled out, any attempt by the Communists to reverse current reforms or outlaw the opposition could provoke a popular revolt and even spark a civil war.

While Albania faces an array of seemingly inextricably intertwined problems and extremist forces on both ends of the political spectrum advocate radical approaches, the ruling party and the opposition have engaged in a constructive dialogue. Although isolated for decades and ruled by a repressive regime that denied them their most elementary rights, the Albanians have undergone significant cultural, social, and economic transformations; they are no longer a largely uneducated peasant population, characterized by a clan mentality, as often portrayed by the Western media. The majority of the Albanians evidently recognize that national reconciliation, a major aspect of the program of the Democratic Party, is the best way for the successful revival of their poverty-stricken country.

Albania is endowed with considerable mineral resources and has a young, dynamic population, eager to join the rest of the world. Albanian émigrés have done remarkably well in the West, especially in the United States, where there are many successful capitalists and small businessmen. There is reason to believe that if conditions were favorable, ordinary Albanians would respond to economic incentives.

The biggest challenge facing Albanian decision makers is how to realize immediate improvements in the standard of living and implement fundamental political and economic reforms that will facilitate the country's full integration into the community of European nations. Traditionally, Albania has been of marginal interest to the world, and particularly to the American public. Now, as it enters the postdictatorship phase, it desperately needs the assistance and friendship of the outside world. Without that assistance, Albania's fledgling democracy may be doomed.

The Leninist Legacy

Ken Jowitt

Conceptual Geography

Eastern Europe's boundaries—political, ideological, economic, and military—have been radically redefined twice in less than a century. As Tony Judt has written, at the end of the First World War, "the disappearance of the Austro-Hungarian Empire (a truly momentous event in European history) left a huge gap in the conceptual geography of the continent. Of what did Central Europe now consist? What was East, what West in a landmass whose political divisions had been utterly and unrecognizably remade within a single lifetime"?[1] In 1989 the Soviet bloc became extinct as Communist parties in every East European country added the loss of political power to their earlier loss of ideological purpose during the phase of "real socialism"; and the Soviet Union, the "stern, . . . impersonal, perpetual Center" of this imperium not only tolerated but instigated its collapse.[2] The result is a no less significant gap in Europe's "conceptual geography" than seventy years ago.

In 1987 Daniel Chirot and I pointed out that

> because of its historical experience, the diversity of its cultural traditions, and its vulnerability to big power interference, Eastern Europe has had, and will continue to have a uniquely creative role in producing

---

1. Tony Judt, "The Rediscovery of Central Europe," *Daedalus* 119, no. 1 (1990): 25.
2. John Le Carre, *The Spy Who Came in from the Cold* (New York, 1963), p. 144.

ideas and experimental solutions for solving the major problems of the modern world. Not only a number of key artistic and literary movements, but also political ideologies such as fascism, socialism, and peasantism received major innovative contributions from Eastern and Central Europe in the first half of the twentieth century.[3]

The mass extinction of Leninist regimes in Eastern Europe in 1989 is a dramatic, promising, and unsettling event whose immediate consequence is a direct challenge to the boundaries and identities of the region and its constituent parts. Whether looked at as an imperative, process, or outcome, Eastern Europe is in the midst of redefining its cultural frames of reference, political and economic institutions, and political-territorial boundaries. Once again Eastern Europe has become a laboratory in which a set of experiments are being undertaken under less than controlled conditions, with the likelihood that most will fail, and of those that succeed many will have predominantly antidemocratic-capitalist features. Whatever the results of the current turmoil in Eastern Europe one thing is clear: the new institutional patterns will be shaped by the "inheritance" and legacy of forty years of Leninist rule.

The "Inheritance"

Confronted with a turbulent environment, there is a quite understandable, predictable, and observable tendency by intellectuals to restore certainty idiomatically. That certainly is the case regarding Eastern Europe. One of its most pronounced expressions is the fetish-like repetition of the phrase "transition to democracy"—as if saying it often enough and inviting enough Latin Americanists from the United States to enough conferences in Eastern Europe (and the Soviet Union) will magically guarantee a new democratic capitalist telos in place of the ethnic, economic, and territorial maelstrom that is the reality today. One is reminded of Mephisto's observation: "Men usually believe, if only they hear words, That there must also be some sort of meaning."[4] From the "transition to democracy" perspective, Eastern Europe resembles a historical blackboard written on with Leninist chalk for forty years, erased (largely) by Soviet actions in 1989, and waiting, a tabula rasa, to be written on now in liberal capitalist script.

3. Daniel Chirot and Ken Jowitt, "Beginning E.E.P.S.," *Eastern European Politics and Societies* 1, no. 1 (1987): 2.
4. *Goethe's "Faust"* (Garden City, N.Y., 1963), p. 253.

Any substantial analysis of the chances for democracy and market capitalism in Eastern Europe, however, must interpret the maelstrom itself, and that means coming to analytic grips with the cultural, political, and economic "inheritance" of forty years of Leninist rule. For Western analysts to treat the Leninist legacy the way Leninists after 1948 treated their own East European inheritance—namely, as a collection of historically outmoded "survivals" bound to lose their cultural, social, and psychological significance—would be an intellectual mistake of the first order. All cultural and institutional legacies shape their successors. Peter Brown's creation of an age—Late Antiquity—rests on his rejection of a simplistic dichotomy of continuity versus discontinuity, on his appreciation of novel, not absolute, transformations of the Roman legacy.[5]

Some historical legacies contribute positively to the development of successor states. Karl van Wolferen presents a powerful (to me, compelling) case to support his argument that Japan's current economic success is directly related "to the authoritarian institutions and techniques dating from the first half of the twentieth century."[6]

The Leninist legacy is currently shaping, and will continue to shape, developmental efforts and outcomes in Eastern Europe—though not in a "Japanese" manner. Regarding the Leninist legacy Timothy Garton Ash says: "perhaps the beginning of wisdom is to recognize that what communism has left behind is an extraordinary mish-mash."[7] The comment is perceptive, suggestive, and self-defeating. The Leninist legacy is a conflicting, confusing, *and*, fortunately, an identifiable one. Otherwise we are left with two inadequate and unacceptable alternatives: the simplistic application/imposition of (a very theoretically thin) "transition to democracy" literature to the East European/Soviet setting, or an acceptance of the Mock Turtle's designation of current events in Eastern Europe as Modern Mystery (not History).[8]

Private versus Public Virtues

In a curious, unintended, and highly consequential way, Leninist rule reinforced many of the most salient features of traditional culture throughout Eastern Europe (the Soviet Union and elsewhere). In my 1974

---

5. See Peter Brown, *The Making of Late Antiquity* (Cambridge, Mass., 1978).
6. Karl van Wolferen, *The Enigma of Japanese Power* (New York, 1990), chap. 14.
7. Timothy Garton Ash, "Eastern Europe: Après le Déluge: Nous," *New York Review of Books,* August 16, 1990, p. 52.
8. Lewis Carroll, *Alice's Adventures in Wonderland* (London, 1973), p. 105.

article on political culture I argued that "through their organization and ethos [Leninist regimes] have stimulated a series of informal adaptive social responses (behavioral and attitudinal) that are in many respects consistent with and supportive of certain basic elements of the traditional political culture in these societies. In turn, these elements are antithetical to the appearance of a regime and society with an ethos and structure predicated on a complementary relationship between the public and private realms, on the viability of impersonal rules and norms, and on the value of egalitarianism expressed in the role of effective participant."[9] In 1991 I would put it more succinctly, but no differently: the Leninist experience in Eastern Europe (and elsewhere) reinforced the exclusive distinction and dichotomic antagonism between the official and private realms.

For forty years, regardless of the quite substantial developmental changes in the Communist Party's relation to its host societies, ruling Leninist parties persistently defined and asserted themselves as the superior and dominant alternative to the nation-state, as the exclusive autarchic locus of political leadership and membership.[10] The political consequence was to reinforce the traditional stark gap between a privileged domineering official realm and a private mutually suspicious realm similar to Montesquieu's description of despotic society.[11] No politically integrating nationwide public realm existed in the greater part of Eastern Europe (or the Russian, then Soviet, empire) before or during the period of Leninist rule. The Leninist experience intensely reinforced and added to the already negative image of the political realm and the insular quality of the private realm. This reality expressed itself in a number of ways during the period of Leninist rule and persists more than inertially throughout Eastern Europe today.

To begin with, the party's political monopoly and punitive relation to the population produced a "ghetto" political culture in Eastern Europe. The population at large viewed the political realm as something dangerous, something to avoid. Political involvement meant "trouble." Regime-coerced political activity (not participation) sustained and heightened the population's psychological and political estrangement. At the

9. Ken Jowitt, "An Organizational Approach to the Study of Political Culture in Marxist-Leninist Systems," *American Political Science Review* 68, no. 3 (1974): 1186.

10. See Ken Jowitt, "Inclusion and Mobilization in European Leninist Regimes," *World Politics* 28, no. 1 (1975): 69–97. I outline the developmental history of Leninist regimes in this article.

11. I thank Veljko Vujović for suggesting Montesquieu's observations to me; see *The Spirit of the Laws* (New York, 1949), pp. 20–115.

same time the party could not be everywhere. So Leninist parties made a de facto trade off: active control and penetration of priority areas in return for de facto privatization in nonpriority areas. This became particularly true during the Brezhnev period when private egoism—personalism not individualism—became the major sociocultural reality.[12] As I argued fifteen years ago in the same piece on political culture, dissimulation became the effective (and ethically as well as politically debilitating) bridge between the domineering official and the societal supplicant during the entire period of Leninist rule. For four decades dissimulation became the central feature of the population's (misre)presentation of its public, or better, visible self. Dissimulation reflected the fear and avoidance responses of a subordinate population: the need to deflect the party's attention from possible or real underfulfillment of tasks and from its unchecked penetration of one's private and social life. Dissimulation also provided the means for an estranged population to interact regularly with a powerful, entrenched, and illegitimate regime.[13]

The absence of a *shared public identity* as citizens, an identity that would have equalized rulers and ruled, and allowed for truthful discussion and debate, had a second consequence: the central place of rumor as covert political discourse. In *The Agricola,* Tacitus suggested that "rumour is not always at fault: it may even prompt a selection."[14] Maybe in Rome; not in Eastern Europe (the Soviet Union, or China). There, rumor had and continues to have a debilitating effect on political life. It divides, frightens, and angers those who participate in what amounts to a chronic mode of semihysterical (pre)political speech. To be sure, its impact is much greater in some countries than others. If Romania could export its rumors, it would be more developed than Germany. But the political psychological impact exists in the entire region, and its substantive thrust is clear: it strengthens the insular privatized quality of social life and obstructs the sober public discussion of national issues. The legacy that continues to shape the character of "civil society" in Eastern Europe and the Soviet Union comprises the neotraditional secrecy characteristic of a ruling Leninist party; its corresponding distrust of an ideologically "unreconstructed" population; the invidious juxtaposition of an elite in possession of the real but secret truth about the polity, economy,

---

12. I distinguish individualism and personalism in the following manner: individualism is ego restrained both by impersonal norms and an internal discipline of deferred gratification. Personalism is ego unrestrained by anything except external obstacle or internal disability.

13. Jowitt, "An Organizational Approach," pp. 1183–84.

14. Tacitus, *The Agricola* (Middlesex, 1970), p. 59.

world affairs, and so on; and a population living in the "cave" of political jokes and rumor.[15] Civil society is more than economic and legal sociology; it is political culture.

In yet another way the organization and operation of Leninist rule contributed to the difficulty East European populations experience now as they try to create frameworks that relate their private, social, and political identities in a complementary, not fragmentary, fashion. Leninist regimes in Eastern Europe, the Soviet Union, and Asia organized their societies around a series of semiautarchic institutions, the *danwei* in China, and *kollektiv* in the Soviet Union and Eastern Europe. Unlike liberal capitalist democracies, Leninist regimes "parcel" rather than "divide" labor. In Leninist regimes the factory was (is) less a specialized institution and school of modernity than a functionally diffuse neopatriarchal provider: of houses, vacations, medical attention, food, and to some extent social activity for its workers.[16] The net effect was a division of labor that in important respects resembled Durkheim's *mechanical* division of labor, a "ringworm" division of labor in which each institution attempted to replicate the self-sufficiency of all the others.[17] Again the consequence was to juxtapose the polity and society antagonistically, and fragment society itself. One corporate autarchic political entity, *the party* hierarchically dominated and connected a set of semiautarchic socioeconomic entities whose only common bond was a distant, different, and dominant official realm—the party, *them*.

The same pattern was created by the Soviet Union in its relations with East European regimes. As Władysław Gomułka's interpreter Erwin Weit noted, "The men in power in the Eastern bloc talk constantly of 'internationalism,' but . . . no friendly neighbour relationship of the type that has developed since the end of the war between the French and the Germans has ever linked the Poles with the Russians or the Czechs or even the people of the DDR. They have remained 'stranger to each other.' "[18] In the bloc, the Soviet regime occupied the same strategically dominant position the party occupied in each society.[19] Regionally and nationally the East

15. See Ken Jowitt, "Soviet Neotraditionalism: The Political Corruption of a Leninist Regime," *Soviet Studies* 35, no. 3 (1983): 282.

16. Alex Inkeles and David Smith, *Becoming Modern* (Cambridge, Mass., 1974); On China see Andrew G. Walder's excellent work (and title) *Communist Neo-traditionalism: Work and Authority in Chinese Industry* (Berkeley, Calif., 1986), chap. 2. Soviet and East European factories are not the "total institution" the Chinese factory appears to be but are more similar than dissimilar.

17. Emile Durkheim, *The Division of Labor* (Toronto, 1964), chaps. 2 and 3.

18. Erwin Weit, *At the Red Summit* (New York, 1973), pp. 190–91.

19. See Ken Jowitt, "Moscow 'Centre,' " *Eastern European Politics and Societies* 1, no. 3 (1987): 296–349.

European polities were fragmented, not integrated: fragmented into mutually exclusive official and private realms bridged by mutually deceptive presentations of their respective "selves." In this respect Leninist regimes fostered the generic features of all despotisms in which people are

> far too much disposed to think exclusively of their own interests, to become self-seekers practicing a narrow individualism and caring nothing for the public good. Far from trying to counteract such tendencies despotism encourages them, depriving the governed of any sense of solidarity and interdependence; of good-neighborly feeling and a desire to further the welfare of the community at large. It immures them, so to speak, each in his private life and, taking advantage of the tendency they already have to keep apart, it estranges them still more.[20]

The party's charismatic modus operandi also shaped the actions and dispositions of East Europe's populations. Leninist parties in this (and every) region were overwhelmingly concerned with targets and outcomes, ends not means; and they acted in a storming-heroic manner to achieve them. During the Brezhnev period, when they had exhausted their heroic-storming resources, capacity, and even inclination, they substituted a corrupt set of personal patron-client relations to achieve their substantive ends.[21] What no Leninist regime ever did under Stalin, Khrushchev, or Brezhnev; Gheorghiu-Dej or Ceauşescu; Bierut, Gomułka, or Gierek, was to create a culture of impersonal measured action. The result is an East European (Soviet, Chinese . . .) population that in its majority has very little experience with regular, deliberate economic and political activity in a context of impersonal procedures; a population that in its authoritarian peasant and Leninist personas is more familiar with sharp disjunctions between periods of intense action and passivity than with what Max Weber termed the "methodical rational acquisition" (of goods or votes); a population that in its majority would find the tenor and operation of Benjamin Franklin's Protestant liberal capitalist way of life boring, demeaning, and in good part unintelligible.[22]

---

20. Alexis de Tocqueville, *The Old Regime and the French Revolution* (Garden City, N.Y., 1955), p. xiii. For those interested in the political evolution of Eastern Europe (and the Soviet Union) I suggest this book's value surpasses anything yet written on "transiting" to democracy.

21. See Jowitt, "Soviet Neotraditionalism," pp. 285–90.

22. It is not enough to point out that most citizens in liberal capitalist democracies (certainly the American) themselves fail to vote and are poorly informed about issues and basic premises of democracy. The institutional framework, the practices and habits of elites, and the sociocultural constitutions in these countries assign critically different meanings to events in Western democracies and East European countries.

Ironically, even the remarkable discovery, articulation, and public expression of human dignity and public ethics by exemplary political figures like Adam Michnik and Václav Havel, and civic movements like Solidarity and Civic Forum, partially reinforce the antagonistic juxtaposition of a suspect political world and one of private virtue and ethics. In 1989, in Eastern Europe, one saw the charismatic efflorescence of public ethics: demands for and expressions of individual dignity as the "base," not the superstructure, of political life. In 1989, in Eastern Europe, ethics moved from the purely personal realm to the public realm; not in the form of an intrusive private standard for public performance (as in the United States today), but as an autonomous political criterion for public action, one that judges leadership in terms of its impact on and contribution to human dignity.

Still, liberal democratic polities do not—for that matter, cannot—rest primarily on the charismatic permanence of politically ethical leadership or the private ethics of its citizens. They rest on "public virtues." Ralf Dahrendorf rightly emphasizes that in a society where "private" virtue is exalted the human personality

> becomes a creature without a public life, and the formation of the nation is left behind. Many may well be quite content with this state of affairs. Their greatest happiness is found in private life, in the heights and depths of friendship, and familial harmony, in the satisfaction of imprecise reveries, perhaps even in the nearly metasocial bonds with others in unstructured collectivities.[23]

Now listen to the Russian poet Andrei Voznesenskii: "In Russia, I think we have . . . spiritual life. We can talk all day and all night long about all kinds of questions, immortal questions. That is the Russian style of thinking. I want our economy to be the same as in the West. . . . But I am afraid to lose this Russian part of our soul."[24] Voznesenskii's reflection, for that matter the entire thrust of Hedrick Smith's recent description of Russian popular culture, speaks to the predominance of private over public virtues in the Russian population; and no great damage is done in generalizing his observations to the majority of people in practically every East European country.

23. Ralf Dahrendorf, *Society and Democracy in Germany* (Garden City, N.Y., 1969), p. 293.

24. Hedrick Smith, "The Russian Character," *New York Times Magazine*, October 28, 1990, p. 30. Practically every observation Smith makes about Russian culture in 1990 is analyzed in Jowitt, "An Organizational Approach."

Eastern Europe's pre-Leninist peasant culture and oligarchical authoritarian elites (at times cosmetically outfitted with Western political facades), the neotraditional features of Stalinist and Brezhnevite rule, *and* the ethical charisma of 1989 for all their qualitative difference combine to provide a remarkably consistent and continuous support for a world view in which political life is suspect, distasteful, and possibly dangerous; to be kept at bay by dissimulation, made tolerable by private intimacy, and transcended by private virtues or charismatic ethics.[25] To return to Dahrendorf: the "inner-direction of those oriented to private virtues is incomplete. *It is inner-direction without its liberal element, the carrying over of interest to the market of politics and the economy.*"[26] To put it bluntly: the Leninist legacy, understood as the impact of party organization, practice, and ethos, *and* the initial charismatic ethical opposition to it favor an authoritarian, not a liberal democratic capitalist, way of life, the obstacles to which are not simply how to privatize and marketize the economy, or organize an electoral campaign but rather how to institutionalize public virtues. East European elites and social audiences have inherited what is for the most part a suspicious culture of mutual envy fostered by a corrupt neotraditional Leninist despotism that in good measure unintentionally reinforced a set of "limited-good" peasant cultures.[27] The charismatically ethical antithesis provoked by the indignities of "real socialism"—Solidarity being the paradigmatic instance—is by its very nature an unstable, inadequate base for a tolerant polity based on the complementarity of ethics *and interests.* Max Weber's observations are quite apt in examining the current fate of Solidarity in Poland and Civic Forum in Czechoslovakia:

> When the tide that lifted a charismatically led group out of everyday life flows back into the channels of workaday routines, at least the "pure" form of charismatic domination will wane and turn into an "institution"; it is then either mechanized, as it were, or imperceptibly displaced by other structures, or fused with them in the most diverse forms, so that it becomes a mere component of a concrete historical structure. In this case it is often transformed beyond recognition, and identifiable only on an analytical level.[28]

25. On the Stalinist period see Vera S. Dunham, *In Stalin's Time* (New York, 1979); on the Brezhnev period see Jowitt, "Soviet Neotraditionalism," pp. 285–90.

26. Dahrendorf, *Society and Democracy in Germany,* p. 291, my emphasis.

27. See Jowitt, "An Organizational Approach," for a discussion of "limited good" cultures and the Leninist impact and for reference to the author of the concept, George Foster.

28. Max Weber, *Economy and Society,* ed. Guenther Roth and Claus Wittich (New York, 1968), 3:1120–21.

The Fragmentation of Eastern Europe

A good place to begin specifying the type of developments likely to occur in Eastern Europe is with a look at a special flag. The most vivid symbol of the Romanian uprising in December 1989 was the sight of the Romanian flag with its Leninist center ripped out. Eastern Europe in 1990 and 1991 is like the Romanian flag: its Leninist center has been removed but a good deal of institutional and cultural inheritance is still in place. In all of Eastern Europe the Leninist extinction was as much a case of regime collapse as regime defeat, nicely captured by Garton Ash's term "refolution."[29]

And what one now sees taking place in Eastern Europe is more the breakup of existing identities and boundaries than the breakthrough to new ones. Before the latter happens political conflict in Eastern Europe will have to get beyond the "many are called" phase to the "few are chosen" stage. To a point where the antagonists are politically organized not simply viscerally identified. Currently, the cleavages in Eastern Europe are neither cross-cutting nor superimposed. They are diffuse, poorly articulated, psychological as much as political, and for that reason remarkably intense. One reason for this is the absence of established successor elites in these countries.[30] With the exception of Solidarity, prior to 1989 most opposition elites in Eastern Europe had minimal insulation from the intrusive punitive presence of their Leninist adversaries, minimal familiarity with one another and "politics as a vocation," and minimal success—for that matter opportunity—to bond themselves with a politically loyal social constituency. Only in Poland over almost a two-decade period did a counterelite enjoy a Yenan-like protective/interactive experience; one that produced a contentious but mutually tolerant and intelligible elite that cohered and even in its current divided and divisive state offered Poland something more important than either marketization or civil society: an "established" leadership. An "established elite" is one that despite genuine party, policy, and ideological differences recognizes the legitimate place of all its members in the policy, has worked out civil and practical modes of interaction, and can identify and organize a sociopolitical constituency in a regular manner. Excepting Poland, no East European country has an established (democratic or nondemocratic)

29. Timothy Garton Ash, "Refolution in Hungary and Poland," *New York Review of Books,* August 17, 1989, pp. 9–15.
30. See Ralf Dahrendorf's contrast of "established" and "abstract" elites in *Society and Democracy in Germany.* Dahrendorf emphasizes the shared socialization of established elites and how this contributes to implicit cooperation.

elite. That means they are fragile polities—highly fragile democratic polities.

We can begin with Hungary. According to Elemér Hankiss, among the new democratic forces "there is a certain confusion. . . . They are rent by inner divisions; they have not yet built up their national networks and constituencies. . . . They have not yet found their identities and their places in the political spectrum. They have not drawn up their detailed programs and have not clearly outlined the sociopolitical model they want to establish in this country."[31] In Czechoslovakia the absence of an established elite is pointedly underscored by the ethnic splits between Slovak and Czech leaders; the dramatic political entry of a religious authoritarian, the Roman Catholic pope, in Slovakia (in April 1990), where one million (out of five million) Slovaks greeted him; and the recent selection of Václav Klaus—a man with little political connection to or affinity with the charismatically ethical Havel—as finance minister. The political flux of Civic Forum's disorganized partisan constituencies completes the picture of an attenuated, diffuse political "constitution" in what many consider one of the most promising candidates for "transition to democracy."

In Romania and Bulgaria, the governing elites do form an established elite. Still, opposition elites (for example, the UDF in Bulgaria, along with the Liberal and Peasant party leaders in Romania) fundamentally reject the legitimacy of the incumbents. In Romania and Bulgaria one has Dutch-like sociopolitical "pillars" without a reconciling consociational political elite.[32] If that is not enough there is evidence of serious fragmentation within the governing parties themselves in Bulgaria and Romania. The absence of democratic or nondemocratic *established successor elites* in Eastern Europe favors and furthers the maelstrom quality of life throughout the area.

The difficulty of creating a democratic established political elite with a tolerant culture is exacerbated by the "*refolutionary*" change that occurred in 1989. Leninist personnel still play a prominent role in administrative, economic (and in the Balkans, political) life. In Eastern Europe one sees a novel evolutionary phenomenon—survival of the first, not simply the fittest.[33] Former party cadres are exceptionally well placed to

31. See Elemér Hankiss's exceptional piece, "In Search of a Paradigm," *Daedalus* 119, no. 1 (1990): 183–215.
32. On the Netherlands see Arend Lijphart, *The Politics of Accommodation: Pluralism and Democracy in the Netherlands* (Berkeley, Calif., 1968).
33. My colleague in astronomy, Richard Muller, uses this phrase in his discussion of evolutionary change.

adapt themselves—and their families—successfully to changes in the economic and administrative order. Evidence of this adaptive ability abounds in Poland, Hungary, and elsewhere in Eastern Europe. Add to this the sizable portion of the population in Eastern Europe who in some significant way collaborated with the party and you have the recipe for a nasty social climate, in fact more than nasty, a climate of sustained, if so far largely contained, psychological rage, which expresses the emotional fragmentation of populations who cannot find an acceptable political solution to the issues of Leninist survivors and collaborators.[34] Fragmentation is the dominant East European reality.

Daniel Bell's observation that "most societies have become more self-consciously plural societies (defined in ethnic terms)" certainly applies to Eastern Europe today.[35] The case of Yugoslavia is compelling. On balance there is more reason to think Yugoslavia will not exist as a sovereign entity in five years than it will. Civil war is a probability in good part because national hate is a reality. The mutual hate of Serbs and Albanians in Kosovo, between Milošević's Serbia and Croatia—for that matter between Serbs and Croats in Croatia—when combined with economic issues and the effective demise of the League of Communists of Yugoslavia favors civil war more than civic culture. The same might be said of the Soviet Union, where in one "East European" republic, Moldavia, the Romanian population is moving closer to union with Romania while trying to suppress a secession movement by the Gagauz Turkic minority in the southern part of the republic, and the efforts by its Russian population around Tiraspol' to maintain Moldavia's ties with the Soviet Union. But the problem of ethnic and territorial fragmentation exists also in the "Orange County" part of Eastern Europe—in Czechoslovakia, where many Slovaks are demanding that Slovak be the official language in Slovakia, something quite unacceptable to the hundreds of thousands of Hungarians living in Slovakia. The Slovak National Party demands full independence for Slovakia.[36] And should anyone need reminding, the territorial issues between Yugoslavia and Albania, Romania and Hungary, and Poland and its eastern neighbors are latent, not extinct. Today, Eastern Europe is a *brittle* region. Suspicion, division, and fragmentation

34. If one takes Czechoslovakia, it has been estimated that some five of the fifteen million inhabitants have had some relation to the former Communist Party. So if one adds survivors and collaborators, one out of three Czechoslovaks are suspect to the remaining two. See Serge Schmemann, "For Eastern Europe Now, a New Disillusion," *New York Times,* November 9, 1990, pp. A1, A10.

35. Daniel Bell, *The Winding Passage* (New York, 1980), p. 224.

36. See Vladimir V. Kusin, "Czechs and Slovaks: The Road to the Current Debate," *Report on Eastern Europe* 1, no. 40 (1990): 4–14.

predominate, not coalition and integration. Sooner rather than later attitudes, programs, and forces will appear, demanding and promising unity.

In response to enduring economic disorder, popular desperation will—and already has—led to large-scale emigration that includes many of the youngest, most skilled and talented parts of the population. According to a recent article in the *New York Times,* 1.2 million people left "what used to be the Soviet Bloc" in 1989. Seven hundred thousand were East German. In 1990 "more than two million are expected." The author of this piece, Serge Schmemann, quite correctly emphasizes that "nobody can predict . . . how the growing hardships in the East, and especially in Romania, Bulgaria, and Yugoslavia, will develop. What is known is that all economists agree that things in Eastern Europe will become far worse before they become better."[37] Like ethnic separatism and antagonism, emigration fragments a nation and will generate nationalist calls to end demographic fragmentation.

Unstable governance by recently formed ruling parties and coalitions—political fragmentation—also favors authoritarian developments. Poland, "tired but exhilarated after 14 months of a Solidarity government, is bracing for a presidential election campaign that threatens to divide the nation and jeopardize economic and political change." The bitter conflict between Wałęsa and Mazowiecki is taking place in a country where "the standard of living has dropped 35%, unemployment is expected to climb to 1.5 million by year's end and there is a recession in industrial production."[38] In Hungary, "the ruling center-right coalition, in power for less than six months, took a beating in local elections. . . . The most severe blow was felt in Budapest, where opposition parties won 20 of the city's 22 electoral districts. . . . With inflation creeping past 30 percent, unemployment on the rise *and the political debate again mired in a barrage of accusations,* the mood in Hungary is grim."[39]

Past, Present, Future

I have presented a "Catholic" not "Protestant" argument regarding Eastern Europe's Leninist legacy and current fragmentation(s). I have

37. Serge Schmemann, "Migrants from Eastern Europe Find Journey Ends Just Short of the West," *New York Times,* November 1, 1990, p. A13.

38. John Tagliabue, "Poland's Elections Threaten to Jeopardize Change," *New York Times,* September 23, 1990, p. 3.

39. Celestine Bohlen, "Hungarian Coalition Is Badly Beaten at Polls," *New York Times,* October 16, 1990, p. A12, my emphasis.

obviously, if not explicitly, argued that the historical differences between countries and their current modes of transition from Leninism are not as important as the similarities. One genuine exception exists—Poland—from its "failure" to carry out a Stalinist antipeasant and church revolution, to the historically momentous emergence of a counterpolity, Solidarity, to its current ability to entertain passionate intraelite conflict *and* sustained governmental action with social support. All but one of the other East European regime "transitions," however, were instances of rapid and peaceful "decolonization" and consequently face the same problems as "Third World" successor elites who rapidly and relatively peacefully transited to independence: a very undeveloped capacity to cohere and govern after taking power.[40]

Now for the necessary genuflection to national differences: they exist. It is clear that different types of fragmentation will predominate in different countries and that some will have lower thresholds of violence. But it should be equally clear that today the dominant and shared East European reality is severe and multiple fragmentation.

Allow me to continue with my "Catholic heresy" and suggest that in this setting it will be demogogues, priests, and colonels more than democrats and capitalists who will shape Eastern Europe's general institutional identity. The future of most of Eastern Europe (as I argued in January 1990) is more likely to resemble Latin America than Western Europe. Irony of ironies, it may be the earlier literature by American academics on the "breakdown of democracy" in Latin America rather than the recent literature on "transition to democracy" that speaks most directly to the situation in Eastern Europe.[41]

East European fragmentation, annexation, secession, and emigration offer a firmer foundation for transiting to some form of authoritarian oligarchy (in response to perceptions of anarchy) than to democracy. One likely area-wide response to fragmentations will be a growing political role for the Roman Catholic church. The pope and national churches are major actors not only in Poland, where Wałęsa and his "Center" as well as

40. In the "Third World," guerilla counterelites who fought (the longer the better) against the colonizer constituted themselves as more cohesive successor elites. In this respect Poland's Solidarity is more like the Algerian FLN, KANU in Kenya, and the Indian Congress Party than the "Ghanaian" rest of Eastern Europe. In Romania, where there was violence, it did not last long enough and was too anomic to generate a counterelite, let alone a cohesive one.

41. See Juan Linz and Alfred Stepan, eds., *The Breakdown of Democratic Regimes* (Baltimore, 1978) and Guillermo A. O'Donnell, Philippe C. Schmitter, and Laurence Whitehead, eds., *Transitions from Authoritarian Rule: Prospects for Democracy* (Baltimore, 1986).

the Peasant Party offer firm political support, but in Hungary, Slovakia, Slovenia, Croatia, and, diplomatically, even Romania. The church offers a hierarchically ordered community quite proximate in organization and ethos to the patriarchal peasant and neotraditional Leninist East European experience prior to 1989; an international presence, something that East European populations and elites need as their claim on West European and American democrats and capitalists loses some of its initial attractiveness; and a legitimating myth for authoritarian political rule in conjunction with a nationally unifying military. I should emphasize that just as the Latin American case might be relevant after all to Eastern Europe (in its experience of breakdown of—not transition to—democracy, in its Peronist more than its Alfonsin-Menem incarnation), so the Spanish case might prove to be equally relevant (in its Franco even more than its González stage of development).[42]

One must be prepared to see East European armies and their leaders become more self-aware, confident, and assertive as the maelstrom develops. The military will offer and receive support if, as is likely, these economies continue to deteriorate; if, as is likely, a clear pattern of "hustler" rather than market capitalism produces an ostentatiously wealthy consuming elite in societies that resent disparities in wealth and remain perplexed as to how one succeeds independently of a benevolent state— precisely the underpinnings of Perónism; if, as is likely, Western Europe fails to provide a massive "democratic subsidy"; and if, as is likely, frontier and border issues become salient in a context of civil violence, even war, in Yugoslavia and/or in the Soviet Union.[43] Already, the Romanian army provides whatever glue exists in holding that country together. The same is true of Yugoslavia. And recently, in Bulgaria a "regional judge in Haskovo registered the Bulgarian Legion 'Georgi Stoikov Rakovski' as an official organization. The group . . . was founded to promote professionalism in the army and to campaign for soldiers' rights."[44]

In contrast to the shared quality of the Leninist legacy and fragmentation(s) of Eastern Europe's successor regimes, the impact of the military

42. I find K. H. Silvert's "The Cost of Anti-Nationalism: Argentina," the most insightful analysis of Argentina's remarkable sixty-year failure to combine political modernity (that is, civic nationalism) with an industrial economy. See K. H. Silvert, ed., *Expectant Peoples: Nationalism and Development* (New York, 1963), pp. 345–73.

43. In explaining Perónism, V. S. Naipaul stresses it was not "the existence of the poor, but the pain about the rich that remained the basis of the popular appeal of Perónism. That was the simple passion—rather than 'nationalism' or Perón's 'third position'—that set Argentina alight" (V. S. Naipaul, *The Return of Eva Perón* [New York, 1981], pp. 176–77).

44. Duncan M. Perry, "A New Military Lobby," *Report on Eastern Europe* 1, no. 40 (1990): 1–4.

and church may vary decisively from country to country. Here we must be more "Protestant." To begin with, even those countries with a pre–Second World War history of army political activity (like Serbia, Bulgaria, Romania, and Poland) have now had regimes for close to half a century that have politically subordinated the army, and denied it both a distinctive national mission and institutional élan. Second, at the moment neither the Czechoslovak or Hungarian armies appears to have any significant place in the polity. As for the Roman Catholic church it is not strong in the Czech lands or the Balkans.

The reality appears then to be decisively "Protestant," diverse. If one adds a factor I have not yet touched on, however, the economic, the situation and interpretation of the area-wide role of armies and church might change substantially. Currently there is a debate in and outside of Eastern Europe as to what type of governance is best suited to deal with Eastern Europe's economic emergency.

> The immediate question . . . is: What variant of democratic politics can, on the one hand, provide sufficiently strong stable, consistent government to sustain the necessary rigors of fiscal, monetary, and economic policy over a period of several years, while, on the other hand, being sufficiently flexible and responsive to absorb the larger part of the inevitable popular discontents through parliamentary, or at least, legal channels, thus preventing the resort to . . . ultimately extraparliamentary means?[45]

Timothy Garton Ash agrees with Alfred Stepan—one of the leading figures in the "transition to democracy" school—that "an unambiguously parliamentary system has a better chance of striking the necessary balance [between economic development and democratic participation] than a presidential one."[46] I don't. The choices are not between presidential authoritarianism, with the president either becoming a "weak president, because he bows to the majority, or a strong but antidemocratic one, because he does not," or Garton Ash's "strong freely elected coalitions."[47] (In fact, given the current maelstrom of ethnic, economic, ecological, and political emergencies, any expectation of "strong freely elected coalitions" might be called utopian liberalism.) A third "option" exists—liberal authoritarianism.

45. Garton Ash, "Eastern Europe," p. 54.
46. Ibid., pp. 54–55.
47. Ibid., p. 54.

In Eastern Europe the immediate political imperative is economic. Any successful response to this imperative is likely to have an authoritarian cast. Take a "good" case for democratic capitalism, Czechoslovakia, a country that has just dismissed its Communist defense minister, Vacek, and where the church is a political force mainly in the minority Slovak area. The economic emergency has led to Václav Klaus's dramatic political emergence. Klaus has an agenda with traumatic implications, comparable to what was attempted in England when the Speenhamland Law was abolished.[48] And he must act on this charge without the advantage of (m)any shared substantive agreements or stylistic affinities within the Czechoslovak governing elite(s), or any well-delineated sociopolitical constituency to offer regular partisan support for his program.

What is likely to happen? Klaus's economic reforms will fail. What would it take to succeed? A Giovanni Giolitti, not a Havel, as president; a Giolitti with a *dominant* parliamentary faction able to draw on a strategically placed and privileged voting constituency, with tacit but evident support from the Czechoslovak military and Roman Catholic church. In short, it will take the type of liberal authoritarianism that existed in nineteenth-century western Europe. Bonapartist presidents who rely primarily or exclusively on the military and the church, and unambiguously freely elected parliamentary coalitions will both be overwhelmed by emergency environments. I suggest that a form of liberal authoritarianism like the bourgeois regimes of nineteenth-century western Europe is a desirable alternative to the religio-ethnic, militant nationalist, even fascist regimes that might emerge from the maelstrom; and it would be a more practical response than the utopian wish for immediate mass democracy in Eastern Europe.[49]

The economic emergency in Eastern Europe is a social emergency, and the political responses to it are likely to draw on institutions, elites, policies, and orientations that in varying but also shared ways define themselves in terms of hierarchy, solidary, and exclusionary practices— like the military and the church. The issue is not their participation but on what terms.

---

48. All of Eastern Europe (and the Soviet Union) are in a "Speenhamland" situation so brilliantly explicated by Karl Polanyi in *The Great Transformation* (New York, 1944), pp. 77–85, 94–102.

49. On political development in nineteenth-century Western Europe see Theodore S. Hamerow, *The Birth of a New Europe: State and Society in the Nineteenth Century* (Chapel Hill, N.C., 1983), part 3; and Eric Hobsbawm, *The Age of Empire: 1875–1914* (New York, 1987).

The "Twain" Had Better Meet

The Leninist legacy in Eastern Europe consists largely—not exclusively—of fragmented, mutually suspicious, societies with little religiocultural support for tolerant and individually self-reliant behavior, and a fragmented region populated by countries that view each other invidiously. The way Leninists ruled and the way Leninism collapsed contributed to this inheritance. Still, the emergence and composition of movements like Civic Forum in the Czech lands, and Public against Violence in Slovakia, of the Alliance of Free Democrats in Hungary, and the Union of Democratic Forces in Bulgaria bears witness to the reality of a modern citizenry in Eastern Europe. But it is one that must compete with anticivic, antisecular, anti-individual forces outside and inside itself. With the possible exception of Poland, no East European country has a predominantly civic established elite and constituency. *Question*: Is there any point of leverage, critical mass of civic effort—political, cultural, and economic—that can add its weight to civic forces in Eastern Europe and check the increasing frustration, depression, fragmentation, and anger that will lead to country and region-wide communal-like violence in Eastern Europe? Yes! Western Europe.

The necessary, though not necessarily forthcoming, West European response to the syndrome of East European fragmentation(s) is adoption of Eastern Europe by Western Europe. Fragmentation of Eastern Europe and the Soviet Union, where recently a district of Moscow attempted to claim sovereignty over the Bolshoi Ballet, is not a neutral, peripheral, self-contained event. It is already affecting political identities and relations in and between the Western and "Third" worlds. The disintegration of the former Leninist world and the ongoing fragmentation of its successor regimes can either be the stimulus for a parallel ethnic/civic confrontation in Western Europe (and the United States), or a stimulus for the West to attempt in East Europe and parts of the Soviet Union what West Germany is attempting in East Germany: adoption.

This would require enormous imagination, coordination, and intrusion on the part of Western Europe (and in a significant way of the United States): a massive economic presence, the provision for major population shifts on the European continent, and intracontinental party cooperation and action, all of which would substantially affect the current definition and operation of national sovereignty. Should Western Europe become Liberal White Fortress Europe and deny its responsibility as its "brother's keeper," developments in Eastern Europe will degenerate in a frightening fashion.

Social and Political Landscape, Central Europe, Fall 1990

Ivan Szelenyi

Central Europe on the Road to Liberal Capitalism

By the fall of 1990 the countries of Central Europe were progressing with great determination toward a "free economy" or toward liberal capitalism. Two or three years earlier, social scientists who tried to comment on current developments and forecast the future of the region had sensed that a window of opportunity was opening up for Central Europe.[1] The economic and political structure of state socialism was beginning to disintegrate. For decades it had appeared that the degree of freedom in these societies was about zero. Their rigid internal structure and the tight Soviet control over them almost completely determined their developmental trajectory. During the 1980s, cracks began to appear in the edifice of state socialism. The Polish socioeconomic order collapsed. Hungary and Yugoslavia were sliding into deepening economic recession and aggravated crises of legitimation. Even the Czechoslovak and East German elites began to lose their grip on power. On top of this the dissolution of the Soviet empire began. Under these circumstances, it appeared by 1986–87 that a wide range of alternative futures were be-

---

An earlier and shorter version of this paper was published in the Hungarian daily newspaper *Magyar Nemzet* on August 20, 1990.

1. In my book *Socialist Entrepreneurs* (Madison, Wis., 1988), completed in 1986, I suggested that by the late 1980s a window of opportunity would open up for the region. Writing on possible futures for Hungary, I speculated that that country, and possibly the whole region, might by the end of the 1980s have the best chance to change its course of development that it had been offered since 1867.

coming possible for the region. These alternative futures ranged from a democratic version of socialism, workers' self-management, to multiparty democracy with a mixed economy. Some believed a Scandinavian style of social democracy was likely or desirable, others advocated a "Third Way" between West European capitalism and the Soviet style of socialism. A few economists began to express their preference for liberal capitalism— either in a democratic, West European form, or a more corporatist, authoritarian Southeast Asian version. All these scenarios were articulated in the emergent opposition movements and by increasingly independent social scientists.[2] The dramatic events of October and November 1989 by and large decided the future of Central Europe. A range of alternative futures still remains possible, but the window of opportunity has significantly narrowed since then. At least three dramatic events have shaped the future of the region:

(1) The most unexpected and probably the most important was the acceleration of the disintegration of the Soviet empire. What was unthinkable just a few months earlier has now become possible and even likely. The Soviet Union may fall apart. The USSR, the world empire, may be replaced by several nation-states, such as Lithuania, Latvia, Georgia, and Russia. Russia, with or without the Ukraine, will have to accept a reduced role as a regional power. While such a dissolution of the USSR is far from a foregone conclusion, the Soviet leadership, faced with internal threats, decided by the end of 1989 to give up its hegemonic role in Central Europe. The Soviets let their puppets, Erich Honecker, Miloš Jakeš, and Todor Zhivkov, fall and persuaded the military in their countries to accept Soviet troops as (from the point of view of national security) a necessary buffer between the Soviet Union and Germany. Eventually the Soviet Union decided to allow East Germany to join NATO and did not object openly when other countries sought neutrality or even membership in NATO. This change happened at an astonishing pace. As recently as June 1989, when, at the reburial of Imre Nagy and other executed leaders of the 1956 Hungarian revolution, a leader of the Alliance of Young Democrats (FIDESZ), Viktor Orban, called upon the Soviet Union to withdraw its troops from Hungary, the issue was generally thought to have been raised prematurely, imprudently. Even my close friends in the opposition, who were regarded by the Communists as radical dissidents, were concerned about what they regarded as Orban's

2. Elemér Hankiss gave a rich account of these scenarios in his *East European Alternatives: Are There Any?* (Oxford, 1990).

irresponsibility. Less than twelve months later the Hungarian prime minister (after the treaty on the withdrawal of Soviet troops was signed and Soviet troop withdrawal began) announced Hungary's desire to become a NATO member. He even criticized Austria for staying out of NATO. The sudden decision of the Soviet leadership to give up Central Europe was one of the most unexpected events in recent history.

(2) In conjunction with the Soviet decision to let Central Europe go its own way during the fall of 1989, state socialist systems fell in the region at astonishing speed. As Hungary was opening its borders to East Germans to cross freely into Austria it was becoming obvious that Honecker could not drag on for long with his neo-Stalinism. The writing was on the wall for Jakeš as well. Signs of the weakness of the Czech ruling elite became visible. The hesitation with which the Czechoslovak authorities handled Václav Havel's imprisonment during the spring of 1989, their flirtation with the "Hungarian model," and concessions to small private business and the second economy by mid-1989 were all indications that some change would be inevitable. But the rapidity of the collapse of the East German and Czechoslovak Communist parties, the changes even in Bulgaria, and in particular the fall of Romanian communism were unanticipated. While the difficulties that Yugoslavia was facing were obvious, still, few would have predicted that by the fall of 1990 Croatia and Slovenia would seriously consider full independence from Serbia and use the term "Yugoslav confederation" so obviously to sweeten the bitter pill of Yugoslavia's dismantling for the Serbs.

(3) During the first half of 1990 free elections held in most countries of the region resulted in a sharp turn to the right. In the western zone of what used to be Eastern Europe, in East Germany, Hungary, Slovenia, Croatia, and even in Czechoslovakia, the country that had the leftmost tradition in politics, the political struggles were decided between center-right Christian-nationalist parties, which, although they tended to be left-wing on social issues, were definitely right-wing bourgeois liberal parties in economic policy. With the exception of Czechoslovakia, where the primarily liberal Civic Forum dominated the political scene and formed a coalition government with the Christian-nationalists, more by choice than necessity, the center-right Christian-nationalist parties won the elections and formed governments. Left parties performed miserably. Former Communists were reduced to minor players, winning only 10–15 percent of the votes. Most surprising, the newly formed Social Democratic parties were humiliated by devastating defeats. Retrospectively this all sounds obvious: after forty years of communism whatever is "left-wing" must be

discredited. Social Democrats, as Communist fellow travelers, should not have a chance either. Let us not forget, however, that days before the East German elections virtually all serious political commentators expected an impressive Social Democratic victory and in case of German unification a shift toward the Social Democrats even in united Germany. We were all left breathless by the election results and by Helmut Kohl's taking of Protestant East Germany, the country in which "democratic socialism" was the main slogan even in the opposition discourse just six months earlier. Most of my Hungarian colleagues who began to consider the possibility of a multiparty democracy by the early 1980s had no doubt for a long time that the first free elections would be won by Social Democrats. Frequently I was told that the system that would follow state socialism had to be a democratic socialist, or a Social Democratic, one. All the Czech colleagues I talked to as late as the summer of 1989 had the same forecast for Czechoslovakia.

The political future of the rest of the region, Romania, Bulgaria, and Serbia, is still somewhat uncertain. In all these countries former Communists still have at least a share of the power. The liberal forces seem to be weaker than in the western zone of the region. It is not unimaginable that these countries eventually will move toward right-wing authoritarian systems, not unlike those that dominated them during the interwar years. In Romania and Bulgaria there has been little "circulation of the elite" in terms of personnel. The change of regime meant that the somewhat marginal former nomenklatura moved into the center of the power and displaced a few, the most discredited cadres. Their political colors, however, underwent a far more radical change. After all, it was the new Romanian elite, almost all of them high-ranking officials in the not-too-distant past, that first considered the banning of the Communist Party. They called communism and Marxism alien to Romanian national character and launched a rather extreme nationalistic campaign. As for Poland, "Peronism," or a return to a system similar to the interwar regime of Marshal Piłsudski is not entirely unimaginable. Wałęsa seems ready to accept the role of a strong leader and to combine left-wing trade unionism with the right-wing Christian, nationalist, law-and-order values. It remains to be seen if either the liberals or the Social Democrats will be able to restrict him to a largely ceremonial role as Poland's president.

On the whole, Central Europe politically turned sharply to the right, or center-right. Even the non-Communist Left, whether populist or Social Democratic in orientation, has failed to play any significant role so far. The new political elite, which came to power in 1989–90, is determined to lead its countries toward a purely liberal capitalist road of development. The window of opportunity, so wide open just two or three years ago, is much narrower now. It appears as if neither social democracy nor some kind of "Third Way" solution can be an alternative. The future of Central Europe is liberal capitalism. I would emphasize "appears as if" in the penultimate sentence. History is never guided by iron laws, the future is never completely determined; it is shared by political practice. The unpredictability of the recent past in Central Europe should warn us not to be too self-confident about the predictability of its immediate future. We can say, however, that in light of international development and the changes of political landscape in 1989–90, development other than liberal capitalist development, while not impossible, is nevertheless highly unlikely.

If one accepts these presumptions, two questions remain for the social scientists interested in the future of Central Europe. First, liberal capitalist development is possible and likely, but it is still an open question what kind of capitalist development we can anticipate in that part of the world. Will the countries of Central Europe be able to "join Europe," to ascend rapidly from their current semiperipheral situation in the world market to the core of the capitalist world system and become full-fledged members of the European Community? Or is it more likely—as a result of their peripheral economic status and the extraordinary difficulties they will face in their attempt to restructure their economies and class structure—that they will remain on the periphery and become dependent capitalist economies? Second, one of the most intriguing questions is, what will the relationship be between the Central European countries and a united Germany? Will the traditional ties with Germany help the region to become an equal partner of other countries of the European Community or is it more likely that the new German empire (empire in the economic, rather than in the traditional military sense) will become the hegemonic economic and political force in the region? If this happens, Central Europe may become a sort of semicolony to united Germany, the functional equivalent of what Central America is to the United States.

On the Road to Europe or Dependent Capitalist Development?

Both ruling and opposition parties hope (and promised their electorates) that in a relatively short period of time—according to some, in three to five years—Central Europe will be able to transform itself from state socialism into a developed capitalist market economy and become a part of the European Community. During the Hungarian election campaign in March–April 1990, each party tried to beat the other by emphasizing its orientation toward Europe: "Vote for us and we shall give you a passport to Europe," was everybody's theme, from the conservative Christian Democrats to the liberal Alliance of Free Democrats.

Still, the task of transition from socialism to capitalism is a formidable one. Such an experiment is being attempted for the first time in history and we do not quite know how it will unfold. As one Polish economist put it, "I know how to make a fish soup from an aquarium, but I do not have the slightest idea how to make an aquarium from a fish soup." The task Central Europe is facing is not unlike this unpromising gastronomic exercise.

One formidable challenge is the task of privatization. In 1989–90 the idea of privatization moved to the center stage of policy debates, replacing earlier concerns with self-management, workers' control, marketization, and so on. Most Central European economists (and the politicians who are advised by them) believe that in order to have properly functioning economies, real markets, economies that can effectively interact with the world economy, there is a need for private ownership. The state ought to move altogether out of the sphere of production and leave it to private entrepreneurs. Most economists have for some time accepted the idea of moving from the reform of economic mechanisms to property reform.[3] Until recently, however, property reform meant basically an increasing diversification of public ownership.[4] The aim of property reform was to replace centralized state ownership with systems of holdings, diversification of cooperative forms of ownership, and workers' self-management. The question of private property was put on the agenda before 1987, but just three years ago private property was assumed to play only a limited role in a sort of "socialist mixed economy," which was anticipated to be dominated by the various forms of public ownership.[5]

    3. Tamás Bauer had already called this shift a move toward "second economic reform" in the early 1980s.
    4. As recently as 1985 a leading Hungarian economic reformer—today he is strongly committed to the uncompromising privatization of the economy—told me that "nationalization of the means of production is an irreversible process." In his view, the Western Left was only serving neo-Stalinist interests by writing about the possibility of "restoration of capitalism": "Under no circumstances can capitalism emerge from socialism." He expressed the views of many, if not most, economists in Central Europe at that time.
    5. I analyzed the most radical reform proposals available during the summer of 1987 (such as Turnaround and Reform and Social Contract) in an article written in the early fall

Suddenly the discourse changed. By mid-1990 the necessity of full-scale privatization was accepted by both the dominant and the opposition political elites. The only questions that remain unanswered are how fast privatization should proceed, how great a role foreign capital should play in it, and how much reprivatization (the return of assets to the former owners, rather than their sale to new ones) ought to be allowed.

Such a radical privatization is not an easy task to perform. Let me illustrate some of its difficulties with Hungarian examples. The total value of all Hungarian productive assets (including agricultural land but excluding housing and other infrastructural investments) is somewhere between twenty billion and forty billion U.S. dollars, or two thousand billion to four thousand billion forints. The task of identifying proprietors is historically unprecedented and socially stressful. One must anticipate greed and jealousy, as well as a feeling in many that social justice is not being carried out, in that some people will become very rich while most will remain propertyless. Moreover, most economists, in Hungary at least, believe that these assets should not be given away free but should somehow be sold on competitive markets. It may not be easy, however, to find buyers who are willing to pay reasonable prices. Domestic savings are limited. At best, the population's total savings amount to about 10 percent of the value of all capital goods. One cannot anticipate that all these savings will be invested. Most will be saved for consumption purposes; people save in order to buy a car, a house, and other large items. If the government is lucky, domestic savings will be used to buy about 5 percent of all public property.

In the absence of domestic capital, foreign investors remain the principal hope for privatization. The present economic adviser to the Hungarian prime minister, Matolcsy, floated the idea of "debt-equity-swap" two years ago. Following some Latin American examples, he suggested that Hungary should offer equity in public firms to banks from which it borrowed in exchange for debts. This indeed could be a rapid way to privatization: the value of all Hungarian debt is twenty billion. Hungary was sold to U.S., West German, and Japanese banks during the Kádár years in order to buy political peace and extend the life of the Communist

---

of 1987. I concluded that these reform programs, though not yet clear in their formulation, foreshadowed an economy in which private property would become legally equal with public property, but in the long run would remain rather small. These economists, in short, were cautiously proposing a "mixed economy" of a socialist type. See my article "Eastern Europe in an Epoch of Transition: Toward a Socialist Mixed Economy," in Victor Nee and David Stark, eds., *Remaking the Economic Institutions of Socialism: China and Eastern Europe* (Stanford, Calif., 1989), pp. 208–32.

regime. There are, however, reservations about opening the country to foreign functioning capital. Both the ruling and opposition parties want to restrict foreign ownership; they do not want it to exceed approximately a third of all Hungarian productive assets. Too much foreign control over a national economy may have destabilizing effects, and suddenly passing a large chunk of the economy into the hands of foreign investors may bring about a rapid explosion in unemployment.

Privatization is not simply an economic but also a sociological question. A developed capitalist economy and a democratic political system are hardly imaginable without a propertied domestic bourgeoisie. There is some evidence that those countries in which the development of a domestic bourgeoisie is blocked tend to sink toward the periphery of the world system. Maurice Zeitlin in his book *Civil Wars in Chile (The Bourgeois Revolutions Which Never Were)*, for instance, argues that Chile was on a successful developmental trajectory during the mid-nineteenth century. He challenges the determinism implicit in the world-system theory and suggests it was far from inevitable for Chile to become a dependent capitalist economy. Chile had its chance to move to the core of the world system. In his careful analysis, Zeitlin tries to document that Chile slid into underdevelopment because its semifeudal landholding class defeated the development of the domestic bourgeoisie in two civil wars with the support of American capital. Zeitlin's case is supported by the accounts of several countries that successfully moved from the periphery to the semiperiphery or from the semiperiphery to the core. These, almost without exception, are countries that promoted domestic accumulation and at least at the early stages of their development were cautious about introducing foreign capital. Sweden was on the European periphery in the late nineteenth century and rose to the top of Europe with relatively little foreign capital and the dynamic expansion of the domestic bourgeoisie. Costa Rica, the most successful country of Central America, differs from Honduras, Panama, or Nicaragua in its social structure. Costa Rica implemented a major land reform, created a propertied, family-farmer class, and a domestic bourgeoisie much more effectively than other countries of the region. Taiwan progressed slowly and cautiously during the 1950s. It reduced public property gradually and offered a great deal of support to its domestic bourgeoisie.

Central Europe can hardly jump into Europe in one big leap. A successful transformation of the statist economy into a private one, simultaneously with ascent from its current peripheral situation to a developed market economy, may very well require the evolution of a whole new class of domestic bourgeoisie, which promises to be an epochal task. The current economic policy in Central Europe is hardly conducive to such development. In Hungary, for instance, the system favors foreign businessmen over Hungarians. Foreign citizens get better tax deals than Hungarians, and in the privatization process those who offer hard currency get priority over those who can pay only in Hungarian currency. Recently I read an interview with a successful Hungarian entrepreneur who had just entered a joint venture with foreigners. The interviewer asked him why he needed foreign partners, as he seemed to have done well on his own already. The answer was that he needed a tax break. The only way he could reduce his tax burden was to find a foreign partner. Such policy may easily lead Central Europe to the Third World rather than to the center of the capitalist world system—Europe.

World-system and dependency theories are nowadays in some trouble. Not only can they not explain the emergence of newly industrialized countries (NICs), but the total collapse of state socialism—the collapse of the economies, which tried to isolate themselves from the impact of the world economy—challenges their basic theoretical and political assumption. Undoubtedly we have to rethink these theories. As somebody put it to me recently, "World-system theory proved to be the greatest failure in theorizing in the recent history of the social sciences. No theory proved to be so wrong so fast as world-system theory." Still, it would be premature to move back to an unreconstructed version of modernization theory: some lessons from dependency or world-system theories better be learned. I still find a proposition of the world-system theory—that capitalism is a complex system with distinguishable core and periphery— quite persuasive. It also makes a lot of sense that this system reproduces itself. World-system theory may not have paid enough attention to the possibility of ascent in the system. It may have overemphasized the vicious circle countries in the periphery are hooked into, but it is absolutely right in reminding us that, while ascent is possible, it is quite difficult, too. There are examples of successful ascent: recently the NICs, the Mediterranean countries, and, most promising of all, the story of Finland after the Second World War. Still, there are more failures than successes. Most countries of the Third World attempted to break out and they failed.

Central Europe has been located on the semiperiphery for centuries. I find it moving now to hear Central Europeans say: "We are Europe. We always were Europe, only the Soviet occupation pushed us eastward." At closer scrutiny, however, this proves to be more fancy than historical truth. It is a respectable political aim, rather than a reliable analysis of facts. Central Europe certainly tried to catch up with Western Europe for a long time, but it fell behind for an equally long time. Metternich is credited with saying that Asia begins at the Landstrasse, that is, at the street that leads out of Vienna toward Hungary. Moreover, the past forty years widened the gap between Western and Central Europe. The crucial question is whether the gap can now be closed. The discouraging condition of Central Europe—a devastated natural environment, demoralized populations, a destroyed domestic bourgeoisie and middle class, no domestic capital, and in many countries unbearable foreign debt—is aggravated by the fact that the breakthrough is being attempted at a time when the Western world is in a recession after eight years of prosperity. The current economic situation—the result of several factors such as the Gulf crisis and accelerating oil prices, the difficulties of transition from a wartime to a peacetime economy, the instability of the international monetary system, and grave domestic debts in the United States and foreign indebtedness in the Third World—may well turn into depression.

During the fall of 1990 the social and economic conditions of Central Europe did not look particularly promising. It may not be possible but it will be extremely difficult for those countries to avoid dependent capitalist development. To ascend in the world economy, a country must have economic and social policies that, while seeking a cautious openness to the world market and to foreign capital, give priority to domestic entrepreneurs. This course does not promise the fast results that the politicians were promising during the election campaigns of 1990. A developed capitalist market economy with a stable bourgeois-democratic sociopolitical system cannot be created overnight. It is an epochal task that usually requires decades, if not centuries.

German Hegemony or Central European Integration

The unification of Germany and the collapse of the Soviet empire—the end of Pax Sovietica—has created a new world historic situation. The last forty years saw the world dominated by the two superpowers, whose competition was mainly ideological and military rather than economic. With the degradation of the Soviet Union, or with its dismantling, the world can become tripolar, that is, a world in which the United States, Germany, and Japan compete to shape the future of humankind.

At this moment the German situation is not easy. Germany has to absorb the costs of bailing out East Germany, and they seem to be exorbitant. Estimates of how large these costs will be are rising by the day. Most recently, an economist-journalist of the *International Herald Tribune* estimated the cost of the reconstruction of East Germany to be as high as $100 billion. According to some estimates, three out of four firms are likely to close down, and unemployment may reach four million, or almost 50 percent of the labor force. It may take twenty years for East Germany to catch up with the West.

Some observers conclude that unification may weaken, rather than strengthen, Germany for quite some time. A Germany that will have to be concerned with absorbing the costs of reconstruction and that is strongly committed to the idea of "Europeanizing Germany rather than Germanifying Europe," as Chancellor Kohl put it, may depend more than ever on the European Community and may serve as a link for Central Europeans to find their way toward Europe.

But one can think of the German unification differently. Are these tens of billions of dollars costs or investment opportunities? Is the defreezing of labor from nonproductive firms from East Germany a major social disaster or a unique business opportunity to lower wage levels, to get rid of Gastarbeiters and to work with cheap German labor instead? I find it quite imaginable that Germany will emerge extremely rapidly from the current unification much stronger than ever and will be ready within two or three years to move into Central European markets, even beyond Poland and Hungary, venturing as far as the Baltic states and the Ukraine. One can think of the unification as a major blood transfusion and not as a drain on West German resources.

There is some evidence that this is happening. Germany is certainly present in Central Europe today. Whereas the United States business community is slow in responding to the opening of opportunities, the English lack the dynamism to fill the space opened up by Soviet withdrawal, and the French send delegations and show signs of goodwill but may not have either the will or the resources to do much about the region, German businessmen and even academic entrepreneurs have flocked to Budapest and Prague. While one has to keep knocking on doors in the United States to interest foundations and universities in research and education programs in Central Europe, the Wissenschaftszentrum from Berlin just approached the Hungarian Academy of Sciences with a request to open a branch in Budapest. This is the kind of initiative one rarely sees from any country except Germany. During the summer of 1990 I talked to a Japanese businessman in Hungary and asked him about Japanese business interests in Central Europe. Japan and Italy are close behind Germany in being economically the most active countries in the region. I was surprised to hear his observations: "Yes, we keep an eye open and do business here, but we are also aware that this is German territory and we shall not be able to compete with Germany for this part of the world."

Central Europe itself seems to be very much oriented toward Germany. It is of symbolic importance to me that the first foreign trip of Václav Havel as president of Czechoslovakia led him to Germany. József Antall, the new Hungarian prime minister, also first went to Germany, though he made a point of visiting François Mitterrand shortly after his trip to Bonn. The idea that Central Europe has to orient itself toward Germany is a dominant one. The current Hungarian government is certainly much more pro-German than pro-American. In debates in the Hungarian Academy of Sciences about the reform of graduate training, a respectable linguist argued that Hungary should not adopt the American doctorate system no matter how good it is, but should instead seek to implement the promotion-habilitation system from Germany. Germany represents our future, not the United States, so went the reasoning. It is quite possible that Germany will emerge very soon, much strengthened from unification. Germany is already the most active foreign country in Central Europe. After it absorbs the East German labor force it may find it attractive to move into Central Europe with massive investments; Central Europe seems to be ready for and even to welcome this penetration.

German interest may have far-reaching implications for the future of a united Europe. If Germany indeed recovers fast from the reconstruction of East Germany it may find it profitable to exploit Central European business opportunities. A united Europe may hold Germany back; wanting to share some of the benefits of the Central European market, it may not want to allow Germany to have special deals with Central European countries, and it may want to direct the flow of people from Central Europe to its own, much weaker markets. German unification and German expansion into Central Europe thus may mean an end to a united Europe. So far, Germans promise the opposite, and they keep reconfirming their commitment to the European Community. I can, however, easily imagine a future in which Germany does not need the rest of Western Europe. Western Europe too may be concerned about excessive German power and influence and hence may want to keep certain barriers between itself and Germany.

If a united Germany were to become an expansionist economic power, then a Central Europe "Balkanized" into small nation-states may have few countermeasures available to German penetration and may thus simply turn into an equivalent of something like Central America for the United States. One can do worse than to swap the USSR for a democratic Germany as a "master-nation." But can this region do without a "master"?

Count József Eötvös, a nineteenth-century Hungarian political philosopher, wrote an essay during the late 1850s that made him very unpopular in most Hungarian circles. At the time of its publication, this essay drew a somewhat conservative-sounding conclusion from the defeat of the 1848–49 revolution and the Kossuth type of nationalist radicalism. (Eötvös belonged to the "centrists," to those who tried to find a middle way between bourgeois nationalist radicalism and aristocratic conservativism.) According to Eötvös the survival of the Habsburg Monarchy in one form or another was desirable for the political equilibrium of Europe. With prophetic insights he forecast that the division of Central Europe into small nation-states would make the region an easy prey of either Germany or Russia. A strong buffer state was needed between the two emergent giants of late-nineteenth-century Europe. Moreover, Eötvös believed that Austria was the key to a viable united Central Europe. Austria was the link that connected the Central European countries to the West.

Eötvös's essay understandably did not gain him popularity. During the years of absolutism, with a failed revolution in the recent past, a Central European cooperation under the Habsburgs was problematic indeed. The history of the twentieth century supports Eötvös's analysis. Germany and Russia have indeed proved to be the major threats to the region—not Austria or the Habsburgs.

The concept of regional cooperation arose during the last half of 1990. Soon after Václav Havel took office he tried to persuade Poles and Hungarians to think about closer cooperation, though it appears from the press releases that this proposition has not met with great enthusiasm. The Hungarian foreign minister, Géza Jeszenszky, came up with the idea of a Tisza confederation, suggesting closer cooperation between Hungary, the "eastern parts of Czechoslovakia," Transylvania, and the "trans-Carpathian Ukraine" (a configuration of countries that on the map looks a bit like the old Hungarian kingdom). In a lecture in Helsinki in August 1990, the Hungarian prime minister, József Antall, also spoke favorably of some regional cooperation among post-Communist societies. Others are dreaming about Adriatic Union, which may include Italy, Croatia, Slovenia, Austria, and Hungary.

In terms of both historical roots and current economic conditions the core of a Central European common market, or community, could be Austria, Hungary, Czechoslovakia, and Slovenia. I am sure that Czechoslovakia, Hungary, and Slovenia would greatly benefit from closer cooperation with Austria. Austria is far less of a threat than Germany. Now, at the end of the twentieth century, it is in no way a potential imperial power, and it could offer a great deal of assistance to those countries in getting access to capital, banking, stock-exchange skills, and networks into Western markets. Austria's application for membership in the European Community was put on hold and—with the emergence of a united Germany— it is not obvious that it is in the best interest of Austria to get too close to Germany. With an expansionist united Germany, an economic and sociocultural Anschluss is quite possible. In an interview published by *Die Presse* in early September 1990, Erhard Busek, the conservative minister of science of the Social Democratic Austrian government, expressed concern about such an Anschluss and indicated that the future of an independent Austria would be better served by foreign policy that orients itself toward Central Europe. He bitterly criticized existing Austrian foreign policy, which was not exploiting these opportunities. During the second half of 1990 Austria started doing the opposite of what he suggested. It not only kept knocking on the still-closed door of the European Community, but it was closing its doors to the East. Busek attacked the decision of the Austrian government to close its border to the Poles and require visas of them, as well as its decision to take Hungary to international court and request compensation for the failed Bös-Nagymaros dam project. Busek also found it quite inopportune for Austria to keep criticizing Czechoslovakia for the lack of safety procedures in its nuclear-energy plants, instead of offering help to clean up Czechoslovakia's environment. As I understood the Busek interview, he sees two futures for Austria: Vienna can either become a sleepy provincial capital of German Europe, the fourth or fifth German city in Europe, far behind Berlin and Frankfurt, and even Hamburg, Düsseldorf, and Munich, or it can become a booming capital city, the center of innovation, banking, international trade, science, and higher education in a Central European community with forty or even sixty or eighty million inhabitants.

I may add—though it may sound far-fetched—that Switzerland, for the same reasons as Austria, may have an interest in "going East." In a united Europe under German hegemony Switzerland, like Austria, may find it very difficult to maintain its identity. In a way a "genuine" Central Europe may need Switzerland as much as, if not more than Austria. An identity linked to Austria and Switzerland, with Zurich and Salzburg, followed by Vienna, Prague, Budapest, Ljubljana, and eventually Zagreb and Warsaw, symbolizing what is "Central" in Europe, would certainly move the region powerfully to the west. While Metternich believed Asia began at the Landstrasse, others thought it began at the eastern slopes of the Alps. In order to make sure that one is not in the oriental part of Europe, one may wish to get to the western slopes of the Alps. More seriously, though the idea of Switzerland's joining of such a regional union may be out of touch with history, it is not unthinkable that Switzerland would have an interest in the role that Busek recommends for Austria. The post-Communist countries of Central Europe could only gain from Swiss participation. Austria may be too small, may not have enough capital and dynamism to drag the region out of its stagnation; Switzerland may help.

Croatia and Poland are also obvious, but a bit more problematic, candidates for a Central European regional cooperation. Poland, deeply trapped in its economic crisis, is the sick old man of Europe. It may be a burden to take Poland on, though in the long run Polish labor and human capital reserves may serve the interests of a Central European community. Croatia's burden is Serbia. An intense Serb-Croat national conflict may shift the whole region politically to ethnic tension and right-wing politics.

The point of this essay is not to redraw the boundaries of Europe or to come up with a blueprint for new types of cooperation or confederation. My point is that a united Germany may pose an economic threat to post-Communist Central Europe, it may play a colonizing role, and cooperation among these small countries may be the only way to resist such tendencies before they develop. It may not be easy to persuade the countries of Central Europe to cooperate. There is a good deal of hostility among them. One sees more signs pointing toward further national splits and conflicts than toward international cooperation. There is a strong Slovak separatist movement, there is some tension between Slovakia and Hungary, Hungarian-Croatian relations were never unproblematic, the Czechs seem to be rather skeptical about the Poles, and so on. The small nation-states at the moment seem also to be more on a competitive course with one another. Though Hungarians greeted with enthusiasm the collapse of communism in the neighboring countries, and claimed credit for it by opening their borders for Germans to cross to Austria, many Hungarians complained that the collapse came at the worst possible time, since now they would have to share with other countries any help coming from the West. When I recently talked to a Croat economist, a leading political figure in the governing party, I asked him what he thought about

Central European cooperation. He said that it was Croatia's second option—the first was to become a member of the European Community.
Many, if not most, politicians of the region may think this way, and if so,
they may try to get behind the European door before the others, especially
before the door is shut. Becoming an equal member of the European
Community is a thrilling prospect indeed, but I am not sure that the
European Community or the Central European states would be best
served by such a development. The gap between the two economic blocs is
too great. A premature influx of former East Europeans may adversely
affect Western Europe, driving up the unemployment rates, pushing wage
levels down, and draining the social welfare system. By becoming a part
of the European Community too soon, Central Europe may experience
"internal colonialism." It may become the backward region of a united
Europe and in the long run may be better served by nurturing its own
economy and social structures before it enters into open competition with
its stronger neighbors.

I may have, for the sake of argument, overemphasized the potential
danger of an economically expansionist new German empire and the
subsequent Latin Americanization of Central Europe. I also may sound
somewhat romantic in recommending international cooperation in that
region of the world, with its history of international conflict and interethnic tensions. It seems to be a fact, however, that in 1990 things were
getting worse, and they will continue worsening before they can get better. A friend of mine observed on New Year's Eve in 1989 that the year
before we had drunk champagne and gotten high. The year 1990 would
be the year of the hangover. He had a point. During the course of it,
unemployment rose in the whole region, industrial production fell, living
standards declined, ethnic and national conflicts reemerged, and the competing political parties often used dirty campaign tactics against one another, something that was looked on with disgust and apathy by the
electorate. At the first free Hungarian national elections in history, in the
crucial second round, only 45 percent cast their ballots. The current
Hungarian government was elected by the majority of the minority. In
recent Polish municipal elections 60 percent did not vote. At the Hungarian municipal elections on October 14, 1990, turnout was below 30
percent. One could get elected mayor with as little as 15 percent of the
popular support. And this all happened when the transition to a multiparty parliamentary system was being viewed as a turning point in history, as
a transition from illegitimate Communist rule to political legitimacy. The
last Hungarian municipal elections were heralded by the competing par-

ties as the crucial event of transition from communism to democracy. The political rhetoric before the elections was focused on "dual power": democracy at the top, in the parliament and the government, versus Communist totalitarianism in the local governments. Seventy percent of the population could not have cared less. Altogether the economic, ethnic, and political problems are formidable. Central Europe is a powder keg that can blow up at any moment. National leaders in the region and the international community will need a great deal of wisdom to avoid such an explosion and to navigate peacefully between the Scyllas of dependent capitalism and the Charybdises of excessive German economic power to more peaceful waters of economic prosperity and political democracy.

Contributors

Ivo Banac is Professor of History and Master of Pierson College at Yale University. His books include *The National Question in Yugoslavia: Origins, History, Politics* and *With Stalin against Tito: Comminformist Splits in Yugoslav Communism*, which was awarded the Strossmayer Award of the Zagreb Book Fair in 1991.

Elez Biberaj is Chief of the Albanian Service at the Voice of America. He is the author of *Albania and China: A Study of an Unequal Alliance*.

László Bruszt is a political sociologist at the Institute of Sociology of the Hungarian Academy of Sciences. Widely published on questions of interest representation and corporatism, he was a pioneer in the analysis of public opinion surveys in Hungary and co-founded Gallup-Budapest. He was a participant in the Hungarian Round Table discussions as secretary of the League of Independent Trade Unions.

Jan T. Gross is Professor of Sociology at Emory University. His books include *Polish Society under German Occupation: The Generalgouvernement, 1939–1944* and *Revolution from Abroad: The Soviet Conquest of Poland's Western Ukraine and Western Belorussia*.

Ken Jowitt is Professor of Political Science at the University of California, Berkeley. His works include *Revolutionary Breakthroughs and National Development: The Case of Romania, 1944–1965* and *Social Change in Romania 1860–1940: A Debate on Development in a European Nation*.

Tony R. Judt is Professor of History in the Institute of French Studies at New York University. Author of several books on French socialism, including

Marxism and the French Left: Studies on Labour and Politics in France, 1830–1981, he is currently researching the history of the Left and dissidence in Czechoslovakia.

Gail Kligman is Associate Professor of Sociology and Anthropology at the University of Texas, Austin. She is the author of *Căluş: Symbolic Transformation in Romanian Ritual* and *The Wedding of the Dead: Ritual, Poetics and Popular Culture in Transylvania.* She is currently working on a project titled "Culture for the Masses: The Homogenization of the Body Politic in Ceauşescu's Romania."

Norman Naimark is Professor of History at Stanford University. His books include *The History of the Proletariat: The Emergence of Marxism in the Kingdom of Poland, 1870–1887* and *Terrorists and Social Democrats: The Russian Revolutionary Movement under Alexander III.* He is completing a monograph on the history of the Soviet Occupation Zone in Germany.

David Stark is Associate Professor of Sociology at Cornell University. He is co-editor with Victor Nee of *Remaking the Economic Institutions of Socialism: China and Eastern Europe.*

Ivan Szelenyi is Professor of Sociology at the University of California, Los Angeles. He is the author of *The Intellectuals on the Road to Class Power* (with György Konrád), *Urban Inequalities under State Socialism,* and, most recently, *Socialist Entrepreneurs.*

Maria Todorova, currently a Mellon Distinguished Visiting Professor at Rice University, is Associate Professor of Balkan History at the University of Sofia, Bulgaria. She has published a work on England, Russia, and the Tanzimat and another on British travelers' accounts of the Balkans.

Katherine Verdery is Professor of Anthropology at Johns Hopkins University. She is the author of *Transylvanian Villagers: Three Centuries of Political, Economic, and Ethnic Change* and *National Ideology under Socialism: Identity and Cultural Politics in Ceauşescu's Romania.*

Index

Library of Congress Cataloging-in-Publication Data

Eastern Europe in revolution / edited by Ivo Banac.
    p. cm.
    Includes bibliographical references and index.
    ISBN 0-8014-2711-8 (alk. paper). — ISBN 0-8014-9997-6 (pbk. :
alk. paper)
    1. Europe, Eastern—Politics and government—1989– I. Banac,
Ivo..
DJK51E265 1992
943'.0009717—dc20   91-57903